DI022162

TRESPASSES

ALSO BY HOWARD SWINDLE

Once a Hero

Deliberate Indifference

TRESPASSES

Portrait of a Serial Rapist

HOWARD SWINDLE

VIKING

VIKING
Published by the Penguin Group
Penguin Books USA Inc., 375 Hudson Street,
New York, New York 10014, U.S.A.
Penguin Books Ltd, 27 Wrights Lane,
London W8 5TZ, England
Penguin Books Australia Ltd, Ringwood,
Victoria, Australia
Penguin Books Canada Ltd, 10 Alcorn Avenue,
Toronto, Ontario, Canada M4V 3B2
Penguin Books (N.Z.) Ltd, 182–190 Wairau Road,
Auckland 10, New Zealand

Penguin Books Ltd, Registered Offices:
Harmondsworth, Middlesex, England

First published in 1996 by Viking Penguin,
a division of Penguin Books USA Inc.

1 3 5 7 9 10 8 6 4 2

Copyright © Howard Swindle, 1996
All rights reserved

Grateful acknowledgment is made for permission to reprint excerpts from the following copyrighted works:
Men Who Rape: The Psychology of the Offender by A. Nicholas Groth with H. Jean Birnbaum. By permission of Plenum Publishing Corp.
Inside the Criminal Mind by Stanton E. Samenow. Copyright © 1984 by Stanton E. Samenow. Reprinted by permission of Times Books, a division of Random House, Inc.

LIBRARY OF CONGRESS CATALOGING IN PUBLICATION DATA
Swindle, Howard.
Trespasses: portrait of a serial rapist /
Howard Swindle.
p.   cm.
ISBN 0-670-85879-X
1. Escobedo, Gilbert Hernandez.   2. Rapists—Texas—Dallas—Biography.
3. Rape victims—Texas—Dallas.   I. Title.
HV6248.E72S93   1996
364.1'532'097642812—dc20   95-21276

This book is printed on acid-free paper.
∞

Printed in the United States of America
Set in Janson
Designed by James Sinclair

Without limiting the rights under copyright reserved above, no part of this publication may be reproduced, stored in or introduced into a retrieval system, or transmitted, in any form or by any means (electronic, mechanical, photocopying, recording or otherwise), without the prior written permission of both the copyright owner and the above publisher of this book.

For those beginning and those passing—

To Jake Anson Swindle,
and to the memory of
Professor Martin L. (Red) Gibson

Author's Note and Acknowledgments

Rape, rape victims, and rapists are persistent mysteries because virtually no one is comfortable talking about them. Unwittingly, members of society —police, lawyers, judges, writers, producers, even well-intentioned self-help and advocacy groups—have forced rape's victims and perpetrators into closets sealed with shame and ignorance.

The resulting environment makes suspect the motivations of everyone in a rape case. Stereotypes still exist in which victims are asked in court about their sexual histories and what they were wearing when they were attacked. Rapists are dismissed as "monsters," "beasts," and "perverts," as Alice Vachss, a prosecutor turned author, recently wrote; they are beyond, or not worthy of, help. Detectives and prosecutors, professions still filled predominantly by men, are attacked for their lack of sensitivity. Writers are shunned for fear they will exploit and sensationalize rape.

Even victim self-help groups send conflicting messages about rape. "You were attacked, for goodness sakes," they tell women who are raped. "You didn't do anything to be ashamed of." Then, as if they were counseling lepers, they say: "Avoid the media. People wouldn't understand."

Not surprisingly, then, gaining access to people with firsthand knowledge of the so-called Ski Mask Rapes that unfolded in Dallas from

1985 through 1990 was difficult. But at critical times when it appeared that this book couldn't be written, various courageous and dedicated people surfaced to resurrect it.

Many of them were women who already had more than sufficient reason never again to trust a stranger, particularly a man who also happened to be a writer. Nonetheless, these women opened private doors to relive the most intrusive and tragic events in their lives in the hope that the public won't continue to regard rape in stereotypes and statistics. Theirs are the real faces, traumas, fears, and hopes behind the more than one hundred thousand rapes every year in this country. I admire and respect their strength, and I am deeply indebted to each.

Common decency and their own individual preferences under Texas law demand that their identities, along with those of all the other rape victims, appear as pseudonyms in this book. (Pseudonyms appear with an asterisk on first reference.)

Gilbert Hernandez Escobedo, the enigmatic, self-professed Christian who finally confessed to being one of the most prolific and brazen rapists in Dallas history, likewise allowed me to visit and correspond with him in prison. We shared conversations and letters for two years. His initial decision to cooperate in my research came, he said, only after hours of prayer in which God ultimately blessed the endeavor as Escobedo's way "to help the people I hurt." In reality, our relationship was, at best, sporadic, interrupted periodically by his own paranoia ("I don't want this to hurt me with the parole board" and "I don't want you having lunch with my wife anymore") and peer pressure from other convicts and his family.

Moreover, his family steadfastly refused to discuss him and threatened to banish him if he cooperated in the research. Representing yet another impact of rape, his brother Alfred Escobedo explained: "It's our family name. He's in prison; he doesn't have to deal with it. We do. Every day."

Shirley Escobedo, who married Escobedo by proxy after his conviction, was especially helpful and supportive during the research of this book, even knowing that few people would understand her commitment to a man who has brutalized so many women.

But of all the people who shared portions of their lives, none was more forthcoming or insightful than a woman who once was engaged to, and unwittingly lived with, Gilbert Escobedo for two years during the midst of his series of rapes. Despite betrayal that made her, too, an emotional victim, she nonetheless was dispassionate in recounting facets of Escobedo unreflected in public records. Because she has relocated to another state and has established a family, she, too, is referred to by a pseudonym at her request.

Detective Senior Corporal (Retired) Marshall Touchton, who for thirty years carried a badge and gun for the Dallas Police Department, was invaluable in sharing his extensive knowledge of Escobedo. Our relationship was hesitant at first, not an unusual occurrence among veteran cops and writers; it prospered over time with mutual respect. He's the kind of cop I'd want on my doorstep if my family called 911.

One of Touchton's colleagues, Detective Corporal (Retired) Evelyn Crowder Allison, not only was helpful, but also was an inspiration. Allison was one of the first women to become a commissioned officer in the Dallas Police Department, bringing with her an unusual blend of toughness and compassion that made her one of the department's most respected detectives.

Likewise, I am indebted to the Reverend Dennis Henderson of Manteca, California, a former reserve police officer and minister in Dallas.

The more pieces I pulled together about Gilbert Escobedo, the more elusive, contradictory, and indecipherable his personality appeared. Dr. Jaye Douglas Crowder (no relation to Detective Evelyn Crowder Allison), an assistant professor of forensic psychiatry at the University of Texas Southwestern Medical School in Dallas, contributed interpretation and analysis, and ultimately clarity, to the facts I gathered. On Thursday nights, Dr. Crowder allowed me to load his dining room table with rape reports, interviews, videotapes, rap sheets, chronologies, and summaries. From the maze of information, Dr. Crowder helped me understand rape in general and Gilbert Escobedo in particular.

This book also depended on the kindness and cooperation of several other experts in rape investigation and counseling: Sergeant Larry Lewis, head of the Dallas Police Department's Sex Crimes Division; Sergeant Bob Rommel, formerly assigned to Sex Crimes; Detective (Retired) Stephen K. Hatchel, also with Sex Crimes; Sue James, executive director of the Dallas County Rape Crisis Center; and Kathy Finch, former executive director of Victims Outreach in Dallas. I also am indebted to Sergeant Jim Chandler, the Dallas Police Department's public information officer, who helped me get access to the voluminous police files.

As with all my endeavors, my friends were there when I needed them: Paul Watler, an attorney, without whose legal expertise I never would have prevailed under the Texas Open Records Act; Tim Wyatt, the best computer researcher and skip-tracer in the country; Judy Stratton, more right hand and heart than secretary; Allen Pusey, a colleague and confidant; Lloyd Harrell, a retired FBI agent and friend of twenty years; Bob Mong and Ralph Langer, my mentors at the *Dallas Morning News*; Carlton Stowers, never too busy with his own books to counsel me on mine; Janet Wilkens Manus, my agent who supports me in sickness and health; and Mindy Werner, my patient editor and literary savior.

And finally, my appreciation to my mother for, among a multitude of things, providing a quiet haven to write; and to my wife, Kathy, and my children, Ashley, Stryker, and, now, Jake, for providing inspiration and forgiving all the lost nights and weekends.

To the extent possible, I have tried to minimize lurid depictions of actual rapes, focusing instead on the events that led to the attacks, the aftermath they created, and, most importantly, the reactions of those involved. At times, however, the rape scenes are explicit and graphic only because the detail is important in explaining the rapist or the victim or a modus operandi subsequently important in the investigation.

Rape, like abortion and religion, evokes strong emotional, political, and moral reactions among most people. This book probably will collide with various of those emotions and beliefs, and, almost certainly, with political correctness.

It is common among some feminists and rape therapists, for example, to teach women to regard themselves as "survivors" rather than "victims" of rape. Presumably, this approach to self-image as a survivor is a form of empowerment that allows targets of sexual assaults to regain control over their lives and to no longer perceive themselves as powerless victims.

However, women who were targets of sexual attacks are referred to in this book as victims, not out of insensitivity, but simply because it is a more journalistically precise term. *Victim*, in the context of this book, is an indisputable fact as determined by the justice system and one that does not depend on psychological interpretation or the degree of a woman's emotional recovery. (Indeed, *victim* is a term used by five of six rape victims interviewed for this book.)

Similarly, and to the consternation of at least one victim of the Ski Mask Rapist, I have made an exhaustive effort to ferret out the rationale and motivation of how Gilbert Hernandez Escobedo became a rapist. This particular victim, identified in the book as Claire Miller, a pseudonym, chose not to participate in my research because I already had spent many hours interviewing Escobedo. She contended the interviews would offer him "a forum for his lies and rationalizations."

Journalism, like justice, should afford everyone the fundamental right to be heard. Informed readers, like jurors, weigh the facts, assess the credibility of the witnesses, and arrive at their own conclusions.

As with the comments, insights, and opinions of other people interviewed for this book, including those of rape victims, I offer Gilbert Escobedo's recollections without opinion as to veracity or sincerity, but rather in an earnest and good-faith effort to understand.

"The writer," novelist-playwright W. Somerset Maugham once wrote, "is more concerned to know than to judge."

Some conversations written in this book have been reconstructed, based on interviews with people who had them. Pseudonyms used in the book are, indeed, fictitious names; any similarities between those characters with pseudonyms and to actual persons by the same name are coincidental and unintended.

Contents

Preface

The genesis for this book actually began twenty-eight years ago, maybe an hour or so before daybreak on a June morning that already was muggy enough to sweat out the armpits of my only good shirt. I was twenty-one, green, scared, and an intern for the *Fort Worth Press*, a tired and thin old tabloid that screamed and raised bare-knuckled hell even as it was dying.

On my first innocent day, it was impressed on me that there was no crime that I wouldn't report, though some might end up in the city editor's trash; making decisions was not a rookie's prerogative. Nor would I rely solely on the police "beefsheets," or offense reports, on which street cops routinely misspelled information and which ultimately made their way hours late to the dingy police press room in the basement. Whenever possible, I would be at the scene as quickly as possible after hearing it on the police radio. Good journalism, I was told, was practiced in the field and based on personal observation.

The scene that predawn morning in 1967 was a brick duplex, one of hundreds of nondescript rentals whose tenants changed with the semesters at nearby Texas Christian University. I was relieved as I drove up, noting that the uniformed patrol officer had beaten me by only seconds, not enough time for him to seal off the crime scene. Equally fortuitous, the officer walked in without shutting the door, allowing me to make my way unobtrusively inside the doorway.

The woman inside appeared much younger than the nineteen that would be written on the offense report. The paperwork wouldn't make note of the fact that she was a freshman at TCU. Nor would the record reflect that her world had collapsed around her less than a week after she had left her parents' home to begin life on her own.

Her name was Lisa and she was sitting in a dining room chair, wearing a plaid flannel robe starkly out of place in the June heat. The heels of her bare feet were anchored in the seat of the chair and her arms were draped around her legs, pulling them up tight against her chest in a fetal position. From within, there was a low anguished moan that made me wince.

The veteran cop turned awkwardly toward the door, but made no attempt to remove me. I remember thinking he, too, appeared pathetic and helpless.

There had been pounding at the door, the young woman finally managed to say, at about three-thirty A.M. She opened it and peered groggily beneath the heavy chain latch her father had insisted on only a few days earlier. Through the crack, a frantic man explained that his wife was in the car at the curb, giving birth in the backseat. He had seen the porch light, and he needed to use her phone to call an ambulance. He was desperate.

When Lisa unhooked the night latch, she said, the look on the man's face changed abruptly. He seized her mechanically by her throat and stiff-armed her backward toward the bedroom. Over his shoulder, she saw a second man come through the door. For the next hour and a half, they did things that no man should do to another's daughter.

The story was the first byline in my career. A week later, during lunch with Dr. Martin L. Gibson, my college professor and mentor, I told him that I wasn't certain I was cut out to be a reporter. The incident had made me a voyeur, I told him. Nothing—not a press card, not the threat of a city editor, not even the vaunted public's right to know—justified my standing in that woman's doorway that morning. Though she barely looked at me, my presence was invasive and dehumanizing for her. *I* could feel it.

"The public does have a right to know," Professor Gibson said, "especially about repugnant things that happen in their society. They can't do anything about it if they don't know about it. If that girl had known there was a rapist in the neighborhood, if she had read it in the paper or seen it on TV, do you really think she would have unlatched the door at three-thirty in the morning?"

Maybe not. Or maybe I was simply embarking on a career in which I always would be infringing on people at their vulnerable worst and rationalizing it as the public's right to know.

But I clung to his logic, weighing it, balancing it, and, finally, accepting it and filing it away. Over the years, when other people's anguish would make me question my own motivation, I would resurrect the conversation and cloak myself in it. Sometimes it helped.

Eight years later, in Fort Worth on assignment for another newspaper, I stopped by the police department. I wondered if Lisa's attackers had been arrested. The official account of whatever happened to Lisa that June morning was contained in six sheets of paper in a manila file folder. The statute of limitations had long since expired and, according to the file, there were never any serious suspects, not surprising since she was able to remember only that the men were "white, middle-aged, average-looking." Nor were there any patterns to indicate that the same rapists had struck again, though common sense and a reporter's cynicism suggested otherwise.

Rereading the pages, it was apparent that Lisa had become only a statistic. On the only official report of the events that shattered a teenager's life, there were no hints of what *really* happened to her. There was no mention of the fear or the hysteria or the panic that I saw that morning. Or of mental images that must have gone through her mind when she called her parents. Or of what her mind saw at night when she tried to sleep.

I don't know if Lisa ever finished college. She would be forty-seven today, maybe married, possibly a mother, conceivably a grandmother. And sometimes, particularly when I read about a rape or draw another invasive assignment, I wonder about her.

The mind's eye is indelible about firsts—first car, first date, first sex, first heartbreak, first anything. As a teenager growing up in rural Texas,

I certainly had read about tragedies in the newspaper and watched them play out on television, but I had never witnessed one personally, not until Lisa.

Newspaper journalism, I would discover, is the almost instantaneous Polaroid snapshot of society's warts and wrinkles, of the unexpected, the pathos, and depravity on a given day. There is precious little time for revisiting those who were caught up in yesterday's headlines and almost no time to chronicle how those spontaneous events changed the course of their lives. Contrary to prevailing opinion, daily journalism isn't nearly as premeditatedly exploitive as it is inherently expedient.

In truth, I forgot Lisa's last name years ago. Over the span of her lifetime, the hour and a half of horror was a nanosecond. But I have wondered many times how that trauma in her last year as a teenager affected the decades she would spend as an adult. Was she ever able to trust a man again? Enough to marry? If she had children, had she passed along to them her paranoia about violence and, perhaps, her anger and frustration? Was she overprotective? Mostly, I wonder if Lisa was ever able to find peace.

More than two decades of journalism made me understand, if not condone, greed, rage, retaliation, even random, unprovoked violence. But not rape. Not the betrayal of intimacy, not an assault on the most personal, inviolate core of our souls.

The question of rape became even more complex and confounding on a February morning in 1977 when I learned that Dallas police finally had arrested the so-called Friendly Rapist, at the time the most prolific rapist in Dallas history.

I had met him years earlier in Lubbock, Texas. He had been a reporter then, an intelligent, understatedly handsome and ambitious guy with an unlimited future. By the time he was arrested in Dallas, he had worked his way to vice president of the largest, most prestigious public relations firm in the Southwest. There had been no obvious flaws, not even any hints of a dark side.

Not until I was studying his photograph did I realize the ambiguity I had felt in Lisa's doorway. My inexperience as a journalist on my first assignment had been only part of my uneasiness. The PR executive, a husband and father, was Everyman. And for no other reason than gender, I realized, I, too, had to be considered a potential rapist. Conceivably, all men are.

From Lisa's harrowed perspective, I doubt I looked substantially different from the men who had ruined her life. And notwithstanding the truths I knew about myself, I didn't warrant any more trust than the other strange man who had pleaded for her help, then betrayed and raped her.

It was guilt, I understood, that motivated me as I stood in the doorway looking at the nineteen-year-old rape victim years earlier. Guilt, based not on predilection and certainly not life experience, but exclusively on biological similarity. Awkwardness stymied the words, but what I had wanted to say was: *Please understand. We're not all like that.*

Some feminists believe that all men are, in fact, alike in their propensity to rape. By inference, they claim that it is only the opportunity for abuse that separates the average male from the rapist. Dismissing all socially acceptable biological functions of the penis—urination, reproduction, consensual sex—these feminists focus on the "penis-as-a-weapon."

"The annihilation of a woman's personality, individuality, will, character, is prerequisite to male sexuality . . ." wrote feminist Andrea Dworkin in *Letters from a War Zone.* "Male sexuality, drunk on its intrinsic contempt for all life, but especially for women's lives, can run wild, hunt down random victims, use the dark for cover, find in the dark solace, sanction, and sanctuary."

Susan Brownmiller, in *Against Our Will,* her 1975 rape book that still is considered the watermark, seized on the vague collective guilt men have about rape and escalated it to blanket condemnation. After divining that "one of the earliest forms of male bonding must have been the gang rape of one woman by a band of marauding men," Brownmiller became even more cavalier:

Man's discovery that his genitalia could serve as a weapon to generate fear must rank as one of the most important discoveries of prehistoric times, along with the use of fire and the first crude stone axe. From prehistoric times to the present, I believe, rape has played a critical function. It is nothing more or less than a conscious process of intimidation by which *all men* keep *all women* in a state of fear. [Her emphasis.]

Dworkin and Brownmiller are the incongruous extreme of the simple truth I had discovered looking at the rapist's picture: that all men are inescapably suspect simply because they have penises. Similar, I suppose, to the premise that all gun owners are potential murderers because they own guns.

But a *conspiracy by all men to scare all women?* Not among the men I know. Would Brownmiller, a white woman, see the irresponsibility in a statement that claims, say, that racism is the conscious process of intimidation by which *all whites* keep *all blacks* in a state of repression? A self-professed liberal, Brownmiller presumably would be incensed to be lumped together with Klan demagogues and ignorant supremacist whites in a conspiracy to deny civil rights to a whole class of people.

Brownmiller's incredible statement made me self-conscious about what women really do think about rape and men. All women couldn't believe that, could they?

I had known a handful of women over the years who had been raped. In none of my conversations with them had I detected Dworkin's or Brownmiller's all-encompassing fear or resentment of all men. All but one of the women, in fact, had trusted men enough to marry them after the sexual assaults against them.

But what was common among all the women even years after the attacks was "Why? Why would a man do that? And why would a man do that to me?"

In April 1990, Gilbert Escobedo was arrested, and later confessed to being the "Ski Mask Rapist," a serial rapist who admitted to assaulting forty-eight women during a five-year reign of terror. Since many rape victims, for a multitude of reasons, don't report the attacks, detectives estimate Escobedo's victims actually could range to seventy-five or a hundred, which would make him perhaps the most prolific sex offender in the Southwest. I wondered if Escobedo and the women he raped could or would help answer the question.

Even anticipating some of the problems, researching rape was more difficult than I had imagined. In academic papers, psychologists and psychiatrists split on causation—every catalyst from childhood abuse to bad genes to premeditatedly evil decision making. Answers eluded even the victims I knew, despite their unfortunate firsthand knowledge.

Being a man only made the research more difficult. When my "gender guilt," as I came to call it, went unchecked, I worried that my questions would plunge a victim into post-traumatic stress, only aggravating the damage another man already had inflicted. Many of Escobedo's victims chose not to be interviewed, a decision I understood and accepted at face value. A few were angered that I even asked, however sensitively I tried. One rape victim, who frequently relived her ordeal for a series of rape support groups, told me that I could never understand what it was like to be raped because I was a man and had never been raped. She appeared defiant and, I thought, curiously smug.

It was a rationale I had heard before. While researching a previous book about a decorated Vietnam helicopter pilot who in the midst of post-traumatic stress disorder embarked on a series of aberrationally bizarre crimes, a Vietnam veteran refused to talk to me until I was able to document that I, too, was a Vietnam vet.

"You ain't been there," he said simply, "you ain't gonna understand it. No way."

I didn't subscribe to the veteran's or the rape victim's logic then, nor do I now. Inherent in the belief that only others who suffer the same trauma will truly understand is a perverse elitism that some wear as a badge of honor. Worse, their my-scar-is-deeper-than-your-scar mentality creates a whole subculture of "professional" victims. Most obvious are the Vietnam veterans who, twenty-five years after the fact, still dress in camouflage and jungle boots and whose lives appear forever gridlocked in 1968.

For them and a small number of others, including some rape victims, their victimization is a crutch, an ever-present way of absolving them of responsibility for divorce, substance abuse, unemployment, and anything else at which they have failed.

Political correctness, particularly as it relates to women and targets of sex crimes, only makes the martyrdom easier for victims to wear and more indelicate for the public to question.

The women who agreed to be interviewed, like the majority of other rape victims, I suspect, will carry their fears and scars with them for a lifetime. But to the individual, they had fought to take responsibility for themselves and their lives. They neither demanded nor expected sympathy or pity. "That which doesn't kill you," one told me, "only makes you stronger. Ultimately."

For his part, Escobedo, a classic "power rapist" save for a few unpredictable twists and turns, asked for no sympathy, either. Nor do his crimes evoke any.

With as much candor and insight as their minds would allow, the victims and their attacker tell their stories here. The facts are heinous, the recollections emotional. This, then, is the portrait of a single rapist and those he attacked, their attempt and mine to make sense of the senseless.

—Howard Swindle
Dallas, Texas
May 1995

And forgive us our trespasses
As we forgive those who trespass against us,
And lead us not into temptation,
But deliver us from evil.

—FROM THE LORD'S PRAYER

Prologue

Fall 1987

Angie Welburne* was glad her fiancé lived with her, particularly on nights like this. The tease for the late-night local news carried an update on a chillingly familiar story: "The Ski Mask Rapist strikes again in North Dallas. Police urge caution. Details at ten."

When Angie first moved from Tennessee, a black man had grabbed a woman in her apartment complex, held a knife to her throat, and raped her. Months later, a white man in a ski mask had struck repeatedly in the neighborhood, apparently without leaving a trace. Now, television was saying he was still out there. Angie had known there was a price to living in the big city and, for the most part, she had paid it. She had learned not to expect an acknowledgment when she spoke in the elevator, that she'd spend forty-five minutes driving the five congested miles to work, and that she wouldn't know her neighbor's name.

But being grabbed in the middle of the night by some pervert in a ski mask? No way. That wasn't part of the price. Each time she heard about another rape, she subconsciously put herself in the same situation. If the guy was unarmed, she knew she would fight like hell. If he had a knife, she'd probably still take her chances, even if it meant getting cut. A gun, she knew, would be different, too much of an edge. She figured she'd have to endure it.

Angie and her fiancé had moved, farther north and west, to a controlled-access apartment complex on the edge of one of North Dallas' most affluent pockets. The apartment was a rock's throw from a picturesque creek that adjoined a lavish golf course. Across the street from her apartment were $400,000 homes with manicured, landscaped lawns and whose garages sheltered the requisite BMWs, Mercedeses, and Volvos.

Not only were there twenty-four-hour security guards at the rambling apartment complex, but her fiancé had become obsessive about her protection. He installed special window locks. Constantly, he cautioned her about locking doors, and if he knew Angie would be working late at her office or going shopping, he'd nag her about looking in the backseat of her car before getting in. Recently, he had become insistent that she get a post office box so that her street address wouldn't appear on her personal checks.

"You never know who you're giving your check to at the grocery store," he told her. "It could be some weirdo or madman who'll get your address."

He was sitting beside her on the couch when the ten o'clock news came on. The Ski Mask Rapist had claimed sixteen victims thus far, and if police had any suspects, they certainly weren't acknowledging it to the media.

"What you think they ought to do with this guy when they catch him?"

Angie pondered only momentarily: "They ought to castrate him. Just cut 'em off. It's what he deserves."

"God, Angie." He grabbed his crotch, feigning pain.

It would be more than two years before police would arrest the Ski Mask Rapist. A dull ache would sweep Angie when she learned his identity, her body shaking uncontrollably.

Behind the mask was the man she had slept with, the man who worried constantly about her safety. It was the man she had planned to marry.

I. The Investigation

Sex is hardly ever just about sex.
—Shirley MacLaine

1

July 24, 1985

Woodbend Lane at two A.M. on any Wednesday is deserted, well-lit tranquillity. Residents of the tidy, tan-brick condo community abutting Richland College are white-collar eight-to-fivers. They sell, type, clerk, and teach; their efforts, on average, reap them per-capita incomes of $21,712 a year. For a very few residents of Woodbend Lane, the figure represents the financial watermark of their careers. For the youthful and upwardly mobile majority, though, the sum is only an earnest beginning that will be amortized with commissions, promotions, master's degrees, and, ultimately, double-income marriages.

Between ten and eleven P.M., in preparation for a fresh assault on the workplace, the lights in the windows go dark through the neighborhood like falling dominoes. For a good seven hours, the only creatures that move on the street are an occasional prowling dog or curious cat, their shadows cast long by the streetlights.

In one of the condos wholly indistinguishable from any other on Woodbend Lane, Camellia Michaels* lay sound asleep. Twenty-five, just shy of five-ten, and attractive, Michaels was a clerk in an office a quarter-turn westerly around Dallas from her home. In a bedroom upstairs, her two roommates, too, were sound asleep. Save for the vigilant thermostat that periodically kicked on the air conditioner against the ninety-degree night, the condo was pin-drop quiet.

By the time Michaels realized she wasn't dreaming, she was totally incapacitated, able to neither move nor make a sound. Already there was a gloved hand tight over her mouth and another, grasping a gun, beside her head. She was groggy and disoriented in her first seconds awake, and the ski mask distorted the voice. But there was no mistaking what the voice said: "Don't scream." Simultaneously and for emphasis, the barrel of the gun pressed hard against her temple.

Michaels' fate lay with a stranger whose face she couldn't fathom. Clothing, conversation, mannerisms, grooming, eyes, *any* clue to his predispositions or propensities was lost in the darkness as he pulled the pillowcase over her head.

For an eternity, she lay like an animal in a trap, dependent wholly on an unseen stalker for her existence. The animal, at least, could scream its anguish. For two hours, Michaels' mind silently fought the uncertainty while her body endured one atrocity after another.

Two hours: Enough elapsed time for a made-for-TV movie, thirty-nine commercials, a trip to the bathroom, sixteen station promotions, a raid on the refrigerator, a news update; long enough to drive one hundred miles without cheating the speed limit; enough time to fly nonstop from Dallas to Atlanta.

At four A.M., his lust sated, he left Michaels' bedroom. She heard the front door open. He slipped unnoticed into the darkness on Woodbend Lane.

By midmorning, the written accounts of Dallas' overnight tragedies, recorded by uniformed officers at five substations throughout the city and transcribed by an army of clerks, begin trickling into the Dallas Police Department's decrepit downtown headquarters. Some of the reports—warning tickets, unlocked business doors, unfounded security alarms—will be filed away in computer microchips for posterity, more than likely too inconsequential ever to be seen again by human eyes.

Others, unfortunately the majority, spawn a daily avalanche of paperwork and loose ends that are never resolved that quickly or easily. Their resolution will require a detective's phone calls, shoe leather, and door-knocking. Hourly, the reports are segregated into generic stacks that chronicle average nights in big cities: burglary, robbery, juvenile, auto theft, missing persons, assault, rape, and homicide. Reports on the latter three crimes ultimately find their way to the third floor at the Main and Harwood headquarters.

The Crimes Against Persons Division—"CAPERS" or simply "Persons," as it's known among its troops—lies at the end of a dead-end hall behind a red sign that says RESTRICTED AREA—POLICE PERSONNEL ONLY.

The three-page report on the rape of Camellia Michaels would end up on one of eight desks shoved together in the open bullpen that constitutes CAPERS' Sex Crimes Squad.

Marshall Touchton, part-time tenant of the cluttered desk, wasn't there to see it land. As he had been a day earlier, he was out looking for a rape victim. He had long since grown accustomed to one of the most predictable reactions among rape victims: Move in the middle of the night, stay with friends or family, check into a motel, catch a flight, anything to avoid another night at the scene of the crime. Touchton understood their fear; that was never a question, not with Touchton. He also understood it sometimes made his job damn near impossible.

Back in the bullpen before nine A.M., a cup of coffee to take the edge off yet another futile search, the graying detective fell into his chair to do battle with the day. It wouldn't get better. It never did. Reaching for the stack of computer-generated paper that always grew higher in his absence, he pulled off the top few sheets. He read the report like most veteran cops, only glancing at the complainant's name. He moved quickly to the blocks of information he needed: Beat, Offense/Incident, Injured Person Information, the MO (or modus operandi), and Suspect Information. Then he read and reread the uniformed officers' narrative, looking for a lead he could exploit or a pattern he could detect. Only then did he return to the top of the first page, taking in Camellia Michaels' name and phone number.

It wasn't an insensitive act; it was a reality in a profession driven more by suspects than victims. The rape victim's name was an unfortunate variable, interchangeable like the temperature on any given day. Rapists, they were the constants, their acts appearing again and again if they weren't identified and taken off the street. Undetected and unapprehended, they almost always became bolder, accounting for more victims filling more blanks.

Touchton sipped his coffee and pondered the man who raped on

Woodbend Lane. This man had raped before, he'd make book on that. This was an experienced pervert, not a one-shot opportunist bolstered by booze and testosterone. The detective returned to the last paragraph: "The suspect never appeared to be nervous during the two hours that this offense occurred. The suspect was very polite and never caused any known injury."

Whoever he was, he had forced Camellia Michaels on a slow trip through hell. After removing the gun from her head, the intruder raped her from behind. He forced her onto her back, pulled the pillowcase over her head, and raped her again. He made her submit to cunnilingus, then forced her to perform fellatio on him. And when his fantasies became even more frenzied, he went to her closet, retrieved a pair of black high heels, and made her wear them while he masturbated. Then he raped her again, ejaculating on her stomach.

Throughout the ordeal, Michaels was convinced by the feel on her body that the attacker had only dropped his trousers instead of removing them.

Touchton knew it wouldn't be pleasant questioning Camellia Michaels. Twenty-one years of probing and intruding on citizens at their absolute most vulnerable moment had not made the task any easier. He still dreaded pulling up at the curb and walking the long walk to the door. He could envision the pained grimace on a woman's face when he asked her to relive her rape.

There had been occasional surprises through the years. Cases that opened and closed in less than three hours. Sometimes, he discovered, he was a hell of a lot more interested in finding the rapist than the victim was. And not all those victims had been streetwalking whores. A few had even told him flat out not to waste his time. They wouldn't testify if he found the aggressor. Touchton never understood them, those that didn't give a damn.

Camellia Michaels gave a damn. Sitting in the living room of her condo on Woodbend, Touchton studied her eyes, at least when they weren't locked on the floor. He felt her angst, and like a thousand times before, he instinctively groped for something to say, anything that would ease her pain. Over the years, his condolences, he was certain, had sounded trite. But regardless, Touchton sensed the women usually appreciated the thought, no matter how clumsy his delivery.

Asking questions, probing, and pushing rape victims, however tactfully, into recollections they desperately want to block is no man's land. It's worse, in fact, if the detective is a man. The questioning is treacherous even beyond the awkwardness and embarrassment inherent to the rape. Increasingly, there's a political dynamic fostered by women's support groups and feminists and bred of complaints about the callousness in which rapes are investigated and prosecuted.

Their frequent allegation of insensitive questioning, embarrassing and impersonal vaginal exams, and exploitation in courtrooms, Touchton well knew, trickled down the food chain until it fell on the only identifiable face in the system—the detective on the case.

There could be no margin in the detectives' questions or comments for misinterpretation by the victim. Like the conversation a squad detective had had with a rape victim who phoned after reading in the newspaper that a multiple rapist had been arrested.

"I was wondering, do you think this is the guy who raped me?"

The woman wasn't necessarily put off that she had to recount the specifics of her case to the detective on the phone. God only knew how many cases he had investigated in the year since her attack. Still, she hadn't had an update since the original investigation. She heard papers shuffling in the background.

"No," came the response. "This isn't the guy who did you."

"*Did* you?" The rape victim was incensed. "*Did* you?" The detective had made it sound casual. People *did* lunch, for godsakes. That's what cops thought? That she had made a conscious decision on her part? By God, no one *did* her. Some sonfabitch *raped* her. And for all she knew, he was still out there, thanks to the damn cops.

Touchton made it a point to leave his cop's vernacular in the car. He spent his time with women who, understandably, were paranoid and distrustful of all men, whether they carried badges or not. Even a wrong inflection the victims sometimes read as doubt or blame. No matter the intent, if a cop wasn't mindful of the semantic pitfalls, his sergeant's phone would ring. Touchton had seen it happen to some of his colleagues in Sex Crimes. Some of the victims' complaints were justified. Others, he knew, were honest mistakes made by cops who simply didn't know what to say to overwrought victims.

The uniformed officers at the scene had done their job well with

Camellia Michaels. Touchton hadn't gotten much more. At some point, another Sex Crimes detective, analyst Evelyn Crowder, would lead Michaels through a battery of detailed questions. She would elicit specifics, like where Michaels shopped for groceries, where she had her hair cut, restaurants she frequented, the name of her pest control service, the route she drove to work, any odors she detected on the rapist, if she noticed any unusual speech patterns, even whether she wore glasses or contact lenses. The data would go into Crowder's files for comparison with other rapes.

En route back to Main and Harwood from Michaels' condo, Touchton searched his own recollection for similarities. The MO on Woodbend sounded familiar: ski mask, victim jolted from dead sleep, long time in the house, no forced entry, polite. Brazen enough to pull it off with two roommates upstairs, if he knew they were there.

Yeah, he knew. He was a serial, all right. That's what Sex Crimes needed. A new serial rapist. It was already crowded.

Ski Mask was going to be a problem. Going through past offense reports and talking with other detectives on the squad, Marshall Touchton and his colleagues suspected Ski Mask already had accounted for three, possibly four sexual assaults before he turned up at Camellia Michaels'. There were major departures in the MO, to be sure, but two decades on the street had honed Touchton's instincts. The first rape had been three months earlier, in Richardson, less than two miles north of Woodbend Lane. The most recent had been only two days before Michaels and barely two miles to the south.

Coordinating rape investigations was not an exact science. Crowder and her reams of grids, segregated by police beat, day of the week, time of day, MO, weapon, method of entry, and description, would be a major asset, no question. But the painstaking analysis also was time-consuming. It could be months before the kinks, literally and figuratively, were shaken out. In the meantime, the process of identifying patterns and isolating serial rapists depended on weekly squad meetings, the detectives' own attention to detail, and talking to each other daily.

Touchton, a senior corporal detective, had been assigned to

CAPERS for the last ten years, originally as a homicide detective. Quietly, as was his nature, he questioned the way rape assignments were made. It wasn't unusual for him to be working a pending rape in the southern part of the city only to be handed a rape that occurred twenty-five miles north. He spent half his time in an unmarked Plymouth Fury, gridlocked in congestion and looking for detours and shortcuts. It was a good thing the eight detectives on the squad talked to each other and pooled their information. A loner or an ambitious cowboy who held out could short-circuit the fragile system.

In fact, each of the three, maybe four cases similar to the Michaels case had been assigned to different detectives. The other case was being worked by the suburban Richardson Police Department.

Two days before Camellia Michaels was raped, a baby-sitter was sitting on a couch with her three-year-old charge. Kimberly Baker* caught a glance of movement from the direction of a bedroom. A man in a ski mask was pointing a gun at her. He ordered the twenty-two-year-old Baker to take the toddler to his room, then motioned her into the master bedroom, where he forced the same sex acts on her that Michaels had undergone.

Once again, there had been someone else in the house besides the victim, there had been no sign of forced entry, he had only dropped his trousers, he was calm, and the description—five-foot-eight, 150 pounds, ski mask, gloves, gun—matched Michaels' attacker.

Touchton also made mental notes of the discrepancies between the MOs in the two rapes. Baker's attacker struck in midafternoon, about three P.M. The attack lasted only fifteen or twenty minutes, and the rapist was talkative, repeatedly asking Baker, "Does that feel good?" Periodically, he would become frustrated and yell, "Get into it!"

There were two other ironic departures that grabbed Touchton's attention. After raping Baker and forcing her to perform and submit to oral sex, the attacker lectured her about keeping the sliding glass door in the bedroom locked. And he expected her to kiss him.

No detail was too mundane in trying to ferret out patterns in rape investigations. Touchton discovered Baker's rape wasn't the first attack in the last three months in which a ski-masked attacker had tried to force his victim to kiss him. Just two weeks before the Michaels attack and not two miles to the south, Vickie Wells,* a seventeen-year-old high school student, opened her apartment door to a man who claimed to be selling candy. Hearing the lock unlatch, he burst through the door, grabbed her, and dragged her through the apartment to the bedroom.

Wells hadn't been jolted awake as Michaels had, nor did she have a three-year-old's safety to worry about as Baker had; the teenager fought like hell. She kicked, clawed, and swung at her attacker as he dragged her through the apartment. Finally, he subdued her, pinning her arms and torso to the bed. And though she saw no pistol, he threatened to shoot her.

He unzipped and unbuttoned his pants, but didn't remove them. "You're good," he told her repeatedly as he raped and groped her. Then, when the teenager believed there could be no lower depth to her repulsion, he tried to kiss her. Her body might be immobilized, but her head wasn't. She turned abruptly, burying her nose and the left side of her face into the mattress, narrowly dodging his lips.

He was scorned and furious. His fist came down hard across her right eye. The blow dazed her, and she braced her body for the onslaught. Surprisingly, she heard rapid, muffled footsteps in the carpet, growing fainter. The door opened and slammed. The thwarted kiss apparently had unnerved him. He was gone.

Touchton locked on two sentences in the officer's report: "It appears the suspect may have noticed the complainant at the pool in the complex and somehow found out she is alone at home during the day. *He seemed to know where her bedroom was, which would indicate he has knowledge of the floorplan.* [italics added.]"

The suspect may have done his surveillance, all right, but he had sorely misjudged the teenager's grit. At five-foot-seven and 130 pounds, the red-haired, freckled high school student not only had fought, but unwittingly and probably more importantly, she had punished her attacker's ego by rejecting him.

Touchton smiled. The bastard. Unfortunately, he had learned from his error. Apparently, now he was carrying a gun.

Touchton continued backward through the stack of reports. He discovered another rape, this one on May 13 and just three blocks west of Michaels' condo.

As in previous assaults Touchton had found, Miriam Maloney,* a twenty-one-year-old legal secretary, had described her attacker as "apologetic" and "soft-spoken." Maloney, like Michaels, had been jolted from a sound sleep to find a gloved hand over her mouth and a gun pointed at her head. Similarly, the attacker had ejaculated not inside Maloney, but on her stomach, later wiping up the semen and the scientific evidence it contained. He left without awakening Maloney's two roommates, but not before warning her to go downstairs and lock the window through which he had crawled.

Barely more than two weeks before the attack on Maloney, Leslie Curry,* a thirty-five-year-old nurse at the sprawling Presbyterian Hospital complex several miles southwest, was awakened by an armed, ski-masked intruder as he groped for a light switch. The sex acts matched the others, but Touchton doubted it was the same man. This attacker was profane and abusive, had forced Curry to take a bath while he watched, and was a couple of inches taller and twenty pounds heavier than Touchton's man.

Touchton, however, had been a cop less than a year when he learned a basic police axiom: Eyewitness identifications were pitiful leads; trauma and fear only made them more undependable.

The nurse's hands also had been tied behind her. The light switch nagged at the detective, too; the guy he *thought* he was chasing had always preferred darkness. And this guy had ejaculated inside the nurse's vagina; his man had been too cautious for that. Still, Curry had said her attacker had brown eyes. That was a constant among the other victims. Doubtfully, Touchton pulled the nurse's file and added it to the others he set aside.

The Richardson case clearly was a match with the others. Bonnie Wyatt's* house had a real estate agent's sign in the front lawn, and for the last month, she and her two children, a preteen boy and girl, had lived there by themselves. Her husband's company had transferred him out of state. Bonnie Wyatt, a thirty-nine-year-old kitchen designer, and the kids had stayed behind to sell the house.

Around one A.M. on April 23, Wyatt was jolted awake by a ski-masked gunman who whispered: "Don't scream or I'll kill you. I'm not going to hurt you if you cooperate."

He pulled off her pajama bottoms and panties, then pulled up her shirt and bra. For what seemed an eternity to Wyatt, he groped at her breasts, telling her, "You're doing okay."

Gripped with fear, Wyatt nonetheless had the presence of mind to try psychology. She wanted him to know there was someone else in the house.

"I have a child."

"What do you have?"

"A little boy," she said, careful not to mention her daughter.

"Well, if you don't scream, then we won't wake him."

He pulled her to the foot of the bed, where he forced himself inside her mouth. Then he spread her legs and licked her vagina. Continually, he asked her, "Are you enjoying it? Do you like it?"

When he tried to enter her vagina, Wyatt could tell he was having trouble getting an erection. Yet he wouldn't stop. Finally, he forced her again to perform oral sex on him. When she tried to use her hand, he grabbed it and forced himself into her mouth. Then he tried to rape her again with his only partially erect penis.

Wyatt could sense he was becoming more frustrated. Wyatt kept trying, searching for any ploy that would make him leave. After he asked again if she was enjoying the sex, Wyatt faked an orgasm. Still he wouldn't stop. Hoping, praying that her children were sleeping through the attack, Wyatt's panic was edging off the top of the chart.

What if his frustration turned violent? She feared he would go through the house, maybe discovering and assaulting her daughter. Maybe he'd be angered that she'd lied about having a daughter and kill them all. Finally, an hour after he had jolted her awake, he ejaculated in her mouth. As despicable and repugnant as the act was, Wyatt genuinely was relieved when he climaxed.

"Don't call the police," he said. "Don't get up and don't move." As soon as she heard the sliding glass move over the metal rail in an adjoining room, Wyatt reached for the phone. It was dead; he must have cut the line. It was dark as coal tar outside.

Could he still be out there watching to see if she went for the police? She locked the sliding glass door, turned on every light in the house, and paced and cried. Periodically, the hysteria subsided long enough for her mind to seize a rational thought.

Methodically, she placed on the bed her pajama bottoms, panties, and bra that she had worn at the time of the attack. She noticed some pubic hair on her socks beside the bed and mud stains on the sheets. She was careful not to disturb them. Anything that would give police a clue about the rapist she desperately wanted to preserve.

Four hours after he left, when dawn had mustered just enough light for her to make out the house across the street, Bonnie Wyatt grabbed her children and bolted for the car. After a drive she wouldn't remember thirty minutes later, Wyatt appeared with her children in the lobby of the Richardson Police Department. It was 6:09 A.M.

"I need help," she told the desk sergeant. "Uh, I've, uh, been assaulted, uh, raped."

Touchton eyed the small stack of rape reports he'd segregated from the files and clutter on his desk. Five probables, one maybe. All within the last three months. All within about a two-mile radius of the city limits that separate North Dallas from southern Richardson. All the victims were white. Vickie Wells, at seventeen, was the youngest; thirty-nine-year-old Bonnie Wyatt was the oldest.

The veteran detective couldn't be sure because Richardson's police report had no block requiring the physical description of the victim, but he'd bet good money that Bonnie Wyatt was relatively tall, at least five-foot-seven, and slim, possibly in the 125-pound range. All the other women had been. He'd also bet that Wyatt was attractive. Camellia Michaels, his case, was striking, and the other detectives with whom he'd checked had described their victims the same way.

Except for the Wells case, the MO for obtaining entry actually was no MO at all; the victim had left a sliding glass door or window unlocked.

This guy, Touchton knew, worked hard at being a rapist. The law of averages doesn't have someone just stumbling happenstance onto an unlocked door or window in the paranoid big city. No, this guy was a prowler, checking windows and doors and making notes. Ski Mask also appeared to have singled out a specific target: tall, slim, attractive white women. That meant he probably also was a stalker. He would be cold, calculating, and methodical.

Touchton's mind seized on his new prey as he made his way home that afternoon through heavy traffic to Seagoville, one of the southern suburbs. The detective couldn't recite the exact figures, but he knew the city of Dallas had almost a million people. Dallas County, with so many suburbs you couldn't tell when you were leaving one for the other, had almost a million more. Together, that was about two million people packed into 880 square miles.

How many of them, Touchton wondered, were tall, attractive white women who lived in North Dallas and southern Richardson and who forgot to lock their doors?

The answer depressed him.

2

Dallas, for all its television romanticism and buckle-of-the-Sun-Belt arrogance, is a prima donna without portfolio. For no apparent good reason, she rises up in opulence from monotonous prairie-land obscurity. Its epicenter is flush with an I. M. Pei mirrored, rocket-shaped building, a skyscraper outlined in green neon, and buildings whose names validate the city's self-image and resolute ambition: the Plaza of the Americas, the International Apparel Mart, and the World Trade Center.

On the southwestern edge of this city that would be internationally important is a developer's tribute to a developer's city. Not to be eclipsed by downtown competitors who bought mirrored glass by the trainload, Ray Hunt, a scion of the legendary H. L. Hunt oil empire, concocted a ball-shaped observation tower atop a fifty-two-story cement stem and implanted it next to his mirrored hotel.

The tour de force of this abstract golf-ball-on-tee is a gently rotating platform, replete with glass-encased restaurant, bar, and observation deck inside the ball. At night, on final approach to the inner-city Love Field, the observation ball, its lights synchronized and pulsating, looks like a hovering interplanetary vehicle on a surreal mission to overtake the city.

Dallas, haughty and glitzy, has no visible means of support. The sparse prairie around it offers no rationale for the phenomenal wealth concentrated within its limits. There are no telltale clues to the city's sustenance, not like the rows of gargantuan aircraft hangars that sustain Seattle, or the smokestacked assembly lines that support Detroit, or the miles of piers that feed New York.

Two hundred fifty miles south of Dallas, Houston, the blue-collar, bare-knuckled big brother, is awash in the fumes of its money. Houston's dollars come from the greatest assemblage of refineries and chemical plants in the nation that, around the clock, churn out petrochemicals, plastics, pesticides, and fertilizers. The stench from the plants along the Texas Gulf Coast may cause Houston perpetual grief with the Environmental Protection Agency, but the city's bankers claim they can't smell it.

Crude alone accounts for $126.5 million a year. Houston's most prestigious buildings bear tribute to those petroproducts, with made-up, neon, corporate bastardized names like Pennzoil, Exxon, Tenneco, and Texaco. So elemental to Houston's fiber is oil that when it came time in 1960 to christen its professional football team, there was no more likely or symbolic name than the Oilers. For good measure, an oil derrick was emblazoned on the side of the helmets. Bottom line, there is no apology in Houston for being the unsophisticated, roughneck brother of the Texas clan, just blue-collar, working-class pride.

Dallas, without a decent producing oil or gas well in the county, is rich without dirt beneath its fingernails. Indeed, Dallas eschews dirt. Sprawled in a flood plain alongside an unnavigable river and atop land whose natural resources are parasitic mesquites and cedar, the legacy of the onetime frontier trading post is one of acquired finesse.

The lifeblood of Dallas is *The Deal*: designing the deal, consummating the deal, packaging the deal, underwriting the deal, insuring the deal, selling off the deal. Paper deals: high finance, insurance, joint ventures, partnerships, holding companies, advertising, public relations. The work product isn't anything you can drill, drive, or dig. It's an avalanche of paper that produces billions of dollars in interest, commissions, and debentures with no sweat, no smell, no grease, and, alas, virtually nothing tangible.

The only real products, semiconducters and computers, are nonpolluting, socially acceptable, and high-tech; besides, they actually are manufactured in Silicon Prairie in the northern suburbs of Richardson and Plano. Inside Dallas proper are 650 businesses worth at least $1 million each and more insurance company headquarters than anywhere else in the nation, including New York and Hartford.

By 1980, after a decade of looting corporate headquarters from defenseless northern cities with nosebleed crime rates and rusted-out economies, a cosmopolitan Dallas pronounced itself as the buckle of the Sun Belt. *Time* proclaimed Dallas as "The City That Still Works," where the lifetime of a pothole was less than three days and city maintenance crews jumped on clogged sewer lines within forty minutes. "Dallas," *Time* gushed, "keeps a computerized inventory of all street surfaces, curbs, gutters, sidewalks and stop lights."

And in the interim, high-rise office complexes and apartment cities sprouted like dandelions in cow patties to accommodate the corporate carpetbaggers.

Seemingly, it was flush times for the wanna-be international city on the prairie, not unlike the episodes on the television series that memorialized the city and embarrassed its residents. If Dallasites denounced J. R. Ewing as the implausible stereotype of the unprincipled, immoral Texas *bidnessman*, privately they had to admit they knew at least one indigenous entrepreneur with the same sly gene for cutting corners. Or, if they didn't move in those charity-ball circuits, the Dallas truck drivers, waitresses, and toll takers had read about real-life J.R.s in the local papers.

Throughout the seventies and eighties, the FBI's Dallas office maintained a disproportionately high number of agents assigned exclusively to white-collar crime, even establishing at one time a bank fraud task force. "Idle money and greed," explained an agent. "Word travels among con men. A three-piece suit, a leased Continental, a flash roll, and a post office box. It's always been a formula for success in Big D."

On the surface, the boom appeared vibrant enough. Developers and bankers opined that the star on the city's flag should be replaced with a dollar sign, that its official bird should be the construction crane, and its new motto: Help Wanted.

Truth be known, in the city where promiscuous Texas braggadocio is revered and even cautious reality is attributed to those weak of knee and short of vision, the boom was as soft as a baby's breath. The developers' city with laissez-faire zoning and the ten-minute, $10 million loan application was no stronger than the paper on which it was built. Over the next few years, the economy would unravel like a cheap suit. It would take with it a multitude of savings and loans that had been infiltrated by developers who predicated their futures more on the good ol' boy network than on hard-and-fast collateral. Apartment cities and office buildings, funded but incomplete and therefore empty, would litter the landscape.

Even the only team in the National Football League presumptuous enough to call itself "America's Team" was in transitory distress. Still hanging on to their image from the Super Bowl heydays, the sacrosanct Cowboys routinely found themselves humbled by the likes of cities their fans held in contempt. (Indeed, if truth in advertising extended to the NFL, honesty would have demanded another logo for Dallas' team. The only known cowboys in Dallas were passing through on their way to Fort Worth and points north. Historical accuracy would have demanded maybe an insurance policy or a computer on the side of the helmets.)

Lost in the media during the temporary frenzy of building permits, home sales, and utility hookups was a statistic that had ominous overtones in a dingy downtown building overshadowed by the sleek new skyscrapers. In the seventy-year-old Police and Courts Building at Main and Harwood, detectives found themselves face-to-face with one of the apparent side effects of a burgeoning city whose population was growing hourly.

Rape in Dallas was occurring at the rate of one attack for every 802 residents, twice that of Philadelphia and New York, two cities that Dallas' corporate raiders particularly enjoyed rebuking and exploiting. In 1984, the FBI showed 103.4 rapes per 100,000 Dallasites, three times the national average of 35.7. By the end of the first six months of 1985, Detective Marshall Touchton and his colleagues had logged 545 rapes—99 more than at the same time a year earlier.

The same sophisticated city that boasted subterranean television cameras to monitor underground sewers also had acquired a less publicized but more crass distinction: Rape Capital of America.

3

Wendy Spense* by mood and temperament was not one to bluff easily. Asleep on her back and under the covers, she awoke groggily under the suffocating feel of weight on top of her.

"Don't move," the man said, grabbing her left arm and shoving it above her head and pinning it there. "I don't want to hurt you, or I'll have to use my gun."

A white cloth, maybe a T-shirt, covered virtually all of his face. She saw that. What Spense didn't see was a gun. With her right hand, she groped for the purported weapon, flailing the free hand over his chest, stomach, and ribs. There was no gun, not that she could make out from the dim streak of light from the bathroom or that she could feel with her hand.

At twenty-nine, Wendy Spense's body offered no hint of the soft, sedentary symptoms that give away some secretaries. Her job at a downtown firm dictated long hours at her desk, but semi-religious jogging and regular workouts at a nearby health spa had left her five-foot-eight frame with 130 well-toned pounds almost devoid of body fat. She was, as her husband had said countless times, strong as a horse. Giving up maybe twenty-five pounds, she was almost as big as her attacker.

Readying her single free hand and concentrating all her body's strength in her lower back, Spense in one adrenaline-charged burst threw off the bedcovers and catapulted the right side of her body off the edge of the bed. There was a can of Mace ten feet away in the adjoining master bath. He was unarmed; if she could get to the Mace, she knew she had a chance.

Her sudden jolt caught him off balance, but he recovered like a cat, grabbing her arm and holding on just as her right foot hit the floor. Her momentum carried them to the floor near the foot of the bed, barely outside the doorway to the bathroom. He clung to her with his left hand and the weight of his body came down hard on his left elbow. With his free right hand, he rained blows to Spense's face.

"You're not cooperating!" He said it over and over again as he fought and pummeled her for dominance. His authority restored, he stared down on her, breathing heavily into her face.

"Relax," he said. "Just cooperate."

There was a calm, reassuring tone to his voice. That and the lull in the violence only unnerved her more. Her left eye was badly cut and her face was swelling into an angry red mound around it. The wound was incidental in context. What, her mind fought to know, would he do next?

Over the next hour and a half, conversation would be important to whomever this stranger was. He wasn't erect, and talking, Spense assumed, was to be his remedy.

"What size bra you wear?" he said, fondling her breasts. Then, "You like sex?"

Consistently, she answered without answering. "My husband's working late," she'd offer. Or, "My husband should be home any minute."

His twisted stream of consciousness continued ad nauseam.

"Why are you asking these questions?" Spense was frantic to know; the questions were making her more and more terrified. "Why are you doing this? You seem like a nice guy. Why . . ."

"You've got a good body. What turns you on?"

Hearing himself ask this unknown woman, a total stranger, about the most intimate parts of her life produced an erection. Finally he was able to rape her. At the last second, he withdrew from her and ejaculated over her stomach, wiping the semen away with a black nightgown he had found.

"When I get up and get ready to leave, I don't want you to scream."

The immediate relief Spense felt at his comment was short-lived and cruel. His eyes had fixed on her diamond wedding ring.

"Gimme the ring," he said.

The battle had carried them on the floor from the foot of the bed until Spense's head lay near the leg of a nightstand.

"Gimme the ring."

Moving both her hands together near her mouth, she removed the ring, momentarily fumbled with her fingers, then returned her hands to the carpet on either side of her face. Watching his eyes through the covering over his face, she slowly opened the palm of her right hand and nudged the wedding ring behind the leg of the nightstand.

"I swallowed it," she said as defiantly as she thought the circumstances would allow.

Her enterprise was more commendable than her sleight of hand.

"Look, just give me the ring," he said firmly. "I won't hurt you, and I'll leave."

She surrendered the ring and asked if she could go to the bathroom for clothes, making it sound as if it were part of the deal.

"Okay," he said, studying her closely. "Go to the bathroom."

Barely inside the bathroom, Wendy Spense grabbed the Mace and turned abruptly for the bedroom. The fear, enough she had thought to scar her soul, was gone. Lightning quick, there was rage enough to kill. She heard the front door shut. He was gone. She wasn't relieved; she was mad.

August 31, 1985

The headline on the front of the metro section of the *Dallas Morning News* was inevitable: RAPIST WORKING GREENVILLE AVENUE AREA.

Yeah? Well, I'll be damned. Detective Corporal Evelyn Crowder opted for another jolt of caffeine before sitting at her desk to read the story. The job was never easy; almost always it was worse in the glare of the media.

The stories would wrinkle brows of men who sat at big desks and who wore gold on their blue collars. There'd be memos, then briefings. Low-level street detectives who normally moved in anonymity even within their own department would find themselves singled out by the brass if the media barrages were embarrassing enough.

Being the sex crimes analyst normally meant unique obscurity; normally Crowder's name never even went on police reports. But not with a serial rapist on the loose and grabbing increasing ink in the newspaper. And not in a city with the highest rape rate in the nation, even if its public didn't notice.

The reporter's story linked six rapes to a ski-masked attacker working a section of the Greenville Avenue district in North Dallas. Known as Lower Greenville at its origination near downtown, the road heads north for a good fifteen miles, passing through about every conceivable financial stratum in Dallas before ultimately making its way into Richardson and Plano. By the time Greenville intersects with Royal Lane, it has left behind the mom-and-pop Vietnamese restaurants, the hole-in-the-wall consignment stores, and The Strip, two miles of jammed and packed singles clubs, fast-food drive-throughs, and liquor stores. Buffered from the busy thoroughfare by the sprawling Moss Park, hundreds of upper-end residences are nestled along the lush, low-lying creek areas to the north and east, barely visible from the six lanes of Greenville Avenue. It had become one of the rapist's favorite haunts.

The article carried a quote from Sergeant Jerry King in Crimes Against Persons, who at best had tread water: "Nobody's been able to identify him. This one's apparently going to be a problem. This guy is kind of sporadic."

The story continued:

While police have begun to inform residents about the serial rapes in their area, some neighbors say they are living in fear.

Crowder groaned.

One man, who asked not to be identified, said he sent his wife out of town for two weeks after the man raped a woman baby-sitting his three-year-old son at his home.

"People in the neighborhood are becoming paranoid," he said.

"We're all putting in security systems. People are writing down license numbers."

Fear and loathing in the community. As bad as the quotes were, it was another paragraph in the middle of the story that made Crowder appreciate the dilemma of the rabbit caught between the headlights.

Police say the rapist's methods are different from those of another rapist—also at large—who has attacked eight women at knifepoint in a concentrated area of East Dallas between Feb. 21 and June 29. Investigators said the rapist in the upper Greenville area may prove even more elusive.

Ski Mask, in fact, was Serial Rapist *No. 3*. FNU LNU (First Name Unknown, Last Name Unknown). Or as cops would put it, they were looking for "FaNuu LaNuu, one of the LaNuu boys." The article was accurate, as far as it went, about Serial No. 1—he had committed at least eight rapes since the first of the year. But he also had been out there maybe five years, sporadically raping at least fifteen that Crowder knew of, but undoubtedly more, since one in four or one in two rapes, depending on the supposed expert, never gets reported.

Serial No. 2 had accounted for another eight cases just between February and June in near northeast Dallas. Within the department, he was dubbed the "M Street Rapist" because he struck in a neighborhood whose street names included Monticello, Mercedes, Morningside, and McCommas and was bordered on the north by Mockingbird Lane. Thus far at least, his work was easily distinguishable from Serial No. 1 and Ski Mask not only because of geography, but because he consistently hit single-family residences instead of apartment complexes.

Ski Mask, or Serial No. 3, as Sergeant King had noted, was going to be a major problem, based on his track record thus far. Six, maybe seven victims in four months. This guy was prolific. Thank God there was a major distinction that separated him from the other two, Crowder thought. The new guy was believed to be white, and the other two were black, a fact not reported in the story. The color differences would help cut down on the confusion, as long as the victims got even a partial glimpse at their attackers. They didn't always. And while the rapists worked different areas, two of their prime neighborhoods were adjacent. Ultimately, there would be overlap and confusion trying to sort them out, particularly if the rapists were smart enough to change something about their MOs.

As usual, Crowder noted as she waded into the last four months of rape reports, Marshall Touchton had done his homework. He had plowed through the other detectives' cases, found some similarities, and fit in his Camellia Michaels case, bringing focus to the bigger picture.

Touchton was as much a creature of habit as the rapist they were tracking. The veteran cop, Crowder knew, would be checking recent uncleared homicides, looking for anyone using a ski mask in his MO. Then he'd sort through the glut of burglary reports in the neighborhood, hoping his rapist had committed a "straight" burglary, not an uncommon occurrence, and left some latent fingerprints. It was monotonous, tedious work in a city the size of Dallas, but the mining occasionally produced a nugget.

In her fifteen years as a cop, Crowder had come to believe that if she ever were raped, God forbid, Touchton was one of two detectives she'd trust on her case. Steve Hatchel was the other. Over the years, Touchton and Hatchel had earned her respect and friendship. Both cops had low thresholds for loose ends. Their uncleared cases might not stay at the top of the stack, but they were never shunted off to file cabinets like some of the other detectives' caseloads.

Evelyn Crowder turned to the Wendy Spense file, the case at hand. Spense's assailant fit the North Dallas pattern. His major MO not only fit the earlier attacks, but he also fit in the minutiae that had become Crowder's professional life as a sex crimes analyst: He wore no jewelry and no distinguishable cologne and spoke with no discernible accent.

He had been violent, all right, leaving Spense with bruises and lacerations on her head. But except for his youngest purported victim, Vickie Wells, the high school student, the other women hadn't fought him. Spense had tried. The violence, Crowder noted, stopped when he regained control over Spense; he hadn't gone out of his way to punish her, not like an anger rapist. Anger rapists inflicted damage without provocation, battering and bludgeoning their victims unnecessarily.

No, Ski Mask apparently was a power-reassurance rapist; he was into control, not punishment, and he needed to be told over and over that he was a man, a *real man*.

What was it in this guy's background that had so threatened his manhood? Sooner or later, Crowder knew, they'd find out. Serial rapists seldom ever just stopped. They were either caught in the act or shot by a pistol tucked away in a nightstand or sent away to prison on another charge. Short of a victim getting lucky and shooting them, time— *decades* of time behind bars—was the next best remedy for recidivist rapists. Rape, Crowder knew, was a young man's crime.

It took energy to prowl and lurk outside bedroom windows at all hours of the night. Put them in jail for thirty years, let them out when they're sixty or seventy, and chances are good they'll be average citizens. Veteran sex crimes detectives called it "broken-dick syndrome."

Thumbing through the rape victim questionnaire attached to the offense report, Crowder stopped and made herself a note. Wendy Spense shopped at the Tom Thumb Grocery at Abrams and Forest. She had seen the store on another victim's questionnaire. Camellia Michaels? She couldn't remember. She'd check with Touchton and go back through the files. It wouldn't be a major coincidence considering that most of the rapes had occurred within a five-mile radius. Still, it was the kind of detail that helped Crowder establish patterns.

The questionnaires were designed to isolate patterns. After every rape, and after a decent interval for the victim to regain her composure, detectives methodically led the victims through the questions printed on the form: where they shopped; where they had their hair cut; the churches, health spas, restaurants, and nightclubs they frequented; the companies that repaired their appliances and cleaned their pools; and the dry cleaners and pest control companies they used.

Portions of the questionnaire focused on the victim herself: physical build, complexion, height, weight, hairstyle, her movements on the day of the attack, whether she had received obscene phone calls, if her neighbors had been recently burglarized, the location of her work, her regular business hours, even the route she normally took to work.

But the most critical part of the questionnaire in Crowder's cryptic world were the three pages devoted to the attacker. Beyond the obvious questions about the rapist's physical description and clothing, the questions centered on voice (educated, accent); speech patterns (profane, abusive, apologetic, stutter); odors (alcohol, aftershave, body odor); characteristics and habits; how he gained access; how he maintained control of the victim; whether he showed concern for the victim; any sexual dysfunctions (erectile insufficiency, premature ejaculation); elapsed time of the assault; description and sequence of sex acts (vaginal, anal, cunnilingus, fellatio, other); any sudden changes in the assailant's demeanor; a description of any property taken during the assault; and whether there had been "any contact with the victim by the suspect since the assault."

The questions, Crowder knew, were emotionally grueling for rape victims. But they also were critical. She had seen that in 1977, when analysis of the questionnaires had helped, in part, take one of the most notorious rapists in Dallas history off the streets.

4

Beginning in July 1974, a man hit heavily in Dallas' booming apartment areas north of downtown, slipping through patio doors and unlocked windows and raping women. Usually he wore a stocking over his head, warping his facial features and distorting his voice. He normally wore gloves and frequently put a knife to the women's throats. But always, he consoled his victims, talking to them in a gentle, calm voice and ultimately apologizing before he left. Beyond the sexual attacks, none of his victims was injured. At first internally within the police department, then later in the media, he became known as the "Friendly Rapist."

Periodically, the intruder would say simply "I'm just a burglar," though he seldom took anything, and would make repeated references to his pickup truck, which no one ever saw. After the assaults, during which he usually tied up his victims, he roamed aimlessly through their apartments, occasionally helping himself to orange juice or milk from the refrigerator, which he sometimes drank while casually perusing one of their magazines. Routinely, he rummaged through the women's purses, looking at their personal photographs in wallets and reading their driver's licenses. Before leaving, he often managed to work their names into the conversation, a fact that many of the victims said unnerved them as much as the actual rape.

The Friendly Rapist case of the 1970s marked a turning point in the way serial rapes were investigated by the Dallas Police Department. He undoubtedly would have been flattered to know he was the focus of the department's first full-scale exercise to analyze and profile a serial rapist. And in the precomputer era, that exercise more often than not was exasperating.

Though computer networking between police jurisdictions one day would help standardize methodology and exchange information, most departments in the seventies and eighties relied on their own devices for detecting patterns and trends in criminal investigations. Sometimes that self-reliance meant large police agencies within the same county— sometimes even within the *same* department—didn't share either methodology or leads. As rookies, most detectives learned from old veterans, added their own experiences, and one day passed the "system" onto a new generation of rookies. And because most officers spent entire careers working toward the twenty-year pension at the same agency, there was little new blood to add a fresh perspective. As that system applied to CAPERS, there was no standardized methodology for investigating rape.

Crowder knew that if detectives were ever going to identify the Friendly Rapist and, equally important, to attribute all of his rapes to him, she needed a real system that went beyond a cop's notebook and bullpen exchanges.

Using a ruler and pencil, Crowder drew grids across a page, with columns for victim and location, date and time, MO, and description of victim. Later, she expanded her rudimentary grids to include columns for fingerprints (most of which said "none"), blood type (all of which said "unknown"), method of entry, day of week, and the police beat on which the rapes occurred.

From these master lists, the detective broke out separate headings, under which she lumped all the victims and addresses in which the rapist said, "I'm just a burglar." Crowder compiled yet another list of all the victims who had heard the attacker mention a pickup truck.

The process was trial and error, and the comparisons were maddening. Other detectives in the squad room made it a practice to avoid Detective Crowder when she had the reams of yellow legal sheets scattered over her desk and strewn along the floor around it.

Eventually, days of the week, particularly Sundays and Tuesdays, and times emerged as patterns. Then, much more quickly than it had taken her to establish the pattern, the sequence would vanish before Crowder's eyes. At one point in 1974, she discovered, he went 212 days without a rape. For 68 days, from December 12, 1975, to February 17, 1976, he lay low again. What the hell, she wondered, did that mean? Had he been in jail, maybe doing misdemeanor time? Did he travel for a lengthy time on business? Was he wealthy enough for extended vacations? Who the hell knew?

Eventually, PES (Physical Evidence Section) found latent prints outside a rape scene. Actually, they may have been the best set of latent fingerprints in the history of the Dallas Police Department. In the middle of the night, the Friendly Rapist had hoisted himself over a freshly painted fence—*before* putting on his gloves—and the prints dried solid by morning. They were there for posterity. But any elation Crowder experienced disappeared when the report came back from the FBI lab in Washington:

> Searches were conducted, insofar as possible, in our main fingerprint file, but no identification was effected.

The most prolific rapist in Dallas history, and he'd never been handled for *anything* by *any* police department in the nation. And despite witness estimates that placed him in his late twenties or early thirties, prime fodder for the Vietnam draft, he apparently had never served in the military, at least according to fingerprint files.

Crowder knew she needed more information. In virtually every case, particularly in stranger-on-stranger sex attacks, questions inevitably surfaced that weren't answered in the uniformed officers' narratives or even the detectives' follow-up interviews. Crowder and other detectives with sex crimes experience devised follow-up questionnaires for victims. They knew it would be rough asking the women for such personal information. They also knew it was the only way to catch someone as elusive and unpredictable as the Friendly Rapist. The questionnaire was implemented immediately.

Frustration, bred by another flurry of rapes, led the detective to yet another innovation, at least within the Dallas Police Department.

Crowder concocted what she called the "Tea Party." She recruited three of the best witnesses from the Friendly Rapist attacks and led them to the office of Dr. S. A. Somodevilla, the department's psychologist. For all of one afternoon, Dr. Somodevilla; Officer C. F. Baker, who had a master's degree in psychology; Crowder; and the three rape victims discussed everything they knew about the Friendly Rapist.

Psychiatric profiling, if still in its rudimentary phase, was not a new concept. Nor, as it turned out, was it always particularly helpful.

In the early sixties, Massachusetts officers, confronted with five grotesque rape-strangulation murders of elderly women by the phantom "Boston Strangler," created a psychiatric committee in an attempt to help identify him. The experts apparently fixated on the one dominant thread in all the attacks—that the victims were elderly. Their hypothesis led them to believe that the gruesome attacker, who sometimes shoved broom handles and bottles up his victims' vaginas and left them with nylon hose tied around their necks, was motivated by hatred for his mother. He apparently was retaliating, the psychiatrists surmised, against his mother's behavior that he probably saw as both sexually seductive and punitive.

When five of the Strangler's next six victims turned out to be young women, it splintered the committee's experts into smaller camps. A few surmised that the elusive rapist-killer, in killing elderly mother figures, apparently had resolved his conflict with his own mother and moved on, for reasons that were vague and unclear, to savage younger women.

Ultimately, Albert DeSalvo, incarcerated in a state mental hospital in 1965 for tying up and abusing a woman, implicated himself and confessed to being the Boston Strangler. The psychiatric profile not only had not helped locate the attacker, but critics claimed it led the investigation far afield.

The eleven women DeSalvo raped and strangled were the culmination of a perverted criminal career that had escalated from his days as the so-called Measuring Man, a bizarre character who posed as a scout for a modeling agency in a ruse to measure and fondle women's breasts and hips. In meticulously detailing DeSalvo's criminal background, author Gerold Frank discovered that DeSalvo had been indicted, but never convicted, of molesting a child years earlier. At the time of his confession, DeSalvo told investigators that he had committed so many sexual assaults that he couldn't remember them all.

DeSalvo was murdered in 1973 by fellow inmates in the Walpole State Prison while serving a life sentence.

Escalation, in fact, always worried sex crimes investigators. Just as DeSalvo had begun by fondling before turning to torture and murder, detectives knew that simply because a rapist hadn't yet killed was no guarantee that he wouldn't. And desperate times, Crowder had surmised in deciding to compile the Dallas department's first psychological profile, called for desperate acts. Friendly Rapist was an obvious oxymoron; he might not remain "friendly."

What emerged from the "Tea Party" was the portrait of a deceptively violent man.

"He has some college and his IQ is about 115, making him of above average in intelligence," the finished profile read.

Socioeconomically, he is middle-class, but his parents are probably upper-middle class. His excellent use of English, lack of profanity and even gentlemanly behavior, as well as his compulsive need for order and meticulousness suggest that this man probably works as a professional. . . . He is probably known as a nice guy, slightly introverted, and someone who doesn't make a strong impression either way, positive or negative.

The "truck" statement can be seen as a way of giving a false lead, however, at a deeper psychological level, the reference to a truck, a masculine symbol, can be seen as an unconscious attempt to convey a sense of masculinity.

Psychodynamically this man is not psychotic. . . . He is an inadequate, passive, masochistic male who identifies with his victims due to his own repressed homosexuality which he has never acted out. Thus the rape itself is a reaction formation against his fear of homosexuality. . . . The victims are not sexual objects, per se, but instruments to fulfill his ritualistic need to feel potent and masculine. This is due to the repressed homosexuality.

It was as if the rapist sensed the officers' intense push to capture him. Overnight, he curiously changed his MO, striking heavily in another highly concentrated area of apartments located almost midpoint between the two areas he had previously stalked. Crowder and other detectives begrudgingly shifted their focus, too, trying to find new patterns.

Two years into his violent spree, the Friendly Rapist turned even more diabolical and twisted. For more than a year, Crowder, as one of the lead investigators in the case, had been assigned to "call back," which meant that anytime a rape fit the MO of the Friendly Rapist, she would be called to the scene immediately. The theory was that evidence and detail from a crime scene wouldn't be splintered over three details of detectives, and that a single detective would pick up on nuances others might miss. Call backs were used on only the highest-profile cases, and most call backs lasted no more than two weeks.

The Friendly Rapist had made Crowder's life hell. A single mother with two daughters at home, Crowder found herself leaving her children alone at three A.M., only to arrive at yet another rape scene the rapist had fled half an hour earlier. She even wondered sometimes if she passed him en route to the scenes.

By July 1976, the Friendly Rapist had raped forty-nine women. He also did something that Crowder believed was designed only to taunt and embarrass the Dallas Police Department. And after spending two years of her life chasing the phantom bastard, the detective took it personally.

He broke into the apartment of a thirty-three-year-old woman, one he had raped seven months earlier. "Since this is my fiftieth time," he told her, "I decided you are going to be twice."

He was keeping track, and now he was celebrating. He was also, Crowder knew, throwing down the gauntlet. In his own mind, he had become invincible.

He also had lapsed back into his pattern: predominantly Sundays, Tuesdays, and Thursdays, generally from nine P.M. to three A.M. Using the questionnaires, pinpointing the geography of his most recent hits, and focusing on the most frequent hours and days, Crowder and the other detectives projected him for another rape in a six-square-mile area that included maybe forty apartment complexes.

For two weeks, nine plainclothes officers from the Tactical Division had worked the overnight shift in deployments of three—one group stationed along the northernmost fringe of the six-mile perimeter, another on the southernmost edge, and the last in the center of the sector. It was saturation policing. If they couldn't catch him in the act, maybe they would at least be close enough to respond when a victim phoned police, and catch him getting in his car or pickup.

The tactical officers broke off from their clusters, roaming alleys afoot, stationing themselves in shrubs, and lurking in apartment parking lots. Two weeks. Nothing. Crowder could imagine what the captains in CAPERS and the Tactical Unit were saying and who they were cussing: It was a wash, just a bunch of crystal ball crap from analysts.

On a clear predawn Tuesday in February 1977, TAC officer Barry M. Whitfield spotted a man walking slowly along a sidewalk beside the Seasons Apartments, almost in the center of the designated sector. It was ten minutes after one A.M. and the man, wearing faded jeans, a gray, hooded sweatshirt, and white sneakers, appeared engrossed by the open windows on the second floor of the complex. He stopped, stared upward at the apartment, then turned and walked in the opposite direction. The physical build, the gray sweatshirt, and the time frame fit. Whitfield approached him rapidly, pulling his badge as he neared.

The startled man in the sweatshirt bolted from the sidewalk and onto the lawn. On his third or fourth stride, he stumbled and fell. The officer noticed that he removed something from the big pockets sewn across the front of the sweatshirt. After he cuffed and pulled the man to his feet, Whitfield saw the objects from the pockets: a pair of golf gloves and nylon panty hose.

The arrest validated the hundreds of hours that had been spent analyzing and profiling. The elusive rapist had been arrested precisely where the analysts predicted he would be, and the department's first profile, generated by Crowder's "Tea Party," had been uncannily on target.

The Friendly Rapist was a personable, handsome, and soft-spoken vice president for one of the most respected public relations agencies in Dallas. At twenty-nine, Guy William Marble, Jr., had enhanced the public images of an impressive list of clients, not the least of which was the Baptist General Convention, for whom he had just completed a new campaign to promote Christianity. Marble had called it the "Good News Texas" campaign.

Marble had married his high school sweetheart, was the devoted father of a seven-year-old daughter, and lived in an affluent neighborhood three miles from where he was arrested. Save for two speeding tickets and an accident—none of which necessitated his fingerprints being taken—his name had never appeared on police records.

Marble pleaded guilty to seven counts of burglary of a residence with intent to commit rape, and was sentenced to sixty years in prison. The plea-bargained sentence, prosecutors figured, was as stout as they would have gotten in court. None of the victims could identify him, and none of the telltale fingerprints was actually found inside the apartments.

The arrest on Valentine's Day reiterated something Evelyn Crowder long ago accepted as fact: Never buy into stereotypes that paint rapists as drooling, unkempt perverts in overcoats. The corollary, of course, was ominous: Never rule out *anyone* as a rapist.

Her veteran cop's cynicism notwithstanding, Crowder was intrigued by Marble. He was courteous, even charming; he asked for no special treatment; and he was smart enough not to jeopardize a potential defense even though he appeared quietly and genuinely remorseful. Except for his glaring personality defect, she figured he was probably a devoted husband and a doting father.

Over the years, Marble and probably twenty other multiple rapists had led Crowder to a paradoxical belief that she knew wouldn't be understood among rape support groups or the Sunday School class she dutifully attended: "I hate what they do, don't understand why they do it, but I've never met a serial rapist I didn't like."

Guy Marble was only the most notorious case in point. His arrest was on television and front pages for a week, not only for what he had done, but for who he was. There were a few incredulous, stunned quotes from Marble's acquaintances and colleagues, but most were too embarrassed to acknowledge publicly that someone they had trusted so implicitly was capable of committing such horrendous acts.

Privately, though, his friends and associates were shattered in their trust and vocal in their disbelief. Not Guy Marble. He was too, well, uh, decent. Said a former colleague who had worked with Marble when both were newspaper reporters in West Texas in the early seventies: "My wife and I went to his going-away party when he left for Dallas. He was a helluva nice guy. I can't believe it. I remember his absolute favorite song was by the Eagles, 'Take It to the Limit.' I've wondered many times if that had some kind of weird significance to him. Maybe he just liked the music.

"But he was so mild-mannered, so understated in everything he ever did. I never saw him riled about *anything*. He's the last person you'd suspect of this. He was a good friend. I mean, this sounds stupid now, but he was the kind you'd trust to be around your wife. Really."

The comments would not have surprised Evelyn Crowder. Now, eyeing her newest challenge, the Ski Mask files, the detective wondered what this guy would be like. She had been pulled into this unconscious game over the years, trying to visualize a phantom she knew only by actions and mannerisms generally confined to paper. She was like a trapper studying footprints in the snow and envisioning the prey.

Things had changed in Dallas since Evelyn Crowder had drawn out the grids and compiled the countless lists to unravel the Friendly Rapist. Sleek new buildings overpowered the distinctive red, neon Pegasus on the skyline. The city council and city manager had moved into another new I. M. Pei creation, a seven-story, heavily windowed and inverted pyramid of a building that looked as if it would topple under heavy prairie winds. Presumably, it was here, somewhere in the bowels of this state-of-the-art architecture, that the surveillance camera system kept track of sewage backups and the computer logged chug holes.

But some things—including priorities, it seemed—were slower to change in the City That Still Works. Six blocks east of the fashionable City Hall, in a decaying building across from a bail bond agency, a parking lot, a plasma donor center, and a gym, Detective Evelyn Crowder would try to catch Ski Mask with the same tools she had used on the Friendly Rapist seven years earlier: A pencil, a ruler, and a yellow legal pad.

5

November 8, 1985

On any given weekday, Preston Road attracts perhaps the highest concentration of blacked-out, chauffeur-driven limos and Mercedeses, Lincolns, and Porsches in Dallas. The Preston Road Corridor is the Money Beltway of North Texas.

It begins just north of downtown in the oldest and deepest pockets of Highland Park. Fittingly, among the first addresses on Preston Road is that of Jerry Jones, proprietor of the Dallas Cowboys, which, valued at $175 million, is the highest-priced and most lucrative sports franchise in America. Along the four-lane road and for several blocks on either side lie enclaves of sequestered multimillion-dollar estates with pillared mansions and vine-covered controlled access gates.

As recently as the 1980s, blacks still couldn't drive through the area without being stopped by the Highland Park Department of Public Safety. The probable cause, surmised one tongue-in-cheek civil rights lawyer, was "probably 'cause they didn't have any business being there."

As Preston Road continues due north, it passes alongside the exclusive Dallas Country Club and on into University Park within a rock's throw of Southern Methodist University, *the* university of choice for old-line residents of the Park Cities. Ten miles farther north, beyond

H. Ross Perot's Strait Lane neighborhood and the fashionable St. Mark's School of Texas and past the perpetually gridlocked Lyndon Baines Johnson Freeway, Preston Road's homes still average in the quarter- to half-million-dollar range.

Just east of Preston Road, on a quiet cul-de-sac whose residents included a stockbroker, a lawyer, a local television anchor, a doctor, and a self-employed businessman, Constance McIntyre* finally had time for herself.

As was his custom, her husband Donald, a doctor, had bolted early for a long day of appointments with patients. Finally, Constance had coerced the kids into downing their breakfasts and had deposited them at school. The pool man had arrived and was cleaning leaves and algae out back, and Leticia, the maid, was busy inside cleaning, washing clothes, and vacuuming, all, it seemed, simultaneously. As Constance McIntyre removed her watch to get into the shower, she noticed it was already 10:15 A.M. She lamented the loss of a perfectly good morning.

The shower restored her, and she stood under the pulsating mist for a good fifteen minutes. The attractive thirty-six-year-old poked her head out of the shower long enough to retrieve a towel, and shut the shower door behind her. With the shower off, she could hear the drone of Leticia's vacuum in the next room.

Constance wrapped the towel around her and emerged from the shower, coming face-to-face with a man in dark clothes pointing a silver semiautomatic pistol at her head. She recoiled against the shock, instinctively moving a half step back against the shower door.

"Do not make any noise." He said it in a low and quiet voice from behind a blue ski mask. Except for the eerie red border around the slits for the eyes in the mask, he was dressed in solid blue—a blue ski mask, blue jeans, a blue pullover sweatshirt.

Constance McIntyre pleaded with him. "Don't hurt me. Take anything you want, but please, please don't hurt me."

"Nobody will get hurt if you do what I say. Your maid doesn't know I'm here. Take off the towel."

She pleaded again. *Pleeease.*

"Give me the towel."

His eyes fixed momentarily on her wedding ring, a brilliant three-carat solitaire with two ring guards, worth an easy $15,000. She surrendered it without question. He admired the ring, studying its reflection against the bathroom light, then stuck it into his right front pocket. He was only temporarily sidetracked by the diamond. He returned to what clearly was his primary mission. "Drop the towel."

She was too terrified to move. Abruptly, he reached out and jerked the towel, leaving her defenseless against the eyes behind the mask, which moved up and down her naked body. His left hand moved to his groin and he momentarily fondled himself through his jeans.

"Get on your knees." When still she didn't move, his voice took a lethal tone and he pushed the gun toward her: "If you don't get on your knees, then you're going to get hurt!"

She collapsed to her knees, more because her legs no longer would support her than because of acquiescence. Unzipping his pants, he thrust himself into her mouth five times. Then he draped the wet towel over her head, pushed her onto her back, and forced his way between her legs. Seconds before orgasm, he withdrew and ejaculated on her stomach, wiping away the semen with his hand.

"Keep the towel over your face," he said, "and give me five minutes to leave. If you call the police, I'll be back. And I'll kill you."

She barely heard the door to the bedroom shut over the noise of Leticia's vacuum cleaner.

Even as the private horror unreeled in Constance McIntyre's luxurious master bath, an oblivious Leticia Gonzales found the ball cap just outside the back fence of the McIntyre home. The maid put her load of trash into the can in the alley and picked up the cap. Where, she wondered, looking up and down the alley, would this have come from? The cap was blue. Embroidered on the front was an official-looking badge. Gold letters above the badge read: DALLAS POLICE DEPARTMENT.

Curious, she carried it into the house. She would show it to her employer when she got out of the shower. Minutes later, when a hysterical Mrs. McIntyre summoned a police officer to the house, the maid would give him the mysterious cap and notice the concerned look on the officer's face.

It was out of his typical neighborhood, it was in broad daylight, and it happened while a maid and a pool man were on the premises, but Detective Steve Hatchel knew Constance McIntyre's attacker was the Ski Mask Rapist. There was the mask, obviously, but the physical description also fit and, once again, the rapist had only unzipped his pants, not taken them off, and he had ejaculated on the victim's stomach, again wiping away potentially valuable evidence.

Hatchel, like the uniformed officer who answered the original call to the McIntyre house, was unnerved by the Dallas Police–issue ball cap discovered at the crime scene. Over the years, Hatchel had accepted that there were, as he put it, perverts who "had a screw loose in their heads" and who raped. But as a deacon in a Baptist church and a committed family man with two young sons, the veteran detective would never *understand* rape.

There were twenty-five hundred officers in DPD; certainly it wasn't inconceivable that one of them could have a loose screw. In the fourteen years he had carried a badge, Hatchel occasionally had seen or heard of cops crossing the line, grabbing a drink on duty or screwing a groupie in a park.

When he was hired, a veteran supervisor told him he would never have friends that weren't cops. "They're the only people you'll be comfortable with or who will accept you," his boss had said. Over the years, his last nine as a detective, Hatchel had proven the old sergeant wrong; his friends were, for the most part, fellow congregants at the Meadows Baptist Church in Plano.

The badge Hatchel carried signified his profession, not his existence. Nor was Hatchel a silent Christian; partners who crossed the line drew his wrath. Word traveled within the Blue Circle. Whatever other cops did beyond the line of duty, they didn't do it in Steve Hatchel's presence.

Listening to Constance McIntyre relive her ordeal, Hatchel didn't want to imagine that any cop could account for this kind of trauma. He knew there were other options. Maybe the ball cap was a rabbit track designed to lead investigators away from Ski Mask. Or maybe it could be Ski Mask working a little mind-screw of his own, intentionally leaving the cap to taunt his own stalkers. Serial rapists were headcases, capable of virtually anything.

Evelyn Crowder arrived at the McIntyre residence later, leading the victim through her traditional list of questions and ferreting out minutiae. The detective discovered another detail, one that had been overlooked in the patrolman's original report and, were it not for the ball cap, seemingly would have been inconsequential. The rapist, the victim told Crowder, wore "black, shiny boots, possibly Wellington-type *police* boots."

Heading back to Main and Harwood, Crowder's mind inevitably gravitated to an investigation thirteen years earlier, one that accounted for one of the most turbulent episodes in her career. She hoped the McIntyre case wasn't déjà vu. Going after one bad cop had almost gotten her killed.

In August 1972, Crowder was not among the most popular officers in the Dallas Police Department. She had been appreciative, no question about it, when she had been chosen two years earlier as one of the first ten women to become commissioned female police officers in Dallas Police Department history.

But unlike her nine female colleagues, she was not content to be a glorified uniformed secretary in the Personnel Department or Youth Division, the only two token assignments open to women police officers. She already had paid her dues, coming up through the ranks as a civilian dispatcher.

Sitting behind the communications console, she had listened hundreds of times as officers—always men, of course—had driven up on domestic battles, robberies, gunshots, and stabbings. She had visualized the scenes as she monitored their high-speed chases, and felt the adrenaline in their voices after making arrests. Even their fear when they called frantically for a backup or to report the most dreaded of all police calls: *Officer down.*

Nothing she heard, or saw in police headquarters for that matter, made her believe she would be anything other than an excellent police officer. The hours were just as bad, but the pay and benefits were better than a dispatcher's. More importantly, she had good instincts that would make her an intelligent cop, an asset that she was convinced would more than offset the physical demands of the job.

Crowder's tenacity about becoming a cop wasn't born of seventies feminism or selfless devotion to improving the collective lot of women. Not that she was blind to the need for improvement; rather, her commitment was distinctly individual. She longed for the adventure, she wanted to help people, and if she had to butt heads in a male-dominated police station, well, that was all right, too.

When finally she pinned on the badge, it was the same badge that everyone else wore. She intended, by God, to be a real cop.

After shuffling paper in Personnel for a year and a half, Crowder walked unannounced into Crimes Against Persons, the toughest and most sought-after detective assignment in the department.

She wanted to be a detective, she told Captain Jack Davis, and there were, in general, things that a female detective could do that men couldn't, particularly when it came to getting information from women victims. And individually, she promised, she'd work harder and longer than any man in the division. Defensive at first, the hard-shelled old detective was clearly bemused, even impressed by the end of the conversation. Three days later, Evelyn Crowder became the department's first female detective.

It was a hollow accomplishment. Except to emphasize their strongest belief that homicides, aggravated assaults, and rapes were no place for a "lady," the previously exclusive men's club in CAPERS refused to talk to her. After six months of silence and without a single case assignment of her own, the division's newest detective was back in Captain Davis' office.

"I don't have to be liked," Crowder told him, "but I do want to do my job. I'm not getting any cases."

Shortly after seven the next morning, a sergeant pitched a single piece of paper across Crowder's desk. It was a fresh case just reported by the uniforms. A black man shot to death in his car in the West Dallas projects. Save for the location, there was no other information on the report.

"Don't I at least get a name?" she asked.

"You know what I know," said the sergeant, a grin widening around the blackened remains of the cigar clenched in the corner of his mouth. "Guess that'll keep you busy until noon." He was still laughing at his own joke when she walked out the door.

The corpse had no ID, and from the looks of him and the decrepit car that contained his remains, the deceased was too down and out to have been shot to death over money. Too poor to have bought or sold drugs. This was a crime of passion, the rookie detective surmised, and there probably was a woman somewhere in the equation.

The public housing complex where his car was parked was ground zero for one of Dallas' highest-crime-rate neighborhoods. Knocking on doors in the projects produced a street name for the deceased. Making her way down the row of ramshackle red brick apartments, Crowder came up with the dead man's real name. Yeah, yet another tenant ultimately confirmed, there had been some bad blood over a girlfriend. The dead man's competitor for the woman, in fact, lived two doors down.

When the man opened the door, Crowder could see beyond his shoulder a .38-caliber pistol lying on a table. Uninvited, she maneuvered around him, brushing his shoulder as she entered. As she asked her questions and he unconvincingly maintained his innocence, both detective and suspect edged their way unobtrusively toward the table, each trying to act unaware of the gun that was in plain sight. The rookie detective realized she was playing high-stakes mental poker that could get her killed. Finally easing her way to within five feet of the table, Crowder lunged, securing the .38 and drawing her own pistol from her purse. Only when she had the suspect handcuffed did she have time to call for backup.

She dispatched the weapon to ballistics with the uniforms, who also hauled the suspect to jail. After a futile canvass of the projects for the female portion of the love triangle, Crowder headed back to Main and Harwood. En route, she got a call from the physical evidence section: The slug in the corpse's head matched the suspect's .38, which, tidily enough, also bore his fingerprints.

At one P.M., Detective Crowder appeared at the sergeant's desk. She handed him her narrative report, a book-in record, and a prosecution report.

"I apologize," she told the surprised sergeant. "I know you wanted this wrapped up by noon, but traffic was a bitch."

The case hadn't won Crowder friendship in Persons, but it had meant instant respect, however begrudging. Given a choice, respect meant a hell of a lot more than friendship to the only woman detective in the division.

Officer Felix Floria Florio would take that away. And for meddling in his affairs, he also would make Evelyn Crowder a pariah in her new world. Word in the department was that Crowder was going after Florio, a fellow cop, to make a name for herself. Worse than the earlier silent treatment, Crowder's phone was ringing in the middle of the night with anonymous death threats. The calls were from Florio's buddies, cops just like her.

Felix Florio was a police recruiting poster boy. He was a favorite patrol partner among his subdivision colleagues and known as a stand-up cop who wouldn't let a few administrative rules get in the way of making an arrest or taking care of his buddies. Lean and darkly handsome, a trendy off-duty dresser and perpetrator of more bullshit than a small herd of Longhorns, Florio enjoyed among his fellow cops an envied station in life as a carouser and aficionado of models and flight attendants. In the clubs near Love Field where flight attendants were thick as five o'clock takeoffs, bartenders and bouncers knew the cop by his first name.

Most recently, Florio had been bound to a desk in Research and Planning, the unfortunate result of what he claimed was the accidental firing of his .45-caliber automatic. More unfortunate, the slug from the automatic struck and killed Karen De Phillips, the twenty-one-year-old Braniff flight attendant he had been dating. After driving the wounded woman to the emergency room at Parkland Memorial Hospital, Florio mysteriously had vanished for eighteen hours.

In the midst of an intensive manhunt, the thirty-two-year-old officer presented himself to colleagues, explaining that he had been so distraught over the accidental shooting of his girlfriend that he had driven to a park where, for hours, he had contemplated killing himself.

The Dallas County grand jury apparently bought Florio's story, one that had De Phillips bumping into him as he retrieved the gun from beneath a pillow, making it discharge accidentally. Grand jurors declined to indict him, and Florio was reinstated and reassigned to a desk in Central Headquarters.

It was only by chance and an uncommonly talented police artist that Evelyn Crowder and her partner, B. B. Norris, stumbled onto Florio ten months later. Crowder and Norris had been assigned to the so-called Police Imposter Cases, two attacks in which a man flashed a badge, convinced women that he had to search their apartments, then sexually assaulted them. In the first attack, he raped the woman, then stole $80 from her purse.

The second attack seventeen days later was vicious and had all the earmarks of a sadistic rapist who went out of his way to hurt his victim. After supposedly searching the twenty-two-year-old secretary's apartment and finding nothing, the purported cop asked if he could use her bathroom before leaving. He emerged naked and brandishing a pistol.

"You told me you were a cop."

"I am," he said. "Do what I tell you or I'll kill you. Don't think I won't. Don't give me any shit, you motherfucker."

Holding the pistol to her head, he forced her to commit oral sex. When the ordeal was over, he waved the gun toward the bathroom and told her to clean up. When she finished, he motioned her back to the bed, where he told her to change the sheets. With her back turned to him and without provocation, he brought the pistol down hard on the back of her head, knocking her to the floor. He straddled her body, wrapped a towel around her neck, and choked her unconscious. Removing a pillow from the bed, the attacker placed it over her head, pushed the barrel hard against it and pulled the trigger. Left for dead, the woman miraculously came to and crawled a bloody trail to the manager's apartment. She survived the gunshot wound to her right temple, but the pistol-whipping cost her her left eye.

Even as she recuperated, the woman met Crowder downtown to help a police artist sketch a composite of her attacker. The woman's recollection was uncanny, and she insisted on meticulous detail that most victims would have overlooked. As the artist added the final touch, both he and Crowder were stunned. Outside the office and out of earshot of the young victim, both officers marveled at how remarkably similar the sketch was to a cop they knew. His name was Felix Florio.

The woman later picked Florio's photo from a stack of mug shots. Still, the victim said, she needed to see him in person to be positive. With no more than a sketch and a tentative ID on the photo, Crowder knew she could never force Florio into a lineup.

Crowder did, however, know the officer's work hours, and she'd seen him several times among the early-morning glut of people emerging from the same bank of third-floor elevators. Crowder arranged for the victim to meet her at headquarters the next morning precisely thirty minutes before Florio normally came to work.

Without telling the woman the meeting actually was an impromptu lineup, the detective gave her a cup of coffee and positioned her on a bench facing the three elevators. Crowder studied the victim's face as maybe a hundred clerks, secretaries, and cops exited the elevators over the next half hour.

Suddenly, the woman gasped, almost spilling her coffee. "That's him!" the secretary said in a loud whisper. "He's got a mustache now and he didn't then, but that's him! That's him!" The man she pointed to was Officer Felix Florio.

With the visual identification, Crowder had enough to force a lineup. The victim didn't falter; Florio was her man. She was stunned when she learned he really was a cop.

Crowder, however, had another hurdle to overcome. Both sexual assault victims had been adamant in their description of a large, ugly, off-white scar on the inside of their attacker's left thigh. Smugly, Florio had readily consented to dropping his trousers; he bore no scar on either leg. How, Crowder wondered, could both victims have been mistaken about seeing the same scar?

Crowder and Norris got a search warrant for Florio's house. The search for evidence was futile until the officers discovered the false-front compartment in the ceiling of a closet. Inside, they found a theatrical makeup kit. Among the fake mustaches, beards, and wigs were several makeup pencils. When she ran the white one over the inside of her forearm, she knew she had the answer to the mysterious scar. And a case.

Even as Florio was being charged with attempted rape, the Blue Circle accommodated its own. Florio, suspended as a suspect for the second time in less than a year for a violent act, was arraigned and booked in an interrogation room in Crimes Against Persons and never was processed through the jail. And while reporters and photographers staked out the front of the jail, Florio's cop buddies slipped him to a rear elevator and unnoticed out a back door.

It was not the only special treatment accorded Florio. In the aftermath of Florio's most recent arrest, the foreman of the grand jury that earlier no-billed Florio in the flight attendant's death claimed police misled his grand jury. According to the foreman, officers told jurors that if they agreed not to indict Florio in the attendant's death, he would be fired from the police department.

In fact, he had been reinstated and reassigned to Planning and Research, a position that ironically had allowed him immediate access to information on Crowder's and Norris' investigation into the so-called Imposter case.

In the nine months it took for Florio's case to come to trial, Crowder's phone continued to ring with anonymous threats from cops. She tried to ignore the ominous glares in elevators, and she was only moderately relieved when a jury found Felix Florio guilty and sentenced him to fifty years in prison.

"Messing with one of our own," she'd been reminded in an anonymous call before the trial, "could get you hurt real bad."

Getting hurt real bad, in fact, was why Evelyn Crowder was a sex crimes analyst. It was not the job she wanted, but it was her only option if she wanted to stay in Detectives. Her days as a detective in CAPERS had been successful even by the most jaundiced, macho measure. But all that ended with the accident.

After a long shift one night, Crowder apparently dozed off on her way home, lost control of her car, and slammed into a utility pole. She lay in a coma for days before she regained consciousness. When finally she awoke, she had lost one eye, had a mangled hip that required replacement surgery, and endured more pain than she believed possible. She had to get medical and civil service waivers to even get the desk job. She was lucky to still be on the force, and she knew it. Still, shuffling paper wasn't why she had become a cop.

Mercifully, some things had changed within the Dallas Police Department since the days of the Florio investigation. Quietly, swiftly, investigators from Crimes Against Persons now assumed the worst; immediately the detectives began treating the Constance McIntyre case as if the suspect were, in fact, a cop. All the information about the McIntyre rape, along with the other assaults committed by the Ski Mask Rapist, would be closely held among selected investigators from CAPERS.

The ball cap the maid had discovered in McIntyre's alley appeared to be regulation police issue. It was an adjustable cap, and the strap in the back was set in the third hole. It was bagged as evidence and sent to SWIFS, the Southwestern Institute of Forensic Science, for analysis. The chances for prints on fabric were nil; if investigators were lucky, they could end up with hair or maybe some substance that had been spilled on it. It was a long shot.

Crowder obtained a sketch and a photo of McIntyre's solitaire wedding ring, along with a description of her husband's Piaget wristwatch, which the attacker apparently took from a dresser on his way out, and passed the information to the pawnshop detail. The ring and watch retailed for $17,725. Most professional burglars used their own fences, not pawnshops where they got about ten cents on the dollar. It was a good heist, but the chances of this guy taking the loot to a pawnshop weren't good. Another long shot.

Under the Texas Open Records Act, the media are guaranteed access to original offense reports. Like the previous Ski Mask offense reports, the beefsheets routinely contained detailed narratives about how the crimes evolved. But the uniformed patrolman who answered the McIntyre call, Officer Scott Towns, included only a terse three-line narrative on the McIntyre attack: "Complainant McIntyre stated that at the listed time and date, listed suspect (an unknown white male, approximately 25) entered the listed location and forced the complainant into the bathroom where the suspect raped complainant at gunpoint. NFI [No Further Information]."

Specific details, including finding the mysterious Dallas Police Department ball cap at the rape scene, were contained in a lengthy supplement which, by Texas law, was not releasable to the public.

Withholding the possible police connection to the rape from the regular reports was not happenstance. Investigators legitimately argued that making public their investigation of a cop's potential involvement would jeopardize their case. And if that consideration weren't enough, police brass no doubt viewed the disclosure as bad press, conjuring up a headline along the lines of POLICE SEARCH OWN RANKS FOR ELUSIVE RAPIST.

Hatchel and Touchton buried themselves in the department's duty rosters, trying to isolate all officers who would have had days off, been on vacation, or taken sick time during the McIntyre assault. It was a gargantuan task considering the size of the department and the fact that two full shifts of officers would have been off duty at ten-fifteen A.M. on any given morning.

The more they immersed themselves in the logs, the more futile the process became. The list of officers off duty at the time of the rape totalled two thirds of the force, about 1,650. Approximately thirty percent of those would be women and minorities, still leaving about 1,155 white male cops. How many of them, the beleaguered detectives wondered, would be under, say, thirty-two, about five-foot-eleven or less, and weigh from 150 to 185 pounds? God only knew. It was a hell of a long shot.

Captain John Holt and Sergeant Jerry King of CAPERS met with the department's computer experts, who devised a trap of sorts that would tell them when any computer terminal was used to call up any of the Ski Mask rape reports. If an officer wasn't assigned to the investigations and he tried to dip into the department's mainframe computer for information on the offenses, he was going to have some explaining to do.

Crowder, meanwhile, began poring over all of the previous Ski Mask Rapist reports yet again for any clue, the use of police slang or terminology, the presence of a walkie-talkie, anything that would indicate the attacker could be a police officer. There had been two other attacks by Ski Mask since Wendy Spense was raped on August 29 and before the attack on Constance McIntyre, making him good for at least nine, maybe ten attacks in less than seven months.

On September 27, he raped Mary Ann Abbott,* a thirty-six-year-old woman who had been separated since April from her husband. Abbott's two daughters, three and five, were asleep in the bed with her during the attack. Almost a month later, on October 26, Janice Matthews,* a twenty-five-year-old buyer for a department store, was raped in her apartment about half a mile from Abbott's house in northeast Dallas.

In both cases, the attacker talked incessantly, asking if they enjoyed the sex and coaxing them to "talk dirty." In each case, he ejaculated outside the women's vaginas. Four days after he attacked Abbott, at about one in the morning, he called her unlisted number. "Do you know who this is?" he asked. The voice was unmistakable. She slammed the phone down and called police.

The phone call to Abbott mildly interested Crowder. Police officers could get unlisted numbers. Or anyone could read it off the dial if they had been inside the house. Nothing conclusive. The call itself was curious, but not unprecedented, particularly for power-reassurance rapists.

The guy, Crowder theorized, wanted a breathless Mary Ann Abbott to say the sex was the best in her life, that she couldn't live without him, and, oh, please, please, come back. His life depended, apparently, on being told that he was a real man, maybe in a class by himself. Power-reassurance rapists were that way.

He was, Crowder knew, a disgusting, perverted asshole. But she'd give her next paycheck to know if he also carried a badge.

We have to recognize that sex and violence are fused for men into domi-
nance; and that not only is violence sexual but also sex is consistently used
to assert dominance.

—Andrea Dworkin, *Letters from a War Zone*

The typical offender's motivation is to express power, dominance, control and
anger. Numerous studies have proven and professionals agree that rape is a
crime motivated by violence or misdirected aggression and NOT SEX.

—From information distributed to rape victims by Victims Outreach, a
nonprofit Dallas support group

6

"I hate it when feminists say that rape doesn't have anything to do with sex, that it's just about power and control. They're full of crap. And when I hear them say it, I know that they've never been raped."

Elizabeth Eckstein, educated, professional, fiery-eyed, attractive, and single at the time, became a victim of one of the handful of serial rapists who plagued Dallas in the late 1980s and early 1990s. She had been on her own for years, and even half a decade after the rape, she can't believe she allowed herself to become a victim.

"He knocked on the door and said I needed to call the police because he had just chased away a man who was trying to get in my bedroom window. I was thankful, and I let him in. I *wanted* him to be there while I called the police. It made me feel safe. I was glad to know there were men like that.

"And while we were waiting for the cops to come, the bastard pulled a gun on me, forced me into the bedroom, and raped me. I think he got an extra charge just knowing that the cops were on the way while he was raping me. And *I'm* the one who let him in.

"I've heard so-called experts tell women that rape isn't about sex, that it's about control. That makes me sick. Let me put it this way. When he came in waving his gun, he definitely was in control, no doubt about it. But he didn't use the control to make me grab my cat by the tail and twirl him over my head. He didn't make me write hot checks. He didn't make me vacuum the apartment.

"He raped me, dammit. He screwed me without my permission, and threatened to kill me if I resisted. And he didn't leave until he got off. From my view—and it seems like I ought to be in a position to know —it damn well was about sex."

It is distinctively human that effect and impact always are more obvious than cause and motivation. A devastated homeowner standing amid the debris that once was his home may not understand the meteorological theory behind a tornado, but he has precious little doubt about the abject destruction left in its wake. The defendant in a divorce suit knows that the outcome will be the end of a marriage. But the years-long path of interminable rough spots and hard falls may blur together with time and defense mechanisms, obscuring a specific reason for divorce.

Groping to explain the inexplicable—another human trait—people are left with answers that they know aren't really answers at all: "I guess I survived because it wasn't my time to go." Or, "We got a divorce because we had grown in different directions."

There are no crimes in the criminal justice system whose causes are more crystal clear than burglary and theft; they are, pure and simple, bred of greed. Greed, in fact, is such a common denominator in crime that the first axiom a new investigator learns is "Follow the money, you'll find your suspect." Burglary and theft are, in prosecutors' vernacular, "throw downs," cases in which motive—greed—always is a given and in which only possession or maybe opportunity have to be proven.

Drug law violations are equally conspicuous: The user pays for the high; the dealer walks with the money. Aggravated assault, even homicide, the heinousness of which society has condemned as a capital offense for its perpetrators, many times can be traced to greed.

Rape, though, is a breed apart and occupies a unique place in the criminal code. Like molestation and incest, rape falls in a skip zone of criminology, as much a morass of morality, psychiatry, and cultural taboo as it is of illegality. Its effect is devastatingly obvious, but virtually none of those closest to rape, certainly not the shamed victim or even sometimes the embarrassed perpetrator, can adequately explain its cause. And curiously enough, it wasn't until relatively recently that the dynamics of forcible rape were even widely investigated by academic researchers.

Perhaps the common thread that runs through all rape research is that, in fact, there is no stereotypical rapist. Most current research is consistent, however, in that rapists tend to be young, generally under twenty-five, many are married, and most have had some kind of socially acceptable sexual relationship with women.

Ironically, rapists frequently are passive personalities to the point of feeling weak and inadequate. They may be slightly above average in intelligence and below average in independence. They possibly may be the product of a cruel and abusive mother or a neglectful or absentee father. And often as not, they may have been drinking immediately before or be drunk at the time of committing the rape. Rapists appear proportionately across racial lines, and their victims generally are of the same race.

But while most researchers may agree generally on who rapists are, their theories on the causes and motivations of rape aren't nearly so tidy. One rationale, particularly espoused by some feminists, is that men hate and fear women; rape merely is a form of punishment and a means of oppression.

Susan Brownmiller terms rapists as "dreary and banal" and refers to them as "punks."

"Rather than society's aberrants or 'spoilers of purity,' " Brownmiller writes, "men who commit rape have served in effect as front-line masculine shock troops, terrorist guerrillas in the longest sustained battle the world has ever known."

By extension, so her global theory of Man vs. Women goes, rape is the masculine conspiracy to force women into social, political, and economic servitude. That conspiracy, apparently, is aided and abetted by male-dominated society and law.

Said feminist Andrea Dworkin in a speech originally given to the Committee Against Sexual Exploitation in Dublin in 1983 and later printed in *Letters from a War Zone*:

The feminist fight against violence against women is also necessarily a fight against male law: because the way the law really works—in rape, battery, prostitution, and incest—women are its victims.

The state, then, keeps women available to men for abuse—that is one of its functions. The dominance of men over women through violence is not an unfortunate series of accidents or mistakes but is instead state policy, backed by police power.

Conversely, another hypothesis has men raping in a symbolic attack against a dominating, castrating mother. Yet another theory is that rapists have so little self-esteem and feel so inadequate about themselves that they are convinced no reputable woman voluntarily would have sex with them. There also is the genetic-based "bad seed" or "born bad" theory in which unusual or defective chromosomes purportedly create criminals, including rapists, at birth.

"Rape," according to Dr. Richard T. Rada, a former professor of psychiatry at the University of New Mexico Medical School and a preeminent rape researcher, "is a crime of control, power, and dominance." He continues:

> The primary motive in the rapist is the desire to control the victim in the specific instance of rape and, by extension, all women. In this sense, the aggressive component appears to be more dominant in rape than the sexual component. In fact, for many rapists the sexual act itself appears to be less important than the ritual of the rape event, which is more often carefully planned than impulsive.

However, there can be distinct differences, according to Dr. Rada, in the basic motivations for rape: "For some the manner of raping is primarily sexual; for others, it is primarily aggressive; and for others, it is primarily humiliating."

Noting that rapists previously were considered as primarily antisocial personalities, recent research by Dr. Gene C. Abel, Dr. Joanne-L. Rouleau, and Jerry Cunningham-Rathner discovered "that many of them have a specific sexual preference for aggressive acts against their victims, and they rape in order to satisfy their sexual arousal."

But perhaps no researcher has a more bare-knuckled or commonsense explanation for criminal motivation than Dr. Stanton E. Same-now, a clinical psychologist who has treated criminal offenders, including rapists, for more than twenty years at a federal psychiatric hospital in Washington, D.C. In his book *Inside the Criminal Mind*, Dr. Samenow debunks much of the existing cause-and-effect explanation that portrays criminals as victims themselves, the unfortunate products of broken homes, alcoholism, unemployment, drug addiction, television violence, poverty, or vague and passionate impulses.

"In short, psychological theory, in its current state," Dr. Samenow writes, "is more misleading than illuminating in explaining why people become criminals. Far from being a formless lump of clay, the criminal shapes others more than they do him."

People commit crime, the psychologist says simply, because they think differently than the majority of law-abiding society and they base those bad decisions on ego and instant gratification. And they feel too impatient and superior to the rest of society to commit their time and energy to working hard at a job or relationship to make them successful.

"People who rape," Dr. Samenow writes,

are irresponsible in other ways and are likely to have committed other kinds of crimes even though they may not have been caught for them. Rape is just one expression of their attempt to dominate others, to seek excitement in the forbidden, and to build themselves up. There is no attempt to punish women, nor does the offender believe that a nice woman wouldn't have sex with him. In fact, he believes that he is irresistible to all women. At stake in a rape is the criminal's affirmation of his image of himself as powerful and desirable. The assailant believes that his victim already wants him or will want him once she gives him a chance. Her attempts to ward him off only heighten his excitement. . . .

A rape or child molestation is a dot on the landscape of the criminal's irresponsibility. . . . Even if one conditioned a criminal so that deviant sex behavior no longer appealed to him, that would not stop him from injuring people in other ways. Sex is only one outlet for the excitement that he seeks at the expense of other people.

Demystifying rape even in academic circles is like trying to put a handle on Jell-O. And because more than a few prosecutors have floundered trying to unravel that complexity for juries made up of average citizens, more than fifty-one percent of accused rapists, according to the FBI's most recent Uniform Crime Reports, have walked from courtrooms free men.

Those are just the rape cases that make it to trial. The Senate Judiciary Committee's report *Violence Against Women: The Response to Rape: Detours on the Road to Equal Justice* found that "62 percent of the reported rape cases never result in the apprehension of an individual for the crime." Worse, the *Violence Against Women* report, released in 1993, discovered that a rape case, once filed, "is more than twice as likely to be dismissed as a murder case . . . nearly 40 percent more likely to be dismissed than a robbery."

Those figures, of course, reflect the disposition of rapes *reported* to the criminal justice system. In 1990, according to the FBI Uniform Crime Report, an accumulation of statistics from all the nation's police departments, 102,560 women claimed to have been raped. That number, virtually all experts agree, is only a fraction of the actual number of rapes committed.

A nationwide survey by the National Victim Center and the Crime Victims Research and Treatment Center of the Medical University of South Carolina estimated, for example, that the number of women raped in 1990 actually was 683,000—*six times greater* than the number reported to police agencies. And even that figure, researchers said, didn't include female victims under the age of eighteen, which would drive the number of rapes even higher.

"Rape remains the most underreported violent crime in America," according to the victim group's report. "The National Women's Study [a component of the main report] found that only 16 percent, or approximately one of every six rapes, are ever reported to police."

The criminal justice system relies on criminal codes that almost wholly are predicated on physically demonstrable evidence of wrongdoing: loss of property, possession of drugs, bodily injury and death. While there frequently is physical evidence in rape cases, some, however, are more obscure and intangible, demanding more sophistication and sensitivity than the black-and-white, garden-variety justice system can sometimes fathom.

By criminal code, rape, like armed robbery, is an assaultive offense committed under threat of bodily harm, frequently with a knife or a gun. But unlike robbery, rape transcends the criminal code. It is a crime not only against the peace and dignity of society, but also against the individual psyche, the theft of well-being so intrinsic and vital that it never can be compensated or restored to its original state.

Rape is the defilement of intimacy, the ultimate invasion and violation of a woman's innermost being. From the time little girls are old enough to remotely understand, their parents tell them there are parts of their bodies that shouldn't be touched by anyone except themselves.

By prepubescence, some parents have extended that warning to include sex: Sex is special and pure, an intimacy to be shared only with someone you love. Under any other circumstances, girls are told, sex is sordid and immoral.

Sex taken violently under threat is an emotional train wreck that derails not only the law but, more importantly, the sanctity of the soul. Rape strips its victim of her power to make determinations about perhaps the single most intrinsic value in her existence: the right to share intimacy. That loss of control and power of self-determination is a scar on the soul, a pox on the spirit.

Save perhaps for homicide, rape more than any other crime defies equitable treatment under the law. If a television set and VCR are worth two years in prison for a burglar, what is the punishment for a man who assaults a human being's very existence? If a dislocated vertebra in a car wreck is worth $500,000 in pain and suffering, what is fair compensation for a shattered psyche?

Not surprisingly, the National Victim Center's *Rape in America* survey showed that rape stigmatizes its victims like perhaps no other crime short of incest and child molestation.

Among the top four concerns expressed by rape victims were their families finding out they had been raped, people believing the rapes were their fault, people outside the family learning that they had been raped, and their names being made public by the news media.

For all those reasons and more, victims of rape frequently don't call police. The notion of telling a police officer, a total stranger, about the depravity they endured, of undergoing a physical examination by yet another stranger, of possibly confronting her attacker in a public court-room, and ultimately of pitting her word against his frequently is as terrifying as the actual rape.

More often than not, the victim of rape simply withdraws into her private anguish, relying on whatever courage she still maintains and on time to ultimately salve the guilt, anger, and shame from a naked mo-ment in her life over which she had no choice.

"If the *stigma* of rape was not *still* a very real concern in victims' eyes, perhaps fewer rape victims in America would be concerned about invasion of their privacy and other disclosure issues," the *Rape in Amer-ica* report said.

Nor are all victims mentally able to face the intense personal scrutiny that reporting rape inevitably entails. The *Rape in America* report reveals that thirty-one percent of rape victims suffer from post-traumatic stress disorder, a trauma-induced mental disorder in which victims' minds involuntarily and realistically relive the trauma weeks, months, even years after the sexual attack. The aftermath of rape, in fact, pushes some to the breaking point.

"The fact that 13 percent of all rape victims had actually attempted suicide confirms the devastating and potentially life-threatening mental health impact of rape," according to the *Rape in America* report.

Theories are like relatives; everyone has them, and some are more ac-ceptable than others. The cop on the street has heard all the theories. Even the most implausible and far-fetched are interesting, but the rape investigator relies on those parts that are compatible with his experi-ence. While helpful maybe in explaining his suspect, the rape detective doesn't have to know *why* the man rapes. His job is simply to catch him before he rapes again.

The rape detective, like a doctor confronted with an unknown virus, focuses on the symptom. Police work is about the manifestation of the crime, not its psychological cause. And in that regard, there's a luxury in the detective's black-and-white existence: If it's a violation of the criminal code, it doesn't matter why.

Still, the best detectives glean what they can from the multitude of psychological data on rape and sex crimes, and mesh it with what they see firsthand at rape scenes and in interrogation rooms.

One of the more valuable tools excerpted from academic research and widely implemented by street cops has been the categorization of rape, as detailed in *Men Who Rape: The Psychology of the Offender*, by Dr. A. Nicholas Groth with H. Jean Birnbaum. Dr. Groth, director of the Sex Offender Program at Connecticut Correctional Institution at Somers, breaks the crime into three distinct categories: anger rape, power rape, and sadistic rape. The Groth model, embraced by police, appears to be widely accepted among other rape investigators and researchers as well.

Using eight indicators, ranging from the amount of aggression used in the attack to the demeanor of the rapist's language, a detective is able to establish broad patterns and characteristics about a rapist.

In anger rape, for example, the rapist appears to be exacting retribution for some perceived wrong or injustice he has suffered, and he uses more physical force than necessary to overpower his victim, often leaving her battered. The attack is impulsive and spontaneous, the rapist is angry and depressed, his language is abusive, and the crimes are episodic.

Sadistic rape, which accounts for the smallest percentage but is most life-threatening of all rapes, is characterized by physical force that often is symbolic and eroticized. The sadistic rapist preplans his attack, he is intensely excited, his language is commanding and degrading, and he may kidnap, torture, and mutilate his victim in ritualistic acts before killing her.

In power rape, the attacker uses threats and only enough force to control his victim; any physical injury to the victim would be inadvertent instead of intentional. The rapes generally are planned in advance and occur after persistent fantasies of rape. The rapist is in a state of anxiety, and he gives orders to the victim and asks her personal questions.

Writes Dr. Groth of power rapists:

Whatever he may tell himself to explain the situation, at some level of experience he senses that he has not found what he is looking for in the offense—something he cannot clearly identify or define is missing or lacking. He does not feel reassured by either his own performance or his victim's response to the assault, and, therefore, he must go out and find another victim, this time "the right one."

His offenses become repetitive and compulsive, and he may commit a whole series of rapes over a relatively short period of time.

No notice is taken of a little evil, but when it increases it strikes the eye.
                                                                    —Aristotle

7

November 19, 1985
To: All PES [Physical Evidence Section] Personnel
Subject: Ski Mask Rapist

Information gathered from the investigation of this individual indicates that at times during the sexual attack, he is removing his gloves possibly leaving fingerprint evidence on the pillows, sheets, or other smooth cloth materials he touches. The Dallas Sheriff's Office recently developed a print on a pillowcase using the laser and are willing to utilize the laser in this investigation.

Investigators answering a sexual assault offense believed to involve the Ski Mask Rapist should collect the sheets, pillowcases or other smooth cloth items from the scene. These items should first be submitted to SWIFS for semen, blood, hair or other body fluid analysis. . . . Once SWIFS personnel have completed their work, the item will be transferred to DSO for examination by the laser.

                            —Capt. Don Whitten, DPD, Identification Bureau

December 13, 1985

"I feel guilty about this. This is all just a fantasy. I've never done this before, and I don't plan on doing it again."

Terrified and naked with two pillowcases wrapped around her head, Billie Jean Rider* had trouble reconciling what sounded like genuine remorse with the brutality of the man in the ski mask. For two hours he had fondled her, examined her body with the lights on, and raped her.

At one point, when Rider had begun shaking violently, the tortured combination of fear and December chill coming from the open window through which he had crawled, the rapist had covered her with a blanket.

When finally he had ejaculated on her leg ("I won't come inside you and get you in any trouble"), he wiped her leg clean with a washcloth from her bathroom.

Before leaving, he browsed through her bedroom like a potential buyer touring a house for sale. "These are beautiful pictures you've got here," he commented. "I like your taste."

Detective Marshall Touchton was neither moved by the rapist's bedside manner nor would he give him high marks for honesty.

" 'Never done it before,' my butt," Touchton told Evelyn Crowder. "Maybe not more than ten or eleven times. That's those we know about. And 'never do it again'? I guarantee you he's out there prowling for another victim before I can get this damned report finished. That devil can spot an open window from across town."

Crowder, who had two daughters of her own, nodded with resignation and a tinge of sadness. She had seen more Billie Jean Riders than she could remember. Young, pretty, ambitious, trusting, always so damned trusting, the Billie Jeans migrated to Dallas, it seemed, like ducks to water.

There were, of course, those rape victims who were born and reared in Dallas and other big cities and who should know they couldn't trust anyone. But it was the women from small towns who seemed doubly shattered by rape. Beyond the assault on their bodies, their values had been attacked, too.

They came to the big city from the Hendersons, Lufkins, and Mount Pleasants in East Texas, and the Glen Roses, Hamiltons, and Stephenvilles to the south, bringing with them their small-town values and trust. Dallas, the nearest major metropolitan area, would be an acid test for both. Dallas was glamour, intrigue, and nightlife, everything their hometowns scattered along the state highways weren't.

Most important, and the major selling point the young women used on their reluctant small-town parents, were jobs. Good jobs in tall office buildings that sometimes paid threefold what the young women could take home from the local phone company or sewing plant. Dubious parents in Henderson and Hamilton could argue the benefits of small-town lifestyles, albeit not very convincingly, but they couldn't dispute economics. With trepidation, parents generally yielded, giving their blessings to their daughters.

Billie Jean Rider, a twenty-five-year-old administrative aide who worked in one of the thousands of nondescript Dallas office buildings, was one of those who had migrated from rural East Texas. Emotionally rattled after two hours of sexual abuse and too scared to stay in her apartment alone, she returned to her parents' house immediately after Touchton interviewed her.

"These girls trust anybody," Crowder said, rejoining Touchton. "They congregate together in apartment complexes in North Dallas. They leave their windows unlatched and forget to lock doors. They never had to worry about that in Bug Tussle. It's sad. I feel sorry for them and you wonder whether they'll ever trust anybody again.

"There's no telling how many rapists go to a place and if it's locked, they go next door. They keep going till they find one that's open. And this guy, he's good."

"He's a stalker," Touchton said. "When he's not raping, he's out looking, scouting, sizing things up. He's doing it right now. He knows how he's going to get in before he ever gets there, I'll bet you that. We're going to have to catch him dirty."

That wouldn't happen anytime soon; Ski Mask took off for Christmas.

January 3, 1986

Detectives chasing the Ski Mask Rapist vowed not to begin the new year the way they had ended the old. If the elusive rapist committed extraordinary crimes, the department would create extraordinary methods of taking him off the street.

CAPERS created the Ski Mask Rapist Task Force, to be headed initially by Sergeant Jerry King. Evelyn Crowder, in her role as analyst and therefore a one-person clearinghouse of all details on the rapist, would help steer the investigation. Touchton, already assigned to two of the eleven Ski Mask cases and one of the squad's most experienced rape detectives, would be a member of the task force, along with Detectives R. S. Gage, J. A. Reeves, Paul M. Lachnitt, and C. P. Harding, all veteran investigators.

Each day, one task force detective was assigned exclusively to each detail, to respond immediately to any rapes that bore Ski Mask's MO. Additionally, Northeast Patrol, the sector hit hardest by Ski Mask, had designated a corporal for special assignment during the rapist's prime time for assaults.

King took unusual care in selecting the detectives for the task force. Not only was it unprecedented to mobilize a team to target one rapist, there was the touchy possibility—never mentioned outside the confines of CAPERS—that the suspect they were chasing might be one of their own.

The task force would be privy to absolutely all the intelligence gleaned about the Ski Mask Rapist. Except for maybe a prison or a beauty salon, the grapevine in a police department is unsurpassed; the information had to be tightly held.

Crowder was reminded of how precious little they knew about the Ski Mask Rapist as she finished her analysis and began her official update to Captain John Holt, head of the Crimes Against Persons Section. The task force faced an uphill crawl through broken glass; this guy could be anybody.

Whoever he was, he took the Sabbath off. And he didn't rape on Tuesdays. Friday was his favorite day, striking three times. Twice he had raped on Saturdays, Mondays, and Wednesdays. He struck once on a Thursday. Those, Crowder thought cynically, were the cases they *knew* about.

In nine of the attacks, he simply entered through unlocked windows or doors, or merely pried a sliding glass door, which, in terms of security, was one of the genuinely dumbest devices ever perpetrated on

the American public. And worse, Crowder suspected you couldn't find
a house or apartment that didn't have one.

Twice, Ski Mask took expensive jewelry. He was a creature of the
night, hitting seven of his victims between midnight and 5:15 A.M. He
had spent as little as fifteen minutes with a victim and as long as two
hours. Never did he ejaculate inside a victim. He was white, from
twenty-five to twenty-eight years old, five-foot-five to five-eleven, muscular, mustached, uncircumsized, and, based on secretion smears left on
sheets, was blood type O, like half the world.

As Crowder reread her memo to Captain Holt, she unsuccessfully
contemplated anything positive she could add; as it was, the memo was
a depressing two pages, to wit:

- "On the 1st two offenses, comparable prints were lifted that have
  a possibility of being the suspect's. These prints, however, do not
  compare with each other."
- "None of the victims can identify the suspect."
- "Progress on these cases is almost at a standstill since we have
  almost nil on physical evidence, or victims' ID of suspect."

Crowder's assessment of what it would take to catch the Ski Mask
Rapist, which she reserved for the final, pessimistic paragraph, was
about as likely as lightning striking between his legs:

"It will be difficult to put a case together on any of these offenses
without a confession, confiscation of the involved stolen items, or catching the suspect in the act."

8

Angie Welburne was in one of the two bedrooms, wedged between packed boxes and a mattress and bed frame that still needed assembly. Short of death, destruction, and famine, she was firmly convinced that moving had to be in the top ten of life's most dreaded events. Once undertaken, though, it was such a repugnant task that it had to be completed immediately. She couldn't endure the clutter, and she knew she wouldn't quit until probably sometime in the middle of the night when the last picture was hanging on the wall.

By comparison, this move was a walk in the park, just a few miles from one apartment complex to the other. Six months earlier, that had been the Move From Hell. She and her mother had loaded their belongings into a rented truck, driven seven hundred miles from their native Tennessee, and arrived in Dallas to makeup-melting temperatures that made them reconsider their wisdom.

Now, Angie heard her mother, Patricia, talking to male voices in the living room. The voices were an interruption in Angie's move-till-you-drop agenda. Picking her way through the debris in her bedroom, Angie maneuvered her way to the living room, where at least the furniture had been arranged, to investigate the intrusion.

One of the male voices, the one with the slow-syrup drawl, belonged to Mike Abrams, a transplanted Mississippian who recently had been dating her mother. The new voice belonged to a Hispanic guy who, apparently, was a friend of Mike's.

"My name's Gilbert Escobedo," the stranger said, extending his hand warmly. "Pleased to meet you."

Mike's friend obviously was along for the ride, and smiled frequently at everyone else's conversation. He seemingly was content to be an onlooker, speaking only when the three friends obligingly pulled him into their conversation. Yet he was affable, in a quiet sort of way.

Escobedo was handsome enough, Angie thought. He was short. Angie was five-foot-four, and from across the room, he appeared only a couple inches taller, maybe five-six or five-seven. His mustache matched his coal-black hair and was meticulously trimmed so that the edges ended exactly at the corners of his mouth.

Throughout the brief visit, those corners appeared in a half smile, as if he knew a joke he wasn't sharing. Once, when the smile broadened, it revealed the whitest, most perfect teeth she'd seen outside the movies. Their contrast against his mocha complexion only accentuated the whiteness. His eyes were the color of coffee and whatever joke his smile concealed, his eyes knew it, too. They were boyish, mischievous even. The portrait was one of a good-natured, easygoing guy who apparently had found a way to enjoy life.

He was simply immaculate from his hair to his feet. Compulsively so, Angie suspected. And on a Saturday afternoon, just hanging out with the guys? There wasn't a black hair out of place in his fashionably styled hair, his jeans were laundry-starched and pressed, you could see the light sheening off his boots, and his green shirt, damned if it didn't match *precisely* the tint in the sunglasses he was holding. It was a helluva mental load for a twenty-one-year-old whose dates regarded Bon Jovi as high fashion.

Abrams and Escobedo didn't stay long. But two weeks later, Escobedo was back, not a totally surprising occurrence considering that Angie Welburne routinely drew appreciative glances from men. They were not leering stares, but rather sincere deference to a distinctively attractive woman. Angie's beauty was not reliant on creams, rinses, or pastes.

Nor did she accentuate her image with clothes that strategically en-hanced her body. If anything, it appeared she conscientiously under-stated her image.

She wore a minimum of makeup. She had blue eyes, and her natural blond hair flowed a good six inches beyond her shoulders. One hundred twenty pounds spread over five feet four inches left her with a well-proportioned body and an unusually tiny waist. She was chic in her dress, with a preference that always favored style over fad. The persona was one of a wholesomely attractive and trim young woman who carried herself confidently with sophistication that belied her youth.

Age, in fact, was one of the primary reasons she initially balked at Escobedo's offer for dinner.

"He's thirty-four," she told her mother. "He really doesn't look it. I thought maybe twenty-five. But that's thirteen years older than I am. Besides, he seems awfully quiet, and he's too conservative-looking."

Escobedo was, however, uncommonly nice, and in a genuine way that Angie equated with respect. He certainly was different than anyone she'd ever gone out with, which heretofore had been an assortment of out-of-work musicians and semi-serious college students with day jobs who, on more than passing occasion, had asked her for help in paying for dinner.

In the end, sincerity overcame age, and Angie relented. When Es-cobedo appeared at the door for her, he was carrying a $60 bottle of perfume in Neiman-Marcus wrapping and wearing a wardrobe the store would have been proud to claim. There was nary a wrinkle in his form-fitting slacks or in his heavily starched shirt; the tailored Italian sport coat had to have cost him $500. And on his left wrist he wore a gold-and-diamond Rolex.

He whisked his beautiful young date off in an immaculate red Por-sche Targa and took her to a trendy, overpriced Dallas restaurant, where he ordered the thickest steak and most expensive wine in the house.

Angie Welburne was moved. Never had any man taken such good care of her or been more attentive. He listened with genuine interest as she made small talk, he opened doors for her, he doted on her. He might be a little obsessive, Angie thought, but he knew how to make her feel, well, regal. It was charm and attention to which she wasn't accustomed.

"How do you afford all this?" she asked at some point in the night. "I mean, what do you do?"

"I work for myself mostly," Escobedo said. "I buy and restore classic cars, then I sell them. Two of my brothers—they're also my room-mates—and I are in the process of trying to start up our own business, you know, expand."

It was an adequate answer for a first date. Over time, Gilbert Escobedo would have so many more answers, and some of them wouldn't ring nearly as true.

March 14, 1986

Even as Gilbert Escobedo was attempting to sweep Angie Welburne off her feet, the Ski Mask Task Force was all dressed up with nowhere to go. Christmas and New Year's were stone quiet; January came and went uneventfully, as did February. It had been almost exactly three months since Ski Mask had raped Billie Jean Rider.

Far from being buoyed by his lapse in activity, the rapist's silence was making members of the task force even more paranoid. Speculation, rooted primarily in the DPD-issue ball cap (on which the forensics lab could find no trace evidence) and Wellington boots (sold in Dallas by the thousands), took over the squad room.

Sergeant Larry A. Lewis, a methodical, intelligent supervisor who only recently had replaced Jerry King as head of the task force, was on strange new turf. The attacks and the subsequent formation of the task force had occurred before he transferred to Sex Crimes. What Lewis knew about the cases he had gleaned from reports and interviewing team members, particularly Evelyn Crowder, who had become a walk-ing encyclopedia on the Ski Mask Rapist.

Lewis' biggest fear was that Ski Mask was, in fact, a police officer who somehow, through direct knowledge or maybe through departmental rumor, had become aware of the task force and gone underground. At thirty-two and already a seasoned sergeant, Lewis had transferred from the department's Tactical Unit, an elite team that handled everything from hostage negotiation and armed standoffs to fugitive apprehension.

Lewis literally had earned his stripes in a unit whose credo was "Assume the worst and be prepared." Quietly, the sergeant began rechecking the integrity of his unit's security and asking surprisingly detailed questions about the department's mainframe computer system.

There was one fact of which everyone on the team was certain: Ski Mask was a power rapist, and power rapists, with their unquenchable need for reassurance, can't stop. Spurred by their sexual fantasies, they generally only became bolder and more prolific. And insatiable.

Three months of inactivity for a power rapist was a long drought. Too long, Marshall Touchton believed, to be voluntary. Maybe Ski Mask was in a position where he *couldn't* rape.

For years Touchton had had a theory about rape, not one necessarily supported by psychological studies or even shared by some of his colleagues. There was, the veteran detective believed, only a thread-thin line between a residential burglar and a rapist. Once crossed, the burglar-rapist moved back and forth across the line with equal ease and guile. In fact, situations that provided him with the opportunity to both steal *and* rape, the burglar-rapist regarded as a bargain, a twofer of sorts.

Touchton had interviewed rapists, some of whom had lent support to his theory. "Yeah," one told him, "I started out with just burglaries. You pull enough of 'em and you get cocky, think you can't be caught. Then you start going in with people there, you know, going through drawers with women's underwear and everything. I mean, it's like you're already there. Why not? I mean, why not do the rape, too?"

"Naw, Touchton, I think you're barking up the wrong tree," a rape detective colleague said. "Professional burglars don't want anybody at home. In fact, the really good ones won't touch the place if there's anybody there."

The rapes in which Ski Mask had taken expensive jewelry—and his ability to distinguish it from cheap imitations—had convinced Touchton once again about his thin-line theory.

Three months off could mean the rapist had been arrested on a nonrape-related charge—say, burglary—and was locked up. In the lull, as was his custom, Touchton searched the book-in logs for burglars, then pulled their offense reports. Hundreds of them.

Marshall Touchton had barked up his share of wrong trees in twenty-two years as a cop; every detective had. But occasionally he found a squirrel. It kept him in the hunt.

In South Dallas, across town from the area Ski Mask had staked out as his own, one rape was adjudicated in the streets, without benefit of police investigation, grand jury, or the courts.

A man broke into a woman's house, pulled a pillowcase over her head, bound her hands behind her, and raped her at knifepoint. After the attack, he took cash from her purse and several pieces of jewelry.

As he prowled through her house, the woman freed her hands and reached a .38-caliber revolver concealed near the head of her bed. Returning to her bedroom, the assailant saw her with the gun and leaped for the open window. Catching him half in, half out the window, the twenty-six-year-old woman fired off three rounds from the .38 at his back.

"I was afraid for my life," the woman told police. "I kept saying a small prayer, the smallest prayer in the Bible, which is, 'Lord have mercy.' "

Four hours later at Parkland Memorial Hospital, doctors confirmed the woman had been raped. Down the hall in the emergency room, Curry Wallace, a twenty-year-old suspect in several other sexual assaults and break-ins, was pronounced dead. He had a single .38 wound in the back.

Evelyn Crowder proclaimed the shooting a rarity in which a rape victim killed her attacker. Some of the other detectives allowed as how it didn't happen often enough.

Like an animal invigorated by rest but starved by the respite, the Ski Mask Rapist returned with a fury. He attacked on March 14, April 5, April 16, April 23, and May 1. He skipped June, but struck back-to-back on July 19 and July 20. The crimes were bolder and more frenzied now: He fought with two of his victims and broke into another's house even knowing that it had an alarm system. And after one attack, when a neighbor saw him leaving the victim's apartment with his ski mask still on, he had chased the neighbor through the parking lot with a gun.

Whatever the reason for the three-month lull, Ski Mask was alive and not very well. The rapist was clearly at the whim of his fantasies, which apparently were escalating and provoking him beyond his previous careful and methodical regimen. The good news, if indeed there could be any in rape, was that he might get sloppy in his heightened frenzy and leave evidence behind that the investigators could exploit. Already there were signs.

In his previous assaults, he almost always managed the element of surprise, generally subduing his victims before they were fully awake. When Sara Meacham* returned home shortly before midnight March 14, she discovered her back door unlocked. Finding nothing amiss in a room-by-room search of the house, she watched TV for fifteen minutes, then went to bed. Almost immediately after Meacham turned out the lights, Ski Mask slammed through her bedroom door, gun in hand, and raped her. It was a major departure in MO; previously, he would have given her time to get to sleep.

Tina Munson,* a twenty-four-year-old sales clerk, became convinced after Ski Mask raped her that he was going to hurt her or maybe worse. Notwithstanding the gun he had forced to her temple, she screamed uncontrollably, pushed him off of her, and flailed at him. He fled without harming her physically. Police found a ripped portion of his sweatshirt and a broken gold chain with a diamond pendant on the floor where the attack had occurred. There was nothing distinguishable about either; more telling was the fact that he had been careless and lost control.

He had been so careless in one of the assaults that, for the first known time, he was seen by someone other than a victim. After raping Sue Ann Strake,* he emerged onto the landing of her apartment still wearing his ski mask. Though it was only 4:20 A.M. and well before daybreak, Melissa Walters,* one of Strake's neighbors, was in the parking lot waxing her car. She and the man in the ski mask, who, she noticed, also carried a gun in his right hand, apparently saw each other at the same time.

"Be quiet or I'll blow your head off," he yelled, moving quickly toward her. Walters impulsively screamed and ran. An upstairs neighbor heard Walters' scream and opened the door for her, slamming and locking it behind her.

A black ski mask and a roll of duct tape were found in the parking lot. Not recovered was the pair of Strake's panties that the assailant had taken, apparently a "trophy" from the assault.

Anne Lancaster* very nearly became one of the thousands of women who don't report rape. A sales clerk who worked night hours, the twenty-seven-year-old was napping in her apartment about 2:45 P.M. on April 23 when a man in a ski mask raped her and repeatedly forced her to commit fellatio.

When she finally felt safe enough to go outside, Lancaster fled to her father's house. It wasn't until May 15, more than three weeks later, that Lancaster reluctantly told Marshall Touchton of the attack. Touchton understood why. Lancaster, emotionally whipsawed and deathly paranoid about all men, was one of those victims he particularly worried about. He was glad she had her father, who, over time, finally had convinced her that reporting the attack not only would help her recover, but also might prevent another woman from being raped.

Like the predator he was, Ski Mask had a sixth sense for sniffing out vulnerability and seizing on it.

Leeza Fanolia's* life was in crisis well before Ski Mask reduced it to chaos. But from outward appearances, the thirty-eight-year-old Fanolia, a strikingly attractive interior designer, was a success story. She lived in a luxurious home, landscaped, with a pool, secluded by lush shrubs and one of the nicest in an affluent neighborhood, and her ten-year-old daughter and six-year-old son attended a well-regarded private school.

Not so obvious was a recently settled, contentious divorce brought by her husband, Mario, who since had moved to San Jose. Most recently, Mario Fanolia's lawyer claimed in court documents that his client was on the brink of bankruptcy and that the "circumstances of . . . providing for support of the children have materially and substantially changed since entry of the decree."

Not only was he behind in child support, Mario Fanolia had not delivered half of the couple's stock portfolio, as directed by the court, he hadn't made the loan payments on the swimming pool, and he was $4,853.16 in arrears on the house mortgage.

On the night Leeza Fanolia would be raped, she was living in a house she couldn't afford that was protected by a faulty alarm system she couldn't pay to repair.

At 10:45 P.M. with a gun against Fanolia's neck, a man in a ski mask motioned to her young daughter lying asleep next to her and said: "Don't move. Don't scream. I don't want to hurt you or your little girl. Take off your rings."

When Fanolia hesitated, the assailant said, "It's not worth your daughter's life." Putting the jewelry in his pocket, he fondled her, commenting throughout the ordeal on the size of her breasts. He forced her to fondle him, then he raped her. Throughout, the little girl slept obliviously on her side of the king-sized bed.

He left with three diamond rings, a gold-and-diamond watch, and two pairs of diamond earrings, all worth $10,000. After the uniformed officers finished their report, they asked Fanolia to accompany them to Parkland for a rape exam. She refused, appearing to be in shock.

"I can't go through any more," she said wearily.

Six days later, early on a Wednesday morning, Leeza Fanolia's phone rang before work.

"It's me," the man's voice said. "I enjoyed you."

"Well, I'll just be damned!"

There wasn't anyone else in the squad room to hear Marshall Touchton. Or to see him drop the report and rummage frantically through the stack of paper on his desk. Finding what he was looking for, he held a report in each hand, his head moving from one to the other.

In his left was a report of an attempted rape. On April 5, a twenty-one-year-old assistant office manager named Ali Martin* fought off a man in a ski mask and chased him from her condo. Hurriedly scanning the text of the report, Touchton found what he was looking for: "Complainant Martin stated that there was something familiar about the suspect's voice and physical description, but was unable to pinpoint who she was reminded of."

The detective turned his attention to the report he had dredged from the stack on his desk. It was the Camellia Michaels case from eight months earlier.

Ski Mask was either stupid or had balls the size of basketballs. He had gone back to the scene of his original rapes, and he had struck some vague but familiar chord with a victim. Rapists *were* like animals. They prowled only where they felt safe.

Ali Martin lived one block from Camellia Michaels on Woodbend Lane.

9

Angie Welburne's first, glamorous date with Gilbert Escobedo wasn't an introductory offer he concocted simply to make a good first impression. Lavishing her with attention, spending seemingly unlimited amounts of money on her, and taking her to the best places, Angie discovered, was simply the way he was.

The couple had been almost inseparable in the two months since their first date. And in the balance, it had been a seductive trip for the young woman from Tennessee who only marginally was old enough to vote or drink. Escobedo's time was flexible, the apparent fringe benefit of working for himself. By mutual consent, a routine evolved: He'd give Angie time to get home from her job at a computer software manufacturing firm, allow her time for a quick shower and a change of clothes, then sweep her into the red Porsche for yet another night on the town.

None of the best movies were released for more than a week without the couple seeing them, and when Escobedo discovered Angie enjoyed dancing, he routinely took her to Dallas' toniest clubs. Many nights, he took her to the best restaurants in town. On occasion, he would surprise her with some gift, usually perfume or flowers. His taste was impeccable, and his money sustained it.

When the relationship turned serious, he appeared at her apartment one day with a mysterious grin. He refused to tell her where they were going, only that he had a surprise. He clearly loved the tease, and drew it out as long as Angie's patience would tolerate. When he finally killed the engine, it was in the parking lot of a fine Dallas hotel where he already had reserved a room. As was his style, flowers and a bottle of chilled champagne awaited them.

Materialism alone wouldn't have swayed Angie Welburne. Her values, the purposeful foundation of strong ties with both mother and father despite their divorce, were too principled to be eroded by money. Gilbert's eagerness to please, which inevitably involved money, was his most obvious trait. But beneath his glitz, Angie found a compassion in little things he did that was refreshing and endearing.

One of Escobedo's favorite pastimes on Sundays was to stop for two boxes of chicken at Henderson's, a greasy legend in Dallas, then head for Turtle Creek on the fringe of the Highland Park mansions. Sitting beneath an antiquated bridge and surrounded by as many ducks as flowers, the couple would have a picnic, chat, and occasionally doze off.

Always en route to Turtle Creek, Escobedo would stop at a street corner where, inevitably, an old black woman in her robe and rollers would be waiting for him. Rolling down the window of the Porsche, he would grab a box of chicken, fold a $20 bill, and hand both to the woman. It was a curious ritual, one he never explained. But Angie figured it was compensation for his own background that he hinted was less than affluent and more turbulent than calm. She appreciated the fact that he never forgot where he came from.

Angie also respected Escobedo. Ambition and hard work were important values in her life, and she had come by them honestly from working-class parents. Escobedo worked constantly, it seemed, when he wasn't with her, even well into the morning hours and every Saturday. He was either restoring old Chevys or detailing cars, a natural outlet, she thought, for his obsessiveness. He had more energy than anyone she ever dated, and he obviously wanted to accomplish something in his life.

When Escobedo asked her to marry him, she was neither surprised nor impulsive. It was a major decision she discussed with her mother.

"Well, I'm not seeing anyone else," Angie told Patricia Welburne.

"I'm only going out with him. He's really good to me, and I think he's somebody who would take really good care of me."

"But do you *love* him?" It was a typical mother question.

"Well, yes, I guess I do," Angie said, sounding surprised at her own words. "I didn't think he'd be the type I'd ever marry, but he kind of grows on you. I've never really ever met anyone just like Gilbert. Yeah, I do. I love him."

Angie accepted his engagement ring, but with a caveat.

"I want us to be engaged," she told him, "but I don't want to get married until next year. Maybe we should live together for a year or so, or maybe just get to know each other a little better to see if it's really going to work before we get married."

If Angie's qualified acceptance of his marriage proposal bothered him, he didn't show it. Gilbert Escobedo was exhilarated. He couldn't wait to share the good news with his roommates, brothers Al and Mondo.

He drove his new fiancée to his town house on Woodbend Lane.

August 23, 1986

Woodbend Lane runs east and west, alongside a creek that separates the well-kept condominium community from the sprawling campus of Richland College to the north. At its easternmost journey through row after row of town houses, the street snakes sharply to the right into a U-shaped bend and resumes in the opposite direction. For no good reason except developers' folly, Woodbend changes its name in the U, becoming Burning Log Lane as it heads back west.

Merilee Watson's* town house was on Burning Log, just beyond the name-change bend. She was outgoing by nature, the single mother of a young son and daughter and, at thirty-six, older than many of the residents in the rental community. Watson not only knew her neighbors, but made it a point to stay abreast of what was happening in the neighborhood.

She knew there had been a series of rapes in months previous, and she also had been hearing disturbing and, as far as she knew, unsubstantiated reports that a man on Woodbend had been exposing himself to children and even talking his way into their town houses before their parents came home from work.

It had been another grind at the office for Watson, except that the day may have seemed even longer than most. She was tired and couldn't wait to get to bed.

The first words she heard in the drowsy darkness were: "I won't hurt you if you're good. I've seen you at work and followed you home. That's how I knew where you lived."

It was one A.M. by the illuminated digital clock on the nightstand. Only after she comprehended that a man in a ski mask was standing by her bed did she feel the gun against her head. He pulled a pillowcase over her head and forced her legs apart. After he raped her, he forced her to commit oral sex. He talked constantly throughout the assault, invading her with deeply personal questions and comments even as he assaulted her body.

Watson felt him leave the bed and heard the light flick on in the bathroom. She could hear drawers being opened.

"What are you doing?"

"Oh, I was just looking," he said casually. "You going to call the police?"

Without awaiting her reply, he added, "It won't do any good. I'm wearing gloves." Ski Mask left with her $1,200 diamond watch.

The assailant, patrol officers theorized, came through an unlocked living room window, a possibility Merilee Watson strenuously disputed.

"I know what goes on in this neighborhood," Watson argued, "and I keep my windows and doors locked. A person would be a fool not to. They were locked. I *know* they were locked."

Officer W. M. Clifton took a closer look at the window, which, he reassured himself, bore no pry marks. In the windowsill, however, lying on its side, was a No. 2 pencil. The window, closed down on the pencil in the sill, would appear from across the room as fully down and locked. Unnoticed at the top, though, the bolt missed, by a quarter inch, meeting the receiver in the lock.

Clifton dutifully noted the intelligence in his report: "Pencil may explain how he gets inside the apts. He talks to . . . victim's children, wrangles himself inside, then sets up a window, then leaves. Children are unaware. Victim comes home and suspect . . . lets himself inside through same window."

Crime search specialists took latent prints off both the window and ledge.

When Detective R. S. Gage of the task force arrived, the immediate shock had passed, and Watson had had time to relive the attack a hundred times—but with recall and clarity she hadn't been able to muster in her interview with the uniformed officers.

Like Ali Martin, who was attacked in April in her town house on Woodbend, Merilee Watson believed there was something familiar about the man who attacked her. Even during the attack, Watson told Gage, she believed she recognized his voice.

"I remember the person's voice real well," she said. "The Sunday before I was assaulted . . . a man who lives near me, but is not a friend or acquaintance, drove up to my car and tried to start a conversation with me. I didn't know him and he didn't know me, but I had talked to him for a short time out at the pool some weeks before.

"Even during the time that the man was in my house attacking me, I remembered the voice of this neighbor. I couldn't see the person, but I thought it was the man who had been trying to have conversations with me on other occasions."

Watson couldn't be certain about the neighbor's last name, but she believed his first name was Gilbert. His house was easy to find, she said. It was around the bend on Woodbend, the town house on the west side of the community swimming pool.

Gage shared his information with Marshall Touchton, who already had pending rape cases in the Woodbend community. They put a trap on Watson's phone and drove to the management company that leased the town houses. There were actually three tenants at the suspect's address, according to the lease contracts, all brothers: Alfred, Armondo, and Gilbert Escobedo.

The detectives took the brothers alphabetically, plugging their names into NCIC, the National Crime Information Center, for criminal backgrounds. Alfred and Armondo drew blanks in the computer. Brother Gilbert, however, was a hit. He had a felony record. Touchton called the Texas Department of Criminal Justice's Pardons and Paroles Division.

Gilbert Hernandez Escobedo, a Hispanic male born September 2, 1951, was on parole, in fact. He had been convicted in Dallas County of burglary of a habitation and sentenced to five years in prison. Only eighteen months into the sentence, he was paroled back to Dallas County. His release date, the detectives noticed, was May 24, 1984—less than a year before the Ski Mask rapes began surfacing in North Dallas, particularly so in the neighborhood where he now lived.

Touchton and Gage contemplated their new lead. It was not uncommon, both knew, for rape victims to name as suspects men who, in their minds, had acted suspiciously before the rapes: a man at the office, maybe, who made a salacious remark about her legs, a first date who grabbed a breast, a repairman who kept thinking of reasons to loiter in her house, or a neighbor who leered at her. Seldom, though, did the suspicions lead to arrest.

Merilee Watson hadn't seen her attacker without his mask—to the detectives' knowledge, none of the victims had. Voice identification, short of a stutter or a distinctive accent, wasn't evidence. It was a hunch. And none of the victims, not Ali Martin who found something vaguely familiar about her assailant, or even Watson, had reported the rapist spoke with even a Hispanic accent. Always, the victims reported their attacker was simply "white."

Still, Watson hadn't flinched in identifying the voice as Gilbert Escobedo's. He had opportunity; he was a burglar on parole. And he lived in the middle of one of Ski Mask's favorite targets.

Detectives pulled Escobedo's prints for comparison against the latents off Watson's window. They were negative. Nor, for that matter, did Escobedo's prints match the precious few others lifted at Ski Mask rape scenes. Touchton had been hopeful, but not optimistic about a match. Many of the victims had reported their attacker wore gloves. The prints lifted at the scene probably were those of husbands, boyfriends, or repairmen.

Five weeks after Merilee Watson was raped, at 11:42 A.M. on Halloween, her phone rang.

"Merilee, are you okay?" It was the same voice.

Southwestern Bell, with a trap on Watson's incoming calls since the attack, traced the call to the Escobedo town house a street away.

"The problem, Merilee," Touchton tried to explain, "is that at least three men live in that house and all would have access to the phone. We can't prove which one placed the call."

Even if, the detective was careful not to say, you're right about the voice belonging to the rapist.

"But I know it's the same voice as the man who raped me."

Suspecting something to be true, Touchton lamented, and being able to *prove* it beyond a reasonable doubt was sometimes as close as New York and LA.

10

November 1986

Marshall Touchton ordered his sandwich and drink through the squelchy remote microphone, picked them up at the drive-through window, and headed north on Abrams Road. Just south of Richland College, he took a right onto Burning Log Lane and followed it through the bend. At the narrow drive that connected with the alley behind the town houses, he turned again. He pulled into one of the rear-entry drives, backed out, and pointed the unmarked Plymouth down the alley toward the swimming pool and the town house just beyond.

Satisfied he could see both the front of the town house and the carport behind it with the red Porsche, he killed the engine and reached for his sandwich. It was not an uncommon luncheon for Marshall Touchton.

Sergeant Larry Lewis would call it work ethic. "Marshall Touchton is an unusual kind of detective," Lewis would say. "He's the type who'll go get his lunch, then drive to a suspect's house or place of business and watch the guy while he's eating lunch. Or he'll drive by his house at six-thirty in the morning on his way to work. He seldom says much, but there's not much happening that he doesn't see."

Marshall Touchton, at forty-six, looked a good five or ten years older, the primary consequence of a head full of prematurely gray hair.

The gray contrasted sharply with the ruddy red face immediately beneath it and gave the appearance of a man who perpetually was embarrassed. Twenty-two years as a cop, the last sixteen as a detective confined to squad rooms, unmarked cars, and interrogation rooms, and with little physical activity to offset the sedentary grind, had pushed his waist a couple of inches closer to the steering wheel.

Dressed in his trademark gray suits and white shirts with stylish but conservative ties, Touchton looked like a prosperous small-town insurance agent who, with little excuse, might unreel a wallet full of pictures of his grandkids.

If his appearance belied his profession as a big-city detective, Touchton's sanguine temperament only made him harder to figure. As a young patrol officer, he had answered hundreds of calls that spanned about every transgression that one member of society could perpetrate on another. He paid his dues as a detective in the vice division, spending as much time with prostitutes and drug dealers as he did with his wife, Cora, and her two young sons from a previous marriage.

In thirteen years in CAPERS, he'd investigated so many homicides, robberies, aggravated assaults, and rapes that they sometimes blurred in recall. Most recently, he, like other detectives in the squad, averaged 150 rape investigations a year, plus another 87 cases of indecent exposure.

But more than two decades of exposure to humanity's vilest acts, and still Touchton had managed to keep his equilibrium. He was easygoing, and probably no one ever told him a joke, no matter how bad, in which he couldn't find humor. His speech was remarkably devoid of street-cop jargon and, with a couple of misdemeanor exceptions, most of what he said could be repeated in a pulpit.

A conversation of ten minutes would guarantee mention of his wife and a reference to the boys. And while he enjoyed good conversation, he fell noticeably silent when the topic turned to himself. In all his years as a cop, which entailed more than his share of headline cases, Touchton's name appeared in the files of the *Dallas Morning News* only four times. It wasn't by accident. When he saw a reporter, he opted for the nearest door.

Marshall Touchton simply managed to hold on to himself in the midst of tragedies and premeditations that devastated people's lives. He negotiated crime scenes and caffeine-charged, smoke-filled interrogation rooms with a practiced detachment that allowed him to go home most evenings without cynicism or jaundice. Detachment was a survival skill, as critical in Touchton's jurisdiction as an immunization shot for the doctor making rounds in a malaria ward.

Remarkably, Touchton's detachment did not preclude genuine empathy and compassion for crime victims, particularly the targets of sex crimes. He had been known to spend as much time with a distraught woman who found a window-peeper masturbating outside her window as he had with so-called major cases. Trauma, the detective discovered long ago, didn't always correlate with life-threatening events or felony offenses.

Similarly, there was little deviation in personality when Touchton had to work the other side of the street, interviewing deceitful, street-savvy suspects in interrogation rooms.

At first glance, he appeared to pose little threat, just a good ol' boy, maybe a little on the gullible side. It was a perception the veteran detective played to. Touchton was deceptively adroit at what he did, more likely to wear down a liar with patience than with accusations and threats.

More than a few unwitting offenders made the mistake of accepting a cigarette and a cup of coffee from the obliging, slow-talking detective across the desk from them. But even as he elicited appalling and damning detail, which he frequently did, Touchton was able to sit poker-faced, resisting, as human nature would have it, not only the impulse to pass judgment, but to register his repulsion. He had been issued a badge, not a clerical collar or a judicial robe. It was that simple and that complex.

Marshall Touchton was not a racehorse, but more like one of the plow horses his father would have kept on the tobacco farm back in south Georgia. The younger Touchton, next to the youngest in a brood of seven, was born twenty-five miles from the Okefenokee Swamp. His father, a onetime revenuer during Prohibition, ultimately couldn't scratch a living from the hardscrabble farm and moved his family south to Jacksonville, Florida. Young Marshall had seen some of the tough times and heard family stories about the others.

Rape investigations were tough, almost always long and drawn out. Touchton approached them like a plow horse works a field, systematically and steady, one row at a time. He didn't dazzle with speed; he impressed with consistency.

Ski Mask was particularly tough because he left no evidence and no one had seen his face. Fingerprints and unwavering eyewitness identification were the bedrock in prosecuting rape cases. Even scientific evidence such as hair, semen, and blood—which the rapist also had been careful not to leave—the district attorney called "associative evidence," and wasn't sufficient to file charges in the absence of witness identification and prints. The hair and body fluids, by prosecutors' policy, were "icing on the cake," additional elements to remove shadows of doubts from jurors.

Absent *any* evidence, Touchton believed you went with what you had. Or, to borrow from a philosophy frequently espoused by Darrell Royal, the legendary football coach at the University of Texas: "Ol' something's better than ol' nothing."

In this case, what Touchton had was a voice, which, if Merilee Watson was right, belonged to a man with a documentable predisposition to crime.

That predisposition, Touchton discovered in a more exhaustive search of the records, was evidenced in not just one prison sentence for burglary, but three. All three had been residential burglaries, consistent with Touchton's "thin-line theory" of burglar-rapists.

More telling, and the reason the detective chose to spend his lunch hour watching Gilbert Escobedo's house, was that Ski Mask, counting yet another attack on October 20, had committed eighteen known rapes. One third of those had occurred within walking distance of Escobedo's house on Woodbend.

Sitting in his car, Touchton fixed on the pool adjacent to Escobedo's town house. Camellia Michaels, his first case in the Woodbend community, had been raped in July. Summer was prime time, he imagined, for traffic at the pool. And didn't Merilee Watson say that Escobedo had tried to strike up a conversation at the pool?

Ski Mask, Touchton and Crowder knew, was a power rapist, consumed and overwrought by sexual fantasy. Escobedo, Touchton had a hunch, started out watching his neighbors in their bikinis at the pool, masturbating from behind his drapes. Over time, Touchton would bet, Escobedo's escalating fantasies wouldn't be satisfied by masturbation, and he began using the pool as a fish barrel, selecting his prey from a front-row seat. Or maybe using the pool to size up potential victims had been his plan from the beginning, which was why he chose that particular town house.

But would Escobedo run the risk of raping in his own backyard? Few rapists in Touchton's experience had been that bold or stupid. Or even frenzied. The detective borrowed the not-so-technical answer from his partner, Steve Hatchel: "These guys just have a screw loose." Anything was possible.

Marshall Touchton wrapped the debris from his fast-food lunch in the white paper sack and glanced at his watch. There had been no movement at the Escobedo town house for more than an hour. Touchton was comfortable with his theory that Escobedo was using the pool to select his victims. When he got back to Main and Harwood, he'd ask Evelyn Crowder to compile the names of all the Woodbend-area victims to see how many had been regulars at the pool.

As he turned the ignition key on the steering column, the detective saw movement from the corner of his left eye. A marked white cruiser with the blue Dallas Police Department emblem stopped at the curb of Escobedo's town house. A uniformed officer emerged, walked up the sidewalk, and reached for the doorbell.

"Well, well, well. What's this all about?" Touchton killed the engine and waited.

The detective's line of sight didn't allow a view of the doorway, but he could see the officer on the doorstep. A moment later, the patrolman began talking, apparently to whomever had opened the door. He was animated and, it appeared to Touchton, jovial and friendly, as if he were talking to someone he knew. Momentarily, the officer disappeared off the door step and apparently into the house.

After fifteen minutes and with the officer still in Escobedo's house, Touchton gambled. He hated the risk of the officer coming out the door and spotting the unmarked Plymouth, but his position in the alley was too far away to make out the unit number painted on the trunk of the cruiser.

Cranking the Plymouth, Touchton pulled from the alley onto Woodbend Lane and accelerated quickly past the cruiser. He committed the six-digit unit number to memory, repeating it to himself until he could get out of sight of the town house. He slowed and wrote the number carefully into his notebook on the seat beside him, turned into the alley on Burning Log, and crept back to his previous vantage point. The cruiser was still there.

Thirty minutes later, the officer, youngish, trim, and dark-complexioned, reappeared on the doorstep, chatted briefly and amicably with some unseen person apparently still in the doorway, walked to his patrol car, and drove away.

With the unit number of the car, Touchton easily could have used his two-way radio to call Northeast Division and find out who was using the car on the day watch. The call, however, would be monitored by every officer on the frequency, including the cop himself.

Touchton waited until he got to Central Headquarters and used the telephone, sounding as casual as he could. When he hung up, he took the elevator two floors up. Personnel, at least the part where an old-time and trusted friend worked, was crammed into a whitewashed, steel-encased corner of what once had been the jail that housed Dallas' two most infamous mentions in history—assassins Lee Harvey Oswald and Jack Ruby.

The driver of the marked cruiser, according to Northeast duty logs, was Officer Roger Garcia. In-depth access to officers' files would take the departmental equivalent of an act of Congress and almost certainly would set off alarms. But confirmation of employment, date of birth, and duty station were easily accessible and shouldn't raise eyebrows.

Roger Garcia was thirty-six and had been a cop for six years. He had an older brother who was a sergeant in the department, and based on other cops' word of mouth, Roger Garcia was an exemplary cop whose by-the-book attitude and ambition probably would propel him far in the ranks.

In fact, in his six years, Garcia had amassed ten commendations from supervisors and citizens against not a single disciplinary action or reprimand in his file.

Asking too many questions inside the Blue Circle about the Blue Circle was guaranteed to get back to the subject of the inquiry. Garcia's showing up at Escobedo's town house posed perplexing questions, all of them sensitive, for Touchton and the Ski Mask Task Force. Not the least of which was the DPD ball cap found at the Constance McIntyre rape scene or her recollection of the assailant's "Wellington-type police boots."

At the minimum, though, Touchton had seen an officer apparently socializing with an ex-con on parole, a violation of departmental policy. That's *if* Garcia even knew Escobedo was an ex-con. Admittedly, rap sheets weren't normal topics of casual chitchat among friends. And that was also if it was Gilbert Escobedo who invited Garcia in. Touchton couldn't see the person inside the door, and three Escobedos, two of whom had clean records, lived in the same house. Like everything else associated with the Ski Mask Rapist, this scenario had warts and wrinkles all over it.

Situations like this were why God created supervisors; Touchton briefed Sergeant Larry Lewis before shift change. After the sergeant briefed Captain John Holt, the word came back down to Touchton and his colleagues on the task force.

"The Garcia situation," as it euphemistically became called, would be handled back-channel, captain-to-captain. Holt would talk to Garcia's patrol captain at Northeast and keep Lewis posted on developments. The strategy was regarded dubiously by members of the task force, but everyone had to admit the suspicious scenario with Garcia had too many holes to handle it any other way.

November 7, 1986

In compliance with the Texas Business and Commercial Code, three new business owners filed their intent with the Dallas County Clerk to use an assumed name. Their business would be known as Ultimate Polishing Enterprises and would be located in the 5400 block of Kentcroft in Garland, an eastern suburb of Dallas.

The owners, each of whom signed the document, were Alfred Escobedo and Gilbert H. Escobedo, both of whom listed the same address on Woodbend Lane in Dallas, and Carlos Santoyo, their cousin, who listed his residence at the Kentcroft address in Garland.

"That's it. *Damn!* He knows we're here. That's twice now he's come out looking around at nothing in particular. He's either really bored with whatever's going on inside or he's checking. He's wise. Lookit, see, he's going back in again. I'll bet you a beer he's back out in a little while. We're blown."

The detective's partner, five years older, a burly mustache offsetting his rapidly decreasing hairline, calmly watched Escobedo retreat from beneath the glare of the porch light back inside his town house.

"Naw," the older officer said, "he's just edgy. Hell, if you did what he did you'd be edgy, too. These people are supposed to have a lot of energy, you know, pacing and everything. 'Sides, he's a con. The joint makes 'em creepy. He hasn't been out that long. Ain't no big deal."

The plainclothes deployment team from DPD's Northeast Division had gotten the surveillance assignment in early November. Crimes Against Persons downtown seemed to think this Gilbert Escobedo could be the Ski Mask Rapist. He was a high priority, not only because of the number of rapes they suspected him of, but because he also was becoming a bona fide media star. The five-inch stories once buried inside the papers were becoming longer and more panicked, making their way to the metropolitan section fronts of both the *Morning News* and the *Times Herald*. One of the television stations recently had done a feature on a neighborhood where residents were installing security systems and women were taking self-defense classes, all because of the elusive Ski Mask Rapist.

The deployment section had juggled its priorities to accommodate the request from headquarters. The detectives downtown had no proof, *nada*, not even a partial print. And they hadn't given a hint in public of their interest in an ex-con named Escobedo. All the newscasts on the serial rapist always included the same *"and police say they have no leads."*

The stakeout was not only an act of accommodation; it was self-defense. The rapist had created hell in Northeast's sector.

The teams, generally assigned in twos, were created to track down fugitives, and they did it better than the Detective Division, which was bombarded daily with so many new cases they couldn't concentrate on the old ones. Sometimes, squad detectives had good locations on fugitives but no time to get them. When the deployment teams proved to be highly efficient at the specialized task, their roles became bastardized and expanded to include primary surveillance and stakeouts in high-burglary areas.

It was tedious, monotonous duty that ended on most nights with virtually nothing to show. But when deployment teams scored, they scored big. And that's what CAPERS, without a shred of evidence, needed. They needed the deployment team to see where Escobedo went and who he talked to. Mostly, they needed to catch Ski Mask in the act.

The mid-November night was chilly but tolerable, and the conversation inside the unmarked police car bounced from the Cowboys to office politics and promotions. Stakeouts were never like the movies. Generally, the biggest concern was where in hell they would piss without missing anything.

At ten minutes after ten, the light in the carport at the back of the town house went on. Momentarily, Gilbert Escobedo, as best the pair of detectives could tell from matching the two-year-old book-in mug shot with the figure in the distance, backed out the Porsche, heading it down the alley in the opposite direction. Running without headlights, the deployment detectives followed. They didn't turn on their lights until they pulled onto Abrams Road, several cars behind the accelerating Porsche.

Escobedo found the LBJ Expressway and headed west, sometimes hitting eighty miles an hour. He exited maybe eight miles later on Marsh Lane, crossed over the expressway, and reentered LBJ in the opposite direction, periodically dropping his speed to below fifty-five.

"The bastard's playing with us," the younger cop said.

The red sports car took the Abrams exit and headed north. The unmarked police car kept him in view until he turned into Woodbend. Turning behind him would have been obvious. The detectives continued on Abrams, turned around in the entrance to Richland College, and parked at the curb in the bend of Woodbend. The Porsche was back in the carport and the outside light was off.

Fifteen minutes later, a man in a stylish red-and-black jogging suit approached on the sidewalk. It was a moment that both angered and humiliated stakeout cops. About three feet from the car, Gilbert Escobedo nodded cordially and said, "Evening, officers, how are you tonight?" and kept walking.

There was momentary silence in the darkened car.

Then, "Some sonofabitch owes me a beer."

II. The Suspect

One deceit needs many others, and so the whole house is built in the air and must soon come to the ground.
—Baltasar Gracián, Spanish writer and Jesuit priest

11

Mid-November 1986

Not until she was confronted with abrupt changes spawned by those closest to her did Angie Welburne realize how charmed her recent existence had been. She had taken for granted the whirlwind courtship by her fiancé, Gilbert Escobedo, and she had counted more than she realized on her mother, with whom she shared the apartment. Now, disturbing news from each of them would change the way she lived her life.

Patricia Welburne hadn't had a lot of choice about her decision to move back to Tennessee. She lost her job, along with thousands of others, when Dallas' propped-up paper economy fell in on itself. Through a friend back in Nashville, she had gotten a good offer from a major hotel. Truth was, Angie suspected her mother was more comfortable back home than she was in Dallas anyway.

Still Angie was not thrilled at the prospect of her mother leaving. The two women were more than just mother and daughter. They were roommates, friends, and confidantes. Angie found herself talking to her mother more and more about her engagement to the charming but increasingly perplexing Gilbert Escobedo. Those conversations, which always made Angie feel better, now would be conducted by long-distance.

By default, Patricia Welburne's departure had created at least one silver lining. Angie had wanted to put her relationship with Gilbert Escobedo to the day-to-day test. The couple had tentatively set March 14 for the wedding, and Angie's plan for their trial run at living together hadn't yet gotten off the ground. She, of course, had lived with her mother; Escobedo shared his house with his two brothers. Neither wanted to displace a member of their family or leave them with all the rent to pay.

Immediately after her mother left for Tennessee, Escobedo moved into Angie's apartment at the corner of Skillman Street and Audelia Road in northeast Dallas.

No question, Gilbert Escobedo was not the man Angie would ever have envisioned marrying. In falling in love with him, Angie had had to negotiate a series of mental adjustments that, cumulatively, had weakened her resolve about marrying him.

Frankly, Angie told her mother, if she had known everything about him earlier in the relationship, she wouldn't have continued to see him, much less consider marrying him.

The thirteen-year age difference she had resolved. Not only did Escobedo pass for ten years younger, he didn't act any more mature than she did, a fact in which Angie at first found genuine humor. He enjoyed the same things she did—music, dancing, movies, dinners out—and he certainly wasn't a stick-in-the-mud. Sometimes, it was Angie who pleaded for a quiet weekend at home.

There were other things about Escobedo, though, much more important than age, that challenged Angie. These revelations he delivered in long, intimate, and emotional conversations separated sometimes by months. And they appeared like bombshells in her mind. When finally she could resolve and accept a heretofore unknown fact about the man she planned to marry, he would stun her again with another. He seemed to know her tolerance and was careful not to push it.

First there had been his acknowledgment that he had two daughters, Rebecca, fourteen, and Martie, a year younger. The girls were one of the main reasons Angie had wanted to live with Escobedo before they were married. She had to get to know his daughters. The extra bedroom vacated by Angie's mother would accommodate Becky and Martie on weekends. At twenty-one, Angie was about to become a stepmother to two girls, the oldest of whom was barely seven years younger than she was. Becky and Martie would be more like little sisters than daughters. Nonetheless, they were part of his life, and Angie knew they'd have to be a part of hers, too, if the marriage was to work.

But in yet another shocker, Angie learned that Escobedo not only was divorced from the girls' mother, he also had had a *second* failed marriage. That fact particularly troubled Angie in the aftermath of her own parents' separation. She remained close to both her parents, but the split-up had made her vow that she would learn from their mistake. Now at twenty-one, she wondered, was she merely naive and unrealistic about the real world? Still, the man she was about to marry had gone through *two* failed marriages; she was about to become his *third* wife.

Each of his disclosures sent Angie, disappointed and frustrated, into retreat. But curiously enough, her fiancé's admissions about his past cut both ways. In spite of the doubt he created, Angie found herself admiring his honesty, if not his timing. She could feel herself being drawn even closer as he laid bare the false starts and wrong turns of his youthful marriages. Courageously, she thought, he accepted an inordinate share of the guilt. He admitted that he not only married too young, but that he really hadn't had a good background for knowing what a solid marriage was supposed to be.

When he was only six, he explained, his mother abandoned his father for another man. She left him and his four brothers, taking only his baby sister. The boys had been shuttled back and forth between father and grandparents until his father finally remarried when Gilbert was a teenager.

Angie could see the anguish in his eyes as he recalled the story. His pain, she thought, was still deep, and she hurt for him.

"I wish I could erase my mistakes," Escobedo said tearfully. "I can't. But I'm older now and I've been through a lot. I know what I want, which is you and a good marriage and a good life, and I know how to get it. I won't make those mistakes again, I promise you."

Among the things he said he wanted was a baby. "I've got two girls and I'd love for us to have a boy, you know, after we get used to each other and settled."

The couple also talked of a house of their own. Not long after he moved into her apartment, they moved to North Dallas to a fashionable but smaller apartment at Preston Greens. The new apartment would allow them to save toward their dream home. And though the apartment was cheaper than the large two-bedroom Angie had once shared with her mother, the sprawling Preston Greens complex, located on the southwestern corner of Preston and Arapaho roads, was on the fringe of the fashionable Prestonwood Country Club, one of three prestigious golf clubs within a four-mile radius.

Preston Greens not only was surrounded by one of Dallas' affluent neighborhoods, it also was a security-controlled complex with guard posts at the entrances and twenty-four-hour security patrols, precautions that appealed to both Angie and Gilbert. One of Angie's neighbors had been raped by a black man with a knife shortly after she moved into her old complex. And since then, the Ski Mask Rapist had struck all around her former apartment. The rapes, routinely reported on TV and in the newspapers, concerned Angie, but no more than Gilbert, who apparently had found a new concern to obsess over.

Immediately after moving to Preston Greens, he bought security locks, which he installed on all the windows and doors in the apartment. He cautioned her constantly about looking in the backseat before getting into her little Nissan in the parking garage after work. If he knew she was going to the mall at night, he warned her about looking through the parking lot as she approached her car.

Privately, Angie loved the concern he showed for her, even if he sometimes did sound like a broken record. She drew the line, however, when he brought up her checks. He didn't want her to list her street address, apartment number, or phone on the new batch of personal checks she was ordering.

"Damn, Gilbert, you're obsessing," she told him, more serious than joking. "Give it up. I'm a big girl and I've taken care of myself twenty-one years without you, thank you very much."

"I'm telling you, you really need to get a post office box. It's just safer, that's all." He rambled on, invoking images of "weirdos" and "madmen" clerks to whom Angie ostensibly would give checks and who subsequently would appear at the apartment while he was gone and rape her.

Obsession, Angie knew, was a dangerous trait. But Escobedo's irrational fixation on her safety was channeled in a positive way. Most of
the time, it was endearing and made her feel secure and loved. Occasionally, though, it could be a drag, forcing her to tell him to drop it
and move on. Even then, he demanded the last word.

"You're a beautiful woman, Angie, and I don't want anything to
happen to you. Men notice you, I've seen them. I'm just saying you
can't trust anyone."

The depth of his concern for her, the lavish little gifts for no reason at
all, the way he talked about someday having a baby boy, the look in his
eyes from across the room, they were all signals that Gilbert Escobedo
had indeed learned from his past, that he was a good risk. Angie was
confident the good signs more than outweighed his baggage. If he could
try that hard, she determined she would help him.

Angie was even more comfortable with her decision to marry Gilbert
when she saw him around his family and friends. She couldn't imagine
anyone not loving Gilbert. She enjoyed watching him work the crowd.

His elderly grandmother would be sitting by herself in the den, temporarily lost in the pandemonium of the Escobedo clan, each talking
over the other, some in Spanish. Angie would watch as Gilbert sidled
up to the old woman, the mischievous, boyish grin appearing on his
face.

Angie imagined it was a look he'd worn a lot as a kid. He'd whisper
something in Grandma's ear, and the old woman would literally glow
and come to life, flourishing under her grandson's attention and offer-
ing up some story that she always related in grandiosely animated
Spanish.

"God," Angie would tell Gilbert, "you're shameless the way you
manipulate the crowd. You're a con man."

He would shrug innocently. "Yeah, well, what can I tell you?" Then
he would grin, exposing teeth like piano keys.

One of the things Angie Welburne loved most about Gilbert was his
family. Hers was in Tennessee, and the Escobedos had adopted her
unconditionally in the ten months she had dated Gilbert. Robert Escobedo, after his divorce from Gilbert's mother, married Betty, who,

like Angie, also was from Tennessee. It became standard fare for father and son to joke about their weaknesses for "Tennessee women" and to tease each other about the women's considerable drawbacks, which, they always ultimately agreed, were worth the grief.

The Escobedos were a tight-knit family that never let a chance for a gathering pass without exploiting it. Christmas, New Year's, Fourth of July, Memorial Day, they were all excuses for food, family, and fellowship. The Escobedo family reunion, Angie's favorite, was chaotic.

Fifty or sixty Escobedos spanning four generations would commandeer a city park early in the morning to stake out the prime spot, dragging along lawn chairs, blankets, fold-up tables, barbecue grills, and radios. Toward noon, some of the men would fire up the barbecue, where they'd grill eighty pounds of marinated, thin-cut slivers of beef and chicken that would be rolled into tortillas with cooked onions and green peppers for fajitas. The party would last until dusk.

Angie envisioned that if you were an Escobedo—or married to one—there was precious little room for anyone else in your life. The clannishness of the family was obvious; Angie was relieved, even surprised, that the Escobedos opened their circle for her.

Even when there weren't holidays to celebrate, it wasn't uncommon for Gilbert, his four brothers, and his sister, their collective clans in tow, to migrate on weekends to his father's house in suburban Irving. The senior Escobedo lived on one of the better streets in a predominantly blue-collar neighborhood, and of all the dwellings on that street, his brick-and-yellow-frame house easily was the most immaculate. Updated inside and remodeled throughout, it sat on a corner lot surrounded by a meticulously groomed lawn with fresh-planted flowers in the beds. When Angie first saw the house, she wondered if there was a gene for obsessiveness.

Gilbert clearly was the levity during the get-togethers, steering conversations to the lighter, funnier side of whatever the topic and always, it seemed to Angie, defusing any family issue that threatened to escalate into full-scale argument. He was neither the firstborn nor the biggest of the Escobedo brothers, but he nonetheless was the unofficial parliamentarian and social chairman, self-appointed roles he probably had assumed in boyhood.

It was during those impromptu gatherings that Angie noticed Gilbert's special ties with his father. Father and son were mined from the same lode. Except for thirty years and the few extra pounds they had deposited around the senior Escobedo's midsection, they were a matched pair. They bore not only a striking facial and physical resemblance, but their mannerisms and personalities, down to their penchant for teasing, sometimes even using the same phraseology, were identical.

It was not surprising, then, that the two men occupied a special place in each other's lives. Robert Escobedo doted on Gilbert, Angie noticed, frequently abandoning an animated conversation in progress to hug Gilbert when he walked into the room. It was clear that Gilbert, even at thirty-four, could do no wrong in his father's eyes.

In turn, Gilbert was lavish in his praise of "Pop," whom he credited with keeping the family together when his mother walked out. His father, he said, had worked staggering hours as an upholsterer, sometimes having to rely on his own parents to care for the boys, while he tried to make a living for the family. He admired his father because he was a self-made man. His father's tidy, well-appointed house, Gilbert pointed out proudly, was a tribute to his father's commitment to hard work.

Curiously, Gilbert's mother, Pauline Hernandez, who lived thirty miles west in Fort Worth, always was a part of the Escobedo holiday gatherings Angie had attended in Irving. And from everything Angie gathered, Pauline Escobedo Hernandez's attendance apparently dated back years. The woman who had walked out on her family, an event twenty-eight years earlier that still brought tears to Gilbert during his private discussions with Angie, was accepted publicly as if nothing had happened. Never had Angie detected a hint of alienation or bad blood toward the woman, either from her ex-husband or from her children. They had either resolved their feelings about her in the two ensuing decades or they, like Gilbert, did masterful jobs of masking those feelings in public. It was a relationship that truly amazed Angie.

Still, except for maybe Mother's Day, Angie and Gilbert didn't drive to Fort Worth to visit her during the ten months they had been together. Nor had she visited in their apartment in Dallas. If the matriarch of the family saw her children, it was at her ex-husband's house, always in the presence of his second wife. The unusual setting, Angie observed, didn't appear to faze Pauline Hernandez.

Angie knew Gilbert still harbored resentment and bitterness toward his mother for the breakup of his family. He acknowledged those feelings occasionally during emotional discussions that left him depressed. He generally tried to change the subject quickly, dismissing the rare recollections by explaining, "But that was a long time ago. We're all grown up now." Time and age, he seemed to say, should be sufficient to heal any wound.

Ever the chameleon, he concealed his ambivalent feelings masterfully, Angie thought. From across the room one night, she watched Gilbert and his mother as they sat at his father's dining room table. Outwardly, Pauline was the concerned, understanding mother and Gilbert the loving and respectful son. Angie doubted that Gilbert had ever confronted his mother about his lingering feelings of her abandoning the family. He sure hadn't mentioned it if he had. Angie suspected he never would. It wasn't the way Angie would have handled a major problem, but she wasn't an Escobedo. Hispanic children, Angie learned, accorded their parents uncommon respect. It was an enviable trait, but not one that necessarily cleared the air or brought resolution to feelings.

Present at every gathering were Gilbert's beautiful daughters, Becky and Martie. Both were daddy's girls, particularly Martie, the quiet younger one, who clung to him whenever he was within reach. Gilbert's penchant for lavishing gifts on his family, Angie suspected, probably had spoiled both girls. Nonetheless, Angie thoroughly enjoyed the girls and looked forward to the weekends they spent at the apartment.

If either girl bore ill will toward her father for the breakup of their parents' marriage, they didn't show it or talk about it. They had either genuinely resolved the divorce in their minds or, as Angie suspected in Gilbert's relationship with his own mother, the girls had merely tucked their pain in some dark corner without public acknowledgment.

When the girls were moody, not an uncommon occurrence for adolescents, Daddy plied them with the same magic he used on everyone else. Escobedo couldn't stand seeing the girls upset, a reaction Angie traced to her fiancé's own splintered childhood or, perhaps, compensation for his role in the divorce from the girls' mother. Their mother, Rosie, had long since remarried. And while she didn't appear at the

Escobedo get-togethers, she and her former husband had an amiable relationship that centered around the girls.

No matter the cause, Gilbert could have his girls grinning almost spontaneously with a funny story, a hug, or plans for an upcoming weekend. If the girls didn't respond to Dad's attention, it was not unusual for him to tuck a folded $20 bill into their jeans for future use at the mall.

Observing him over time in intimate moments, Angie surmised Gilbert must have had an unusually sedate day the first time she met him at her apartment. The same quick humor and deferential manner that made him the center of his family also allowed him to make friends easier than anyone Angie had ever known. She had seen it from the owners of businesses where they shopped to the customers at his auto detailing shop, which he recently had moved with major success to a prime downtown parking garage.

Everyone, it seemed, liked Gilbert Escobedo, inquired about him, and joked with him. A vice president of the realty company that owned the parking garage, a wonderful location on North Akard in the midst of high-traffic downtown office buildings, took a liking to Escobedo and even cut the rent so he could get his business off the ground. And since Gilbert's brother and cousin had gone their own ways, Ultimate Polishing Enterprises was solely in Gilbert's hands.

Attorneys, secretaries, and businesspeople left their cars with Escobedo before work, picking them up in the evening. Escobedo's inherent obsessiveness guaranteed the cars would be meticulously washed and polished—no car was released until he personally inspected the inside of the doorjambs—but Angie suspected his newfound success was just as attributable to his personality.

Escobedo would offer his customers Cokes or coffee and chat while one of his employees was dispatched to the higher levels of the garage to retrieve the cars. He made it a point to remember a fact about each customer—something about the person's job, family, or car—and mention it during the conversation. The personal attention almost ensured repeat business and, equally important, Escobedo would say, word-of-mouth referrals.

One of Escobedo's new friends was a vice president of Republic National Bank who himself had been a customer. Recession had slapped

Dallas hard, particularly myopic yuppies who had christened their short-term successes with lavish new houses and flashy new cars. The Republic loan officer now had task forces of repo men out in the driveways of quarter-million-dollar homes, hauling off hundreds of cars whose buyers had defaulted on loan payments.

Impressed with Escobedo's outgoing personality and attention to detail, the bank officer offered him the contract to ready the bank's repossessed cars for auction. It meant sixty additional details a week. Virtually overnight, Escobedo's employees increased to six, and he had so many cars that they filled almost an entire level in the parking garage.

But of all the friends Angie met through Gilbert, the Garcias were her favorites. While the guys barbecued in the backyard and watched the Garcias' two children, Angie and Karen Garcia concocted huge pitchers of margaritas with tequila and limes. On other occasions, the couples would go out for dinner, grab a movie, or just visit.

Karen was a good mother, down to earth and easy to talk to. And Roger Garcia was so easygoing and laid back that Angie had trouble envisioning him as a police officer.

Escobedo's revelations about two broken marriages had been difficult enough for his twenty-one-year-old fiancée. Reaching deep into maturity beyond her years, Angie had accepted the fact that their pending marriage would be his third. Marrying a man thirteen years older who had twice been divorced was as far from her goals as she could imagine.

Angie, however, was not through making adjustments. Being engaged to Escobedo, she discovered, was living on the emotional edge. Just when she regained equilibrium, she would learn another dimension of her lover's background that would challenge not only her patience, but her commitment.

Just short of being together for a year, Angie noticed one night from the kitchen that he was sitting dejectedly in a chair in the living room. His face was somber, and he appeared on the brink of tears.

"What's the matter, darling?" she said, making her way to his side. "You look down in the dumps about something."

"I think I'm just going to have to move out." He made the startling pronouncement without looking at her. The news sent Angie reeling.

She sat on the floor beside the chair and put her hand on his. His watery eyes were locked on the floor and his lips quivered.

"Move out? What on earth are you talking about, baby? *Tell me.*"

"I've just got to straighten up, you know, straighten my ways," he said vaguely. "I'm going to be a Christian. I want to make my life right."

"What's wrong with your life? Why are you feeling this way? Have you done something? Please, tell me. I've got a right to know. I'm going to be your wife."

The answer wouldn't come quickly or easily, and he labored under some unknown anguish. Angie had never seen him this way and it frightened her.

"You need to know and, God, I hate to tell you this," he said shakily. "I, uh—oh, just forget it. It's best that I just leave. You don't deserve this."

Angie, bracing herself for the unknown, was steadfast.

"You're right. I don't need this. I need to know. Whatever it is. Tell me *now.*"

He had been in trouble, he finally said. He had stolen a car when he was a teenager and gotten into trouble with the law. The admission stunned her. Considering his turbulent upbringing, Angie concluded it was conceivable, maybe even likely that he would have run afoul of authority. But there was more.

"Then when I was twenty or twenty-one, back when Becky was just baby, I got into trouble again for attempted burglary. I was young and stupid, but they sent me to prison. I, uh, just didn't know how to tell you. I wanted you to love me. What you must think about me now. . . ."

Angie ached for her fiancé. Even when he had spoken about his mother deserting the family, she had never seen him in such disarray.

Unconsciously, Angie found herself reaching up to him and hugging him in a long, tight, silent embrace. His admission shocked her. An ex-convict? She was living with someone who had been to prison? Her mind tried to picture a twenty-one-year-old Gilbert in prison. My God, what had that done to a kid who already had had more than his share of trauma? What little she knew about prison she had seen in movies. Envisioning a terrified kid in the midst of hard-core prisoners—in the movies, they always had scars and tattoos—the young woman found herself holding her fiancé even tighter.

Curiously, any anger she felt wasn't directed at Escobedo. Instinctively, she felt empathy for him. His head and shoulders grasped in her arms, she was protecting him against tragedy he had endured years before they met. But his family and friends? She had visited with them regularly for nearly a year and had felt comfortable with them. No one, not once, had given her so much as a clue about Gilbert's background.

In all the informal gatherings at his father's house, with two dozen relatives carrying on a myriad of conversations and no one had confided—or even slipped—something as important as this about the man she loved and planned to marry? Did they merely assume he had told her? Or was it yet another piece of bad history, like his mother walking out or his own two failed marriages, that was off limits for discussion in the Escobedo family? Roger Garcia, a police officer, was Gilbert's best friend. Did Garcia know? Did they think that she'd never find out?

In the best scenario, she had been misled by omission. In the worst, she knew, she had been consciously betrayed not only by Gilbert, but his family and friends. His tearful admission, which *had* to be common knowledge among just about everyone who knew him, had left Angie feeling isolated and unaccepted. Clearly her acceptance by the Escobedo family had not been as unconditional as she had believed. Outwardly, they were loving, trusting, and sincere. Could his family, which obviously had accorded special and unusual considerations to the matriarch who abandoned them, be in denial about Gilbert, too? Did they truly think that if they didn't publicly acknowledge his prison background, it didn't happen at all? That she wouldn't find out? In any event, it left her feeling lonely and betrayed.

The sobbing man in her arms returned her to more immediate issues.

"I know you're not like that now, baby," she said finally, reassuring herself as much as him. "I know how hard you try to be a good person. I see you every day. I'm here. I'm going to be here.

"That was a long time ago. Everyone has skeletons in their closets."

His prison sentence was the last secret he had kept from her. He promised her.

12

"That's well and good, Gilbert, we both said some pretty strong things. I told you you can come back, and we'll live together and see how things go, and see whether we can make this relationship work or not.

"But we're not getting married in March. I'm not ready to marry you by any means. You lied to me on New Year's. You were a butthead. That's why we fought and that's why you left. Because you damned sure weren't telling me the truth. I know it and you know it. This isn't going to work if there's no honesty."

Escobedo had shown up back at the door to their Preston Greens apartment, repentant and conciliatory after storming out on New Year's. Where he had been for two weeks, God only knew. Angie Welburne had cooled only marginally in his absence, and she received his apologies about as warmly as cockroaches in the flour canister.

In the face of Angie's anger, Escobedo fell to pieces, simultaneously sobbing and begging for her forgiveness. It wasn't enough that she agreed to let him come back, he wanted total absolution. That wasn't, at the time, among Angie's options.

The catalyst for the battle had been building well before New Year's. Angie suspected he was seeing another woman. One day, he left for work without his beeper. After it went off several times that afternoon, always with the same message, Angie dialed the number. She hung up the phone when a woman answered. Angie didn't jump to conclusions. The woman could have been a secretary or receptionist for whomever placed the call. But then she caught her fiancé in an outright lie.

When he announced one morning that he would be restoring a car at his brother's house after work, Angie made plans to visit a girlfriend when she got off work. On impulse, she had decided to drop by Gilbert's brother's house on her way home. It wasn't far. He wasn't there.

Confronted when he finally came home, Escobedo said he simply had changed his mind about working on the car. But he couldn't—or wouldn't—tell Angie where he had been. Under Angie's challenge, he became angrier and angrier until finally he stormed into the bedroom. When he emerged, he was carrying his shaving kit and an armload of clothes. He slammed the front door behind him. Now, two weeks later, he was back.

"Well, Gilbert, are you willing to tell me the truth now?"

The truth, he reluctantly confessed, was that he was attracted to a woman who worked at the dry cleaners where he dropped off his shirts. He had gone out with her a few times.

Angie didn't ask her name. She didn't care.

After he was back a few days, Escobedo apologized profusely. Never, he said, would he see the woman again. Or any other woman. What he wanted, he said, was to marry Angie.

The Ski Mask Rapist hadn't struck in more than three months, but according to burglary reports, a thief was hitting the rapist's same favorite neighborhoods, apparently trying to haul off all the jewelry in the Northeast Division, gold pendant by gold ring.

The series of break-ins began the day after New Year's. One resident, a banker who lived just east of Woodbend Lane, lost $2,215 in jewelry, including a West Point class ring that had sentimental value. Two burglaries, however, drew special notice at the Ski Mask Task Force.

One thirty-five-year-old woman, who lived on Burning Log Lane just two blocks from Merilee Watson's house, apparently had been in the house alone on January 16 when the burglar entered. She was in the kitchen cooking dinner about seven P.M. when her dog began barking and headed for the den. The woman followed the dog, discovering her sliding glass door standing wide open. Missing from the adjacent bedroom was $3,000 in gold jewelry.

The break-in, Marshall Touchton proclaimed when he saw the burglary sheet, was a near-miss. It was Ski Mask looking for a twofer, an opportunity probably aborted by the woman's barking dog. He was restless again, caught up in whatever fantasies drove him. Another rape, Touchton predicted, was imminent.

The offense on Burning Log was all the more chilling considering that the deployment team swore that Gilbert Escobedo, the prime rape suspect, had blown their cover in the same neighborhood—a neighborhood in which he already had raped six women. Police had been even more convinced that Escobedo was on to their surveillance when he abruptly moved from his town house on Woodbend Lane to an apartment, apparently leased by his girlfriend, Angie Welburne, at Skillman and Audelia.

After only a brief stay, the Northeast deployment team, supplemented by plainclothes tactical officers, had followed Escobedo and Welburne to the apartment at Preston Greens. The frequent moves, coupled with his hypervigilance—surveillance cops said he used the rearview mirror of the Porsche more than its windshield—made the stakeout officers certain Escobedo had made them.

The burglary report split the task force on Ski Mask's MO. About half the detectives thought his return to the old neighborhood was proof positive that he was out of control; still others believed he had ice water running through his veins, maybe even mindscrewing the cops by rubbing their noses in the fact they couldn't stop him even though they suspected who he was. Only a few held out hope that he was just stupid.

"If he's so stupid," Sergeant Larry Lewis wondered aloud, "how come we've been chasing him for nearly two years?"

The supervisor's comment momentarily quelled the speculation.

Another burglary victim, investigators noted, a forty-one-year-old legal secretary, lived on Audelia Road just a few blocks north of the apartment complex where deployment briefly had found Escobedo in

November before he moved to Preston Greens. Perhaps more importantly, the woman worked for a law firm located downtown in the Republic Bank Tower, just two blocks east of Ultimate Polishing Enterprises.

Touchton had read Ski Mask well. On January 30, just one day short of another silent month from the elusive rapist, at least in terms of sexual assaults, he raped again. The victim, Holly Adams,* a twenty-four-year-old telephone operator, lived across Arapaho Road from Preston Greens, close enough to Escobedo's new apartment that you could throw a rock and hit his front door.

The brazenness infuriated task force detectives, including the normally placid Touchton. They were only angrier at Escobedo, and admittedly more paranoid, when they discovered that Adams had been raped on one of the few nights when neither TAC nor division deployment teams had Escobedo under surveillance. No officer had been watching to record his movements.

How in hell could he have known? Some on the task force, convinced Escobedo was in fact Ski Mask, were equally certain there was another, less obvious motivation behind his crimes: He was an arrogant stalker bold enough to prey on virtual neighbors, but who got an additional thrill by taunting the detectives who stalked him. If they were right, he was playing an icy, high-stakes game that revealed an even darker dimension of his personality.

In fact, there were always more requests for stakeouts than there were detectives to carry them out. Stakeouts worked on priorities, which in Dallas were as jammed as triage lines after a major plane crash. Ski Mask had gone more than three months without a reported attack before he struck at Adams' apartment. It was a sad fact of life, one that even veteran detectives had trouble accepting, that the squeaking wheel gets the grease.

Holly Adams had gone to bed shortly after her boyfriend left at about 11:30 P.M. Around 3:10 A.M., a man in a dark ski mask held a knife to her throat and pulled a pillowcase over her head. Spreading her legs, he removed a tampon and raped her as she lay on her back. Then he rolled her onto her stomach and forced himself inside her from the rear. The woman's hysterical sobs didn't deter him. Pulling her from the bed, he forced her onto her knees and bent her torso over the side of the bed, raping her a third time, from the rear.

Throughout the hour-and-a-half ordeal, the attacker appeared insecure about the size of his penis, asking Adams if it was big enough and whether it was as large as her boyfriend's.

He was calm and gentle, Adams told investigators, and she didn't think he really wanted to hurt her physically, even though during the attack he ripped an earring out of her ear, tearing her earlobe.

Vaginal swabs and smears, taken during the rape exam and analyzed by SWIFS, showed no evidence of seminal fluid or spermatozoa. However, acid phosphatase, a component of seminal fluid, was found on Adams' nightgown, indicating that the rapist ejaculated outside her body, then apparently used the gown to wipe off the semen.

Perhaps because she didn't sense she would be killed during the attack, Adams was more observant than some rape victims. She noticed, for example, that her attacker wore good cologne, maybe Gray Flannel, a scent she had encountered before. The tidbit, read by experienced rape investigators like Evelyn Crowder, meant that the rapist probably bought cologne at a department store rather than off the grocery store shelf, indicating he possibly had at least average, if not above average, income and possibly that he took pride in his grooming or appearance.

Similarly, Adams recalled, the attacker had body hair, an uncommon amount, she believed, at the base of his back, just above his buttocks.

Most importantly, the young woman said the rapist spoke with a "South Texas accent." It was the first time any Ski Mask victim picked up on an accent. Adams couldn't elaborate. She just instinctively associated his accent with South Texas.

Crowder regarded the intelligence a couple of ways: The attacker could be Hispanic, the predominant ethnicity in a region that stretched from San Antonio south into the Rio Grande Valley, who spoke English with a slight Spanish inflection or cadence. Or less likely, in Crowder's opinion, the rapist could be an Anglo who possibly was bilingual and spoke Tex-Mex, a bastardized version of Spanish common in South Texas.

Because there was virtually no physical confrontation during the rape, maybe the rapist felt comfortable enough to lapse into his normal conversational tone instead of a calculated and contrived speech pattern he might adopt for a sexual attack.

Holly Adams' vivid recall during her interview with rape detectives was all the more impressive considering her emotional state immediately after the attack. The uniformed officers, in their report, had noted that Adams "was very hysterical and was unable to give officer(s) much more information."

The scenario, Crowder grimly acknowledged, showed the devastating impact of rape on victims, even when they weren't beaten, stabbed, or shot during the attacks. Holly Adams apparently had remained relatively calm during the attack only to collapse as soon as it was over.

Yet, as her statement to detectives reflected, her mind later recycled every tiny detail, even down to smell and touch, that occurred in an hour and a half of agony.

Defense attorneys had loathsome habits of twisting attacks like Adams' and turning the victims' own reactions against them in court.

"Did you scream?" they'd ask. "No?"

"Well, did you fight or resist?"

"You're telling this jury that a man forced you against your will to have sex, and you just laid there and took it without lifting a finger or uttering a word?"

Motorists suspected of driving while drunk in Texas routinely are videotaped during their arrests so that juries can see every stagger and stumble and hear every slur. Maybe, Crowder sometimes thought, juries needed to see videotape of rape victims immediately after they were violated, to witness firsthand the hysteria and the involuntary convulsions.

The film would be horrifically invasive, undoubtedly only adding to victims' trauma. Still, Crowder would defy any of the good citizens of Dallas County not to be moved by what they saw. To hell with the defense's rationalizations and motivations. Let them see the indescribable, godawful result.

Word trickled down the chain of command to the task force. The patrol officer Touchton had seen chatting amicably on the doorstep of Gilbert Escobedo's town house was a "social acquaintance" of Escobedo's. According to Roger Garcia's captain, Garcia wasn't aware that his friend was an ex-con currently on parole and he certainly didn't know that Escobedo was the key suspect in the so-called Ski Mask rapes.

Further, the word was, Garcia was one of the most respected officers in the Northeast Division and had an absolutely impeccable file. As a result, he enjoyed the full support of his sergeant, lieutenant, and captain. The officer had been cautioned about his selection of friends and specifically instructed not to visit with or talk to Gilbert Escobedo.

"You'd look great in that one," Gilbert Escobedo said, pointing to the blue-and-white floral print in the corner of the show window. Taste was never one of her fiancé's shortcomings. Angie Welburne agreed it was a classy dress.

"This place is overpriced," she said.

"But you need some new clothes for work. Let's just go in long enough for you to try that dress on." He grabbed her by the arm and steered her inside the shop.

The dress, silk, looked even better once on Angie's trim frame, and she obviously was in love with it. The price tag dangling from the sleeve read $116. It was too expensive, she said, revealing another of her basic values. She'd been brought up not to blow money.

She was, however, enjoying the experience of trying on clothes, modeling them for Escobedo, then strolling to the floor-length mirrors for her own assessment. The couple left an hour later, after Angie had fallen in love with, but refused to buy, four more dresses, two sweaters, and a couple of pairs of really dressy slacks.

The couple strolled aimlessly through Prestonwood Mall, holding hands and chatting, a pleasant and comfortable moratorium on the New Year's turmoil and its strained aftermath. At a Mexican restaurant inside the mall, Escobedo insisted they stop for an early dinner. Before the food arrived, he glanced at his watch and excused himself, saying he had to call a guy about a car. He was gone an inordinately long time,

Angie thought, but he returned in a good mood and they enjoyed dinner.

In the parking lot, Escobedo typically opened the door for her. Scattered across the front seat were boxes and bags from the women's store they had visited earlier. He had gone back and bought everything she had fallen in love with.

But evil men and seducers shall wax worse and worse, deceiving, and being deceived.

—2 Timothy 3:13

13

April 3, 1987

Had it not been for his unusual background and eccentric work habits, Dennis Henderson probably wouldn't have even noticed the little red Nissan at the edge of the darkened parking lot, much less cruised past it.

But by most measures, there was little ordinary about the Reverend Dennis Henderson, pastor of the Marsh Lane Baptist Church in North Dallas. He was a night owl, for one thing, sometimes showing up at his office in the church well past midnight to work on a sermon or peck away on one of his new ministerial projects.

He was not, as his congregants well discovered over time, a preacher who merely extolled the virtues of God and the righteousness of the Bible from the sanctum of his pulpit twice a week. When the Reverend Henderson saw an opportunity to carry the message into the real world, well, he couldn't imagine that he was ordained to do otherwise. He was not fearful of getting his hands dirty in the furtherance of the Lord's work.

Such had been the case five years earlier, when the pastor had had an opportunity to spend time with Gilbert Moroney, one of his regular members and a sergeant in the Dallas Police Department. Reverend Henderson admired policemen and empathized with them in the midst of soaring crime rates that made their jobs more and more difficult. In the face of the chaos, Sergeant Moroney told the minister, many officers, particularly the younger ones, were demoralized and frustrated.

Reverend Henderson recalled the verses from Romans 13, scripture that frequently has been used to demonstrate the biblical underpinning of the role of police officers:

> Let every soul be subject unto the higher powers. For there is no power but of God; the powers that be are ordained of God. Whosoever therefore resisteth the power resisteth the ordinance of God; And they that resist shall receive to themselves damnation. For rules are not a terror to good works, but to the evil. Wilt thou then not be afraid of the power? Do that which is good, and thou shalt have praise of the same; For he is the minister of God to thee for good. But if thou do that which is evil be afraid; for he beareth not the sword in vain; for he is the minister of God, a revenger to execute wrath upon him that doeth evil.

Moved and concerned by what he had heard, Reverend Henderson began riding with Sergeant Moroney on patrol every Friday night. What he witnessed was a world alien to his, and he saw firsthand the staggering challenge officers faced. After a year, the Baptist minister applied to the Dallas Police Academy.

When he graduated, he become a reserve officer, wearing a badge and a gun just like regular commissioned police officers. The only difference was that Dennis Henderson was a full-time minister and a part-time cop who didn't get paid for it.

It was two A.M. on this particular Friday morning when Reverend Henderson drove to his office at Marsh Lane Baptist. Were he merely a minister, he probably would have dismissed the Nissan in the parking lot by the alley as a disabled car. But the vigilant part that was police officer figured the car could belong to a burglar.

Turning short of the parking lot, he cruised close enough to take the plate number. He jotted it down with the notes for his next sermon and drove to his office. He'd check the burglary sheets later to see if there had been any break-ins in the neighborhood. If there were, he'd have a rock-solid lead.

Thirty minutes later, Dennis Henderson heard a helicopter over his church. Outside in the parking lot, he saw several cruisers running a grid pattern through the neighborhood to the east. The helicopter was illuminating the alleys with its searchlights. The minister flagged a cruiser. They weren't looking for a burglar. They were searching for a rapist who had struck three blocks from the church.

The red Nissan had vanished from the church parking lot; the reserve officer bolted to his office for the plate number.

Finding the victim's house was not a problem as Dennis Henderson walked through the upper-middle-class neighborhood from his church. Parked at the curb of a substantial rambling brick ranch-style house on the corner were two marked police units and three unmarked cars. It was well after three A.M., and every light in the house was on, a predictable reaction, he had learned, in the aftermath of rape. As he walked up the steps, the minister/cop couldn't help but wonder how the family inside would explain the commotion to neighbors. As small a footnote as it was in the gravity of the situation, explanations always created anxiety among rape victims.

Inside, Henderson found the detective in charge and handed him the piece of paper with a physical description of the Nissan and its plate number. While they awaited the return on the plate, Henderson pieced together what had occurred.

The twenty-seven-year-old daughter of the couple who lived there, Suellyn Teal,* had been raped by a man in a ski mask who apparently came in through her bedroom window. He wore gloves, and the physical-evidence officers were dubious about lifting any latent prints. Predictably, the victim wasn't much help.

A phone call produced the information on the car: The registered owner was Angela Welburne, a twenty-two-year-old white female with an address in the 5900 block of Arapaho Road in Dallas, about three miles from the rape scene. There were no warrants or outstanding tickets on the car.

The on-call detective, not one regularly assigned to the Ski Mask Task Force, was nonetheless familiar with Ski Mask. He radioed for a patrol unit in the vicinity of Arapaho Road to drive by Welburne's address to see if her car was there.

"This may be reference to the serial Ski Mask Rapist. If you locate the car, please sit on it and advise."

A dispatcher relayed a message from a patrol unit within minutes: "Ten-four, got your red Nissan two-door in a carport outside the apartment in the 5900 block of Arapaho. They'll watch it until you advise otherwise."

Henderson accompanied the detective and his partner to Preston Greens, where two uniformed patrol officers were parked in the shadows fifty feet from the Nissan. Following behind the officers, the minister placed the palm of his hand on the hood.

"It's still warm," Henderson said. "It's been driven recently."

A groggy and confused Angie Welburne answered the pounding at the door and, unless she was dreaming, she thought she heard a voice yelling, "Police!" It was barely five A.M. She opened the door to three men in plainclothes and two uniformed officers.

As officers were explaining that her car had been seen by a police officer near a rape only a few hours earlier, Gilbert Escobedo walked up behind Angie. He was zipping up a pair of pants and his hair was disheveled. He yawned and stretched as he approached the men at the door.

"You're crazy," Angie yelled. She stood angrily in the doorway, hands on her hips. "My car's been in the carport all night. It's where I left it. What's this about?"

Once inside, the officers asked her if Escobedo had been at home throughout the night.

"Of course he has. Last night was Thursday night. *Knots Landing* was on. I watch it every week. It came on at nine and Gilbert got in bed beside me. He fell asleep while I was watching it. And until you banged on the door, I hadn't heard another noise."

The questions were directed to Angie, but they all focused on Escobedo. He sat in a chair listening to the exchange, periodically yawning. He appeared bemused by the process, as if it must have involved someone else.

"Well, Miss Welburne," the detective tried again, "is it at least *possible* that he could have gotten up and left in the night without your noticing it?"

Angie hesitated. The fact was, she slept like a corpse, a habit that her mother teased her about. You could taxi a 737 into her bedroom and she wouldn't hear it.

"Well, I guess anything is possible," she answered honestly. "He could have tiptoed around and got back in bed, I suppose. But was it likely? No. He was right here beside me. I'm certain of it."

Escobedo was nonchalant when the detective asked him if he'd go to headquarters with them and answer their questions. "No problem," he said, heading for his clothes in the bedroom. Angie noticed that one of the officers followed him into the hallway where he could watch him dress.

Before leaving the apartment, the detective asked Escobedo's permission to look around. "Not at all," the suspect said expansively. "Look around. I've got nothing to hide. I didn't do anything."

One of the officers uncovered a pair of gloves and, unless he was mistaken, the smudge on one of them was makeup. He put them in a bag.

Evelyn Crowder's reaction was immediate when she was told Escobedo had agreed to be interviewed and was en route to the station: "What a fool. Maybe he *is* stupid."

Not necessarily. Through much of the day a succession of rape detectives would emerge from the interview room, shaking their heads, rolling their eyes, or cursing under their breaths. Their colleagues didn't have to ask. It was not going well. Everyone was frustrated and agitated except Gilbert Escobedo, who acted more like he was applying for a job than being questioned about first-degree felonies.

"He's a likable guy with a lot of personality," Sergeant Lewis said. "He's calm and you can't rattle him. He's talking about everything. Except rape."

Escobedo was impenetrable, like a bunker in a hurricane.

On the car:

"We have Angie Welburne's car three blocks from a rape in progress. An officer takes the plate number. It's gone immediately afterward. The hood's still hot when we get to your place. C'mon, Gilbert."

"That's Angie's car. Maybe you should ask her. I don't drive it.

Maybe the officer took the number down wrong. I wasn't in the car last night. I was in bed with Angie. All night. She told you that."

On the rapes in his neighborhood:

"There weren't rapes in Woodbend until you paroled there. Then there were six and some attempts. You move to Preston Greens, bam, there's one across the street."

"I guess it's just a coincidence. Look, I *used* to be a burglar. Check the sheet. You guys know me. I was a *burglar*, not some kind of sex fiend or deviate. But I don't do burglaries anymore. It took me three times down, but I learned, okay? I mean, that's the point, right, to learn? I'm a Christian. I have a good business. I'm about to be married. I don't do criminal stuff anymore. I don't need to."

On taunting the stakeout officers:

"If you haven't done anything wrong, why did you lead the surveillance officers on a wild-goose chase down LBJ, then walk over to their car and talk to them? You being a smart-ass?"

"I remember running the Porsche out on the expressway, but, you mean, like I was being followed by officers? These sports cars, you have to blow the soot out every once in a while. Builds up, driving around town. I saw some guys later I thought were officers, yeah. I admit that. But, man, I didn't think they were there for me, you know? I mean, they were just sitting there right in the street. I spoke to 'em."

Then a tougher approach:

"What if we told you the gloves we picked up at your apartment contain makeup that matches the young lady you raped last night?"

"I'd say you're mistaken. But if that's what you think it shows, I mean, file the charges. I didn't do any rapes. I'll be able to prove it. But, you know, file the charges."

In fact, the gloves had been at SWIFS all day. Detectives were praying they could stall Escobedo until the analysis was completed. The preliminary report was hopeful. The tiny makeup smudge appeared to be a base manufactured by Mary Kay Cosmetics, the same makeup Suellyn Teal was wearing.

The call from the forensics lab dashed all hope for the gloves. The lab couldn't do the final, definitive test because the chemicals would break down the smudge, and there would be no evidence left to present in court.

The questioning was going nowhere. The task force detectives huddled in Sergeant Lewis' office for a last assault on Escobedo. Try to get at least some standards from him, Lewis said.

Back in the interview room, the detectives tried the strategy:

"Gilbert, we don't believe you, not for one minute. But you keep telling us you didn't do the rapes. We'll work with you. Maybe you're right. If you're innocent, we'll help you prove it. That's our job, too. Will you agree to give us samples of your head and pubic hair? We'll compare them with those at the rapes. I mean, if yours don't match, great. You're telling the truth. We'll leave you alone."

Escobedo didn't flinch, not for a moment.

"Sure. How do we do it? I mean, I want to cooperate, but I just don't know the procedure, you know. I've never had to do this before."

The detectives called technicians from SWIFS to collect Escobedo's hair. The suspect was on his way home within the hour.

When he opened the door, Escobedo found an agitated fiancée who for hours had paced herself into a frenzy. Cops pounded on her door before daybreak, put her car in the middle of a rape investigation, and asked her fiancé if he was a rapist. Her fiancé a rapist? That was bullshit.

Not for a heartbeat did she believe that. Ol' good-looking, charming, deep-pockets Gilbert Escobedo, *her* fiancé, a rapist? Hell, he didn't have to rape. Women beeped him in the middle of the day, female customers at his shop flirted openly with him, even the woman he tossed his dirty shirts to at the laundry couldn't wait to get him in bed. No, if the bastard slipped out in the night and used her car, it was to screw around. Again.

"We're going to sit down and talk," she said, taking the fight to him. "You did use my car last night, didn't you? You slipped out while I was asleep, you bastard, and fucked around. Didn't you?"

The man who only hours earlier had been stoic in the midst of cops who could lock him up for life imploded in the onslaught of Angie's accusations. He buried his face in his hands and his body shook under the sobs. The tears appeared genuine, but Angie was too angry to care. Gradually, Gilbert regained enough composure to break the silence.

"Remember what I told you about my past, you know, getting in trouble with burglary? To be honest with you, I was riding around thinking about that again, looking at places, scoping places out.

"I didn't actually do anything, but I was in your car riding around looking."

"No, Gilbert, I'm not going to live like that," Angie said. "I'm not going to live day to day without knowing what you're doing. If you need help to get straightened out, we'll see that you get some help. Otherwise, we're just going to break it off right now."

Before their blowup on New Year's postponed it, the couple had planned to be married in March, a month before police banged on Angie's door in the middle of the night. Had they stayed with the original plan, she would be *Mrs. Gilbert Escobedo*, a thought that now petrified Angie in the midst of their deteriorating relationship and police accusations that Escobedo was a rapist. The police claim was garbage; much more likely, she knew, her fiancé was cheating on her.

Angie had said what she needed to say. Her anger subsided, and now she was crying, too.

"It was just something in the back in my mind," Gilbert said, breaking the silence. "It didn't happen. It'll never happen, I promise you that."

April 13, 1987

Evelyn Crowder received the reports on the hair comparisons from SWIFS. The lab compared the samples Escobedo had volunteered with head and/or pubic hair collected from beds, pillowcases, and underwear of rape victims Miriam Maloney, Kimberly Baker, Mary Ann Abbott, Janice Matthews, and Billie Jean Rider.

None of the hairs from the rape scenes matched with Escobedo's.

Easter, April 19, 1987

The couple was striking, sitting midpoint in the chapel near the main aisle, she in a delicate silk dress with white heels and bag, he in an expensive suit, lizard shoes, and a shiny Rolex on his left arm. They had arrived early at Prestonwood Baptist Church even as Sunday school classes were trickling into the elegant chapel for the main Easter service.

Escobedo had talked for a week about going to church on Sunday, casually mentioning that he was a member at Prestonwood. His church membership had surprised Angie; mercifully, though, it also was one of the few recent revelations about her fiancé that hadn't forced major mental adjustments on her part.

Prestonwood was a cavernous, wealthy church less than a mile from their apartment, on Arapaho Road. It drew its members from the upper-middle-class residents of the North Dallas neighborhoods that surrounded it, and due to the largesse of influential members, it had expanded aggressively, consuming parcels on both sides of Hillcrest Road, the street that ran beside the church. Chief among its major benefactors was cosmetics-creator Mary Kay Ash, an ironic coincidence considering detectives had found a smudge of Mary Kay makeup on Escobedo's gloves.

The members who passed down the aisle beside Escobedo and his fiancée were doctors, independent businesspeople, lawyers, investors, stockbrokers, consultants, executive officers, and CPAs. Escobedo couldn't contain his intrigue.

"Do you have any idea how much money is in this place right now?" he asked, not waiting for Angie's answer.

"I know that's a thousand-dollar suit.

"I'm going to buy you a dress like that one over there. What do you think she paid for it?"

His conversation was a replay as they filed out after the service.

Walking from church to his red Porsche, Angie was certain they had gone to the right place for the wrong reasons.

14

There was Gilbert with his damn vacuum cleaner. He was so unforgivably predictable. Every day, *every day*, he vacuumed the entire apartment, always winding up with a flourish, steering the vacuum so that it made some goofy design in the carpet near the foyer. Angie walked from the bedroom into the living room, putting as much weight in her footsteps as possible.

"Baby, you're tracking the carpet! Look behind you, for godsakes!"

There it was, almost verbatim every time.

"How do you expect me to get from one room to the next, butthead? You know, you're gonna hurt yourself with that vacuum cleaner one of these days."

Angie considered herself an orderly person. She couldn't go to bed with dinner dishes in the sink; clothes strewn on the floor would run her up the walls. But a neatly folded newspaper on the coffee table, she could live with that. Gilbert would sweep the paper off the table and head for the trash as if he had just walked ankle-deep through pig shit.

The first ray of sunshine after a rain sent him scurrying to vacuum, wash, and wax both cars, which he did every week whether it clouded or not.

He wasn't meticulous; he was obsessed. He was more color-coordinated than any woman Angie had ever seen. On Saturdays for work or just knocking around, it was color-keyed gimme cap, sweatshirt, and socks. And Angie's personal favorite: He coordinated his toothbrushes to match the wallpaper in the bathroom.

Originally, she dismissed his peculiar habits as funny little idiosyncrasies that were distinctively cute and sweet. Over time, they wore at Angie like a rock in her shoe.

Angie Welburne hadn't wanted to make a major mistake in her life. It was why she wanted to live together before getting married. She loved Gilbert. She grew to accept the fact that he had been in prison and that he had violated the trust of their relationship with another woman. Ironically, perhaps, they were mistakes that Angie, thirteen years younger than he, attributed to her fiancé's lack of maturity. She hadn't made any decisions yet, but more and more there were facets of his life she could neither understand nor tolerate.

He was obnoxiously compulsive, to be sure, but there were other quirks that troubled her deeply. They were problems that so fundamentally worried Angie they couldn't be offset or diminished by the shopping sprees, the ankle-length mink, the snakeskin shoes, or the gold watch he'd given her.

What she had seen gradually through the tiny cracks in his controlled demeanor was jealousy and possessiveness. She couldn't remember if the possessiveness had always been there and she had just dismissed it in the euphoria of new love or if the control was getting worse.

One recent afternoon Angie had gone to lie by the pool. It was a Saturday and the pool was crowded. Several college-age men were milling around. Gilbert appeared momentarily, telling Angie she shouldn't be at the pool until the apartment had been cleaned. It was an excuse he had used before, and Angie knew it had nothing to do with whether the apartment was clean or not. It had everything to do with his jealousy. She had had enough.

"Look, to hell with you," she told him. "If you want it clean, clean it yourself. It's my day off. I'm laying by the pool. If you want to join me, fine, and if not, shut up and leave me alone."

When he pushed the point in hushed, embarrassed tones, Angie got in his face again.

"If you're looking for a meek, mild Mexican housewife," she said, "then you need to look somewhere else because you're not going to find it here."

Her defiance, Angie suspected from family conversations, was in marked contrast to his previous wives, neither of whom apparently ever challenged his authority. Rosie, from the picture Angie had drawn, had been the stereotypically dutiful Mexican-American wife, busying herself with rearing the two girls, cooking, and catering to Gilbert's every whim. Angie had noticed the same subservient trait among other women in the extended Escobedo family and surmised that the women's submissiveness probably extended to most traditional Mexican-American families. Mary Lou, Escobedo's second wife, though married only a short time, also had been quick to please, from everything Angie could gather. Mary Lou, who worked full time and apparently collected antiques, was by nature quiet and docile. Neither wife, though, apparently had seen fit to question the authority of the person she clearly regarded as the head of the household. Assuming he had been the same Escobedo Angie knew, she imagined both of his former wives had fallen into a go-along-to-get-along attitude in the marriage, allowing him to come and go as he pleased and always acquiescing.

Curiously, Angie also believed her willingness to speak her mind actually was one of the things that attracted him; he just didn't know how to handle it.

The incident at the pool was part of an emerging and dangerous pattern of jealousy, paranoia, and double standard. She called Escobedo one afternoon to say she was having a drink with a girlfriend after work. When she came in shortly after eight P.M., he accused her of going to the bar to hustle men.

"When you tell me you're going to work on a car, I supposedly have to trust you," she said, pointing indelicately to his own self-confessed affair. "How in hell can you expect me to trust you when you make all these insinuations about me? Tell me. You think that's fair?"

His uncontrollable jealousy led him to say things that Angie knew were intentionally calculated to hurt her. On more than one occasion that jealousy was targeted at one of Escobedo's younger cousins, Charlie, whom she barely knew.

Angie had first noticed Escobedo's reaction one Saturday when she was at the shop doing some bookkeeping. The cousin came in and was making casual chitchat when an obviously agitated Escobedo came in. When Charlie left, Escobedo told Angie he didn't want her to be around him.

"Why, Gilbert?"

"I just know how he is."

Weeks later, the cousin called the apartment asking for Escobedo. Angie told him he wasn't there, and they exchanged idle conversation. Escobedo came in during the conversation, and she passed him the phone. When he hung up, he exploded in a rage, grabbing Angie by her crotch.

"If you're going to act like that, if you're going to be a slut just like he is," Escobedo yelled, "we'll just put you out on the street and sell it."

He never explained his problem with Charlie, nor, for that matter, did Charlie ever say anything suggestive during the few brief conversations with Angie.

Almost always, Escobedo would apologize an hour or so later.

"I'm really sorry," he'd say. "I just lost my temper for a minute. I'm sorry."

Sometimes events that appeared innocent and innocuous to Angie launched Escobedo into tirades that, once begun, he wouldn't let go of for hours. En route to his brother's house on a Saturday, Escobedo bought roses for Angie from a roadside vendor. At Al Escobedo's house, while the brothers were out back piddling with a car, Angie took her shoes off and lay on the couch, dozing off.

Gilbert shook her awake, chastising her for putting her bare feet on his brother's couch.

"It doesn't look right for you to do that in somebody else's house," he told her. "You know what that makes people think about you?"

"God, Gilbert, Al's family. We're over here all the time. I don't understand what the big deal is anyway."

But she clearly had committed a felony in his eyes. On the way back to their apartment, with his brother in the backseat, Gilbert continued to berate her about her indiscretion.

"Look, just give it up, Gilbert. I'm tired of hearing about it. This is stupid."

"It's not stupid," he said. "It makes you look like a bitch."

Angie couldn't tolerate being called a bitch, and she threw the roses in his face. Escobedo reached across the seat and slapped her on her left cheek.

August 1987

The anticipation of going home to Nashville made Angie optimistic. Getting out of Dallas would be good for her and Gilbert. She wanted him to see where she'd grown up and to introduce him to her friends. Her best friend had had a baby in July, and Angie missed her mother and father.

She couldn't wait to see everyone, and staying with her mother would be like old times. It was a beautiful drive, and she and Gilbert would take turns at the wheel. The trip would invigorate their fraying re-lationship.

On Saturday night in Nashville, the couple joined five others, all friends from Angie's teenage years, and went drinking and dancing. At some point, the entourage, by near acclamation, decided to move on to another club. Escobedo balked, telling Angie it was time to go back to her mother's.

"Aw, come on, Gilbert, it's only eleven o'clock," she said. "I want to go on with my friends. I only get to see them once or twice a year. It'll be fun."

"Well, I'm not going. Do you think you could spare the time to take me back to your mother's?" His tone was caustic. It only added to Angie's resolve.

"You got it."

The argument continued in the car as she drove him to her mother's and it spilled into the bedroom where they were staying. Escobedo took his clothes off and got in bed. As she walked from the room, he deliv-ered an ultimatum.

"If you leave now, you might as well not come back."

Angie kept walking.

"Be sure to take your birth control pills with you."

When Angie returned at one-thirty A.M., Escobedo and his suitcase were gone.

Angie woke her mother. She had heard him slamming his suitcase around. He was madder than hell, Patricia Welburne told her daughter.

"He said, 'I'm not putting up with this. I'm leaving.'"

He had asked her to call him a taxi. Angie's mother tried to talk him out of leaving.

"You go back to bed and you guys work it out in the morning," she told him. She went back to bed, but she heard him leave in the night.

August 24, 1987

Gary Whitehurst* was watching the ten o'clock news when his wife, Allison,* screamed from the bedroom. Bolting to the doorway, he found her in her lingerie, cowered in a corner away from the French doors leading to the backyard. She had been sitting on the bed, talking on the phone to a friend, when she saw a pair of men's feet through the bottom of the French doors.

Gary Whitehurst grabbed his pistol from the nightstand and sprinted around the house to the backyard, blindsiding a man as he was easing away from the bedroom window.

Staring down on the smaller man, Whitehurst yelled to his wife to call the police. Then he told the window-peeper: "You make one move before they get here and you'll be a dead motherfucker. I promise you."

When officers arrived, they demanded the voyeur's identification. Even as a nervous Gilbert Escobedo produced his driver's license, he told officers he had been looking for his lost dog. It was a lame excuse, even before officers checked the driver's license, which bore an address on Arapaho Road, more than ten miles northwest. When they asked where his car was, Escobedo told them he didn't have it with him.

Officers told Whitehurst they couldn't charge Escobedo with any offense because no one had actually *seen* him peeking through the window. Whitehurst was incensed at the technicality; his wife had seen his feet beneath the French doors. He still wanted to kill him.

The officers filled out an Intelligence Division Information Card and a Sex Offender Card, standard procedures for anyone suspected of window-peeping. If they knew he was a suspect in the Ski Mask Rapes, neither officer made reference to it.

On the card they noted: "Husband detained subject until officers arrived. No one saw subject looking through the window and there is no fence around the back of the apt. The back of the apt. is an open area easily accessible to the general public. Subj. was taken home for his own self-preservation."

Angie was in Tennessee. The window-peeping event was the most recent, but not most significant, of many that she wouldn't know about.

Our system is too costly, too painful, too destructive, too inefficient for a truly civilized people.

—Chief Justice Warren E. Burger,
the Supreme Court of the United States

15

On the day in April that he deflected detectives' accusations that he was the Ski Mask Rapist, Gilbert Escobedo possessed the unfailing confidence of an innocent man. Or one who, like an assembly-line worker, knew the process by rote.

As he sat in the small interrogation room, Escobedo owned as many years' experience in the criminal justice system as any detective who questioned him. At age thirty-five, his firsthand knowledge of police and court procedure spanned nineteen years, more than half his life. His Texas Department of Public Safety rap sheet listed twenty-two close encounters.

Given his exposure to law and punishment, as documented over the five computerized pages of his criminal history, Escobedo had enjoyed a relatively charmed career as a recidivist criminal. Of all his encounters, three burglaries—not just the single conviction he tearfully acknowledged to Angie Welburne—had sent him to the institutional division of the Texas Department of Criminal Justice in Huntsville.

Cumulatively, the courts had sentenced him to eighteen years in prison. Given deductions for "good time," he actually served only a quarter of that amount. Escobedo was off Dallas streets for four years, eight months, roughly the amount of time people spend in college,

133

perhaps lending support to philosopher Friedrich Wilhelm Nietzsche's observation that punishment is "a sharpening of the sense of cunning."

That he had been convicted even three times was less a tribute to the well-oiled efficiency of the criminal justice system than it was a shabby indicator of the sheer volume of crimes he had committed.

Among the prison population, inmates actually convicted for the commission of their first offense approximated a meteorite striking the same place twice. And save perhaps for killing someone, even if they were caught while committing their first criminal act ever, the courts almost always granted them a benefit of the doubt that amounted to a free pass.

Escobedo was no exception. There were notations in his file that noted "released," "probation," "no charges filed," and "dismissed."

When finally he did fall, Escobedo was locked away more by the law of averages than by the competency of the law of the land.

Indeed, in 1982 when a twice-convicted Escobedo faced his third conviction, for attempted burglary, prosecutors responded by giving him the biggest benefit of the doubt in his criminal career. Texas for decades had an equivalent to the "three strikes and you're out" law.

The Habitual Criminal Statute—the "Bitch," as convicts call it— gives prosecutors the discretion to seek life sentences against recidivists who show up in the system after having been convicted of felonies twice before. At the time he was staring at yet a third trip to Huntsville, Escobedo was, in fact, still on parole from his second trip.

His criminal background apparently had raised no red flags because when prosecutors exercised their discretion, they agreed to a five-year sentence on Escobedo's new conviction. Magnanimously, they also allowed him to serve his new sentence at the same time he finished the remainder of his second sentence.

A life sentence as a habitual criminal, with time off for good behavior, equated to twelve and a half years, which would have put Escobedo back in society in March 1994. Instead, he served the five-year sentence in two years four months and was back in Dallas by May 1984—eleven months before the first of the Ski Mask rapes was reported.

There was nothing in Escobedo's criminal files to indicate why prosecutors had given him the benefit of the doubt on a life sentence. Most of the pages, in fact, were faint fifth- or sixth-generation photocopies of fill-in-the-blank forms, indications of a deluged and beleaguered criminal justice system forced to cope with numbers instead of people.

As reflected in his rap sheet, Escobedo was a specialist, devoting his criminal enterprise to stealing other people's belongings, generally from their homes while they slept or while they were gone. Not noted in the file, because juvenile offenders enjoy a unique secrecy in the legal system, Escobedo actually had run afoul of the law a twenty-third time.

At the age of sixteen, he had been sent to the Dallas County Boys Shelter for stealing a car. His résumé as an adult offender would begin a year later, a month after his seventeenth birthday, when he was arrested for investigation of burglary. It was then that he received his first freebie from the system and was released without charges.

The criminal histories, veteran detectives like Marshall Touchton knew all too well, told a fractured reality. Their entries recorded only those occasions in which the offenders' crimes were flagrant enough to pierce the system's multitudinous safeguards against violating suspects' civil rights: probable cause, eyewitness accounts, and physical evidence. The rap sheets did not record the times a person was apprehended and released, for a lack of probable cause or evidence, *before* going to jail.

That Escobedo had been caught in the middle of the night outside Allison Whitehurst's bedroom window while she, clad in sheer nightclothes, was inside that bedroom would never be recorded on his rap sheet. And since it hadn't resulted in an actual arrest, there would not even be an incident report to be pulled up from a computer. The incident would exist informally, only on two cards filed away in the intelligence and sex crimes offices of the Dallas Police Department.

Even when legal affronts were logged, the official criminal accounts generally didn't reveal the crime for which an offender *originally* was arrested, only the bottom line of the crime once it had been twisted, manipulated, and, always, diluted by plea bargains.

Escobedo's file showed that virtually every time he had been arrested, he hired his own lawyer rather than roll the dice with a free, court-appointed attorney. Yet, never had he chosen to exercise his privilege under the Sixth Amendment to cast his fate with a jury on his innocence or guilt. In each case, he had relied on a plea bargain.

Plea bargains are the oil that greases the wheels of criminal justice. They are the handshakes that consummate a defense lawyer's best efforts on behalf of his client and a prosecutor's acknowledgment that he probably couldn't do any better before a jury. Or, more likely, that the prosecutor simply is too deluged in backlogged cases to try.

Homicides, for example, frequently appear on rap sheets as manslaughter; drug trafficking becomes simple possession of narcotics.

But in no crime are the plea-bargained differences between original charges and final disposition more skewed or misleading than sex offenses. A break-in to commit rape, in the absence of extraordinarily strong physical evidence, damning testimony from the victim, and a relentlessly committed prosecutor, inevitably ends up on a rap sheet as merely a conviction for residential burglary.

Plea bargaining to the lesser offense is so common, in fact, that experts like Dr. A. Nicholas Groth estimate that when these so-called hidden offenders are added, sex offenders really account for up to twenty-five to thirty percent of prison populations throughout the country.

No sex offender wants to go to prison, particularly behind a rape or child molestation conviction. Pleading guilty to a lesser charge—say, burglary—immediately reduces his exposure to prison by ten to twenty years. But there are long-term considerations, too.

Even in a twisted prison social order that affords the greatest respect and deference to murderers, the rapists and child molesters still are the bottom-feeders in the food chain, making them moving targets for the rest of the inmates. Equally important to sex offenders, they know they're more likely to get early parole if officials are looking at burglary on their rap sheets instead of rape.

Not surprisingly, then, Touchton and his colleagues on the Ski Mask Task Force read the rap sheets with the same jaundiced eyes reserved for supermarket tabloids that printed only partial truths.

There were no arrests or convictions for rape on Gilbert Escobedo's sheet. But his odyssey through the criminal justice system had left more than a few indicators in the yellowed, archived records about his criminal propensities and escalating boldness:

· **December 1968**

Susan Burman,* a flight attendant for Braniff Airways, returned to her apartment near Love Field shortly after midnight December 5. She noticed a young man loitering near the front of her apartment complex. When he noticed she was looking at him, he ducked his head and walked away.

About three A.M., Burman was awakened as someone was easing the covers off her bed. She screamed, and the intruder bolted from her bedroom, taking a Neiman-Marcus diamond-and-emerald watch, a diamond Hamilton watch, and three diamond dinner rings worth $8,950.

Police arrested Gilbert Escobedo a week later as he was trying to break into another apartment. Burman's jewelry was recovered the next day from a North Dallas apartment leased by one of Escobedo's female cousins. The flight attendant picked out the seventeen-year-old Escobedo from a photo lineup. Though it had been too dark in her bedroom to see the intruder, Escobedo, she said, was the same teenager she had seen loitering around her apartment nearly three hours before the break-in.

Escobedo, by that time, already had done time at the Dallas County Boys Shelter for car theft. Two months before the break-in at Burman's apartment, he had been arrested for investigation of burglary and released without charges. He was sentenced to a probated three-year sentence for the Burman burglary.

· **April 14, 1972**

Five months short of completing probation for stealing Burman's jewelry, Escobedo was convicted of two residential burglaries in Dallas. The original three-year probation for the flight attendant's burglary was revoked, and the court sentenced him to serve the remainder of his old sentence concurrently with the new three-year conviction.

Escobedo, twenty, father of a three-month-old daughter, began his first tour in the Texas Department of Criminal Justice, assigned to a minimum-security prison for youthful offenders. He was paroled back to Dallas County on January 26, 1973.

- **April 6, 1975**

  Escobedo, in Dallas County Jail since February 4, pleaded guilty to evading arrest. The circumstances of the incident, a misdemeanor, were not retained in official court records. He was sentenced to sixty days in county jail, but was released after serving less than thirty.

- **December 3, 1975**

  Escobedo, twenty-six, recently divorced and now the father of two daughters, pleaded guilty to two counts of burglarizing the homes of two women, both of whom lived alone. He was transferred April 8, 1976, to Huntsville to begin his second prison sentence, this one for ten years.

  Board of Pardons and Paroles records show that on June 9, 1977, Escobedo's first parole review date, his father, Robert, and a brother, Alfred, appeared on his behalf. Parole was denied until November 1, 1978, when Escobedo was returned to Dallas.

- **December 7, 1981**

  Officer Jim Duckworth of the Mesquite Police Department was called at 4:23 in the afternoon to the automotive department of Sears at the sprawling Town East Mall, just east across LBJ Expressway from the Dallas city limits.

  Sears employees reported that a man had been exposing himself. As they pointed to the suspect in a blue 1981 Corvette, the man sped from the parking lot. After a high-speed chase, first westbound on LBJ Expressway, then back eastbound on the freeway through rush-hour traffic, Duckworth, with the aid of a backup patrol unit, finally curbed the Corvette.

  The driver was Gilbert Escobedo. He listed an address in northwest Dallas and said he worked as a stock clerk at a nearby grocery store. The new Corvette was listed in his name. He posted $200 bond and was released.

  Notes, handwritten apparently by the prosecutor, were jotted on the case file: "4 conv. burg, now on parole, parole off. has been notified."

In August 1982, nine months after the incident at Town East Mall, Escobedo pleaded guilty to a misdemeanor of disorderly conduct, "knowingly exposing his genitals in a public place," and was sentenced to sixty days in county jail.

Escobedo, thirty, and married to his second wife for more than a year, was released in thirty days. He was still on parole from his ten-year burglary conviction.

• **September 1982**

Sisters Melanie and Julie Rawlings* were hysterical by the time the patrol unit arrived at their Oak Lawn duplex shortly after midnight on September 11. Several times in previous weeks, they said, a prowler, who sometimes appeared nude, had been lurking outside their windows during the night.

He had returned, this time tapping boldly on a rear bedroom window and asking the younger sister, Julie, twenty-seven, where her sister was. Melanie yelled from another room that she had phoned police; he was gone when officers arrived.

Thirty minutes later, giving the officers barely enough time to leave the block, the intruder was back. By the time Julie Rawlings noticed him, he already had slashed the bottom of the screen with a knife.

As she ran from the room, she heard the sound of breaking glass. She returned quickly from the kitchen with a butcher knife, the only weapon she could find. The man was half in, half out the window, and the terrified young woman fended him off with the knife, but not before he slashed her wrist. Within minutes, the officers were back, but could find no sign of the intruder.

Stunningly, in less than an hour, the knife-wielding prowler returned a third time, apparently to be frightened away by a patrol car slowly cruising the alley.

Several times in the next two weeks, the prowler returned, sometimes nude, with the legs of his khaki pants tied around his neck.

Around midnight on September 25, plainclothes officers Steve Minnis and Edward O'Bara of the Tactical Squad joined the Rawlings sisters inside the house, careful to stay away from the rear windows. According to the report the officers would file:

Officer Minnis, while sitting in a dark, open doorway, observed Escobedo walk from the next-door house to the complainants' driveway. Escobedo then stopped, leaned forward and looked into the complainants' window. Officer Minnis could only see one of Escobedo's hands as he was parting the shrubs, peering into the window.

Officers Minnis and O'Bara exited the door and caught Escobedo as he attempted to flee. A struggle ensued and Escobedo was apprehended. Officers identified themselves as police officers and Escobedo continued to struggle.

Melanie and Julie Rawlings identified Escobedo as the man who repeatedly had exposed himself, who had masturbated while peeking through their window, and who had tried to break into their house. He was charged with investigation of burglary, a first-degree felony, and disorderly conduct, a misdemeanor.

Escobedo, thirty-one, a three-time loser and on parole, had committed the most outrageous and violent felony of his career. Even knowing that police were watching the Rawlings sisters' house, he compulsively reappeared, stabbing Julie Rawlings while trying to come through her window and ultimately battling the two officers who arrested him.

Beyond statutory doubt, Escobedo more than met the provisions of the Habitual Criminal Statute and the mandatory life sentence it carried.

For reasons that are not apparent in his criminal file, the charge was never filed. Three months after his arrest, Escobedo pleaded guilty to attempted burglary of a habitation, a second-degree felony, and was sentenced to five years. It wasn't until February 25 of the next year, after he had been in prison for three months, that the Texas Board of Pardons and Paroles revoked his parole from his third sentence.

Any significance of the parole revocation existed only on paper; he was allowed to serve the remainder of his third sentence at the same time he served his fourth.

On April 16, 1984, a Dallas district judge granted Escobedo's second wife a divorce, in which she claimed "irreconcilable differences" that made their marriage "insupportable."

Little more than a month later, on May 24, 1984, Gilbert Escobedo, thirty-two, was released on mandatory parole. His family met him at the prison release center in Huntsville and drove him back to Dallas.

Within months, he and two brothers moved into the condo on Woodbend Lane.

16

November 1987

Out of necessity, Marshall Touchton had fallen back on his old bread-
and-butter ways, periodically surveilling Gilbert Escobedo's apartment
at Preston Greens in North Dallas and randomly watching Ultimate
Polishing Enterprises in downtown Dallas. Nothing he had seen or
heard from the questioning of Escobedo in April had ruled him out as
a suspect.

Quite the contrary. The ex-con's brassy attitude, weighed in the historical context of his criminal background, only solidified the veteran
cop's gut feeling that Escobedo was the Ski Mask Rapist.

That instinct had been borne out in the last seven months, in Touchton's opinion. Taking Escobedo through the drill after the Suellyn Teal
rape—while in reality it hadn't moved officers even a smidgen closer
to charging him—had at least dropped Escobedo in the grease; he was
hot and he knew it.

Not surprising to Touchton, there had not been a single rape attributable to Ski Mask since. Which, unfortunately, also meant that surveillance, at least anything beyond sporadic peeks, couldn't be justified.

There were other indications, however, that Escobedo's command
performance at Main and Harwood had not scared him totally straight.
The fantasies and his inclination to act on them could have gotten him

killed outside Allison Whitehurst's apartment, not a totally unaccept-
able resolution among some members of the task force.

Power rapists—and there was no doubt among any of the detectives
that Ski Mask fit the category—operated on obsessional thoughts that
triggered masturbatory fantasies. The fantasies *had* to be carried out;
inevitably there would be more rapes.

Researcher A. Nicholas Groth, in *Men Who Rape*, described the typical fantasy experienced by power rapists: "The characteristic scenario
is one in which the victim initially resists the sexual advances of her
assailant; he overpowers her and achieves sexual penetration; in spite of
herself, the victim cannot resist her assailant's sexual prowess and becomes sexually aroused and receptive to his embrace."

But in reality, of course, the scenario never plays out like his fantasy.
The power rapist knows that the woman didn't fall in love with him.
"Therefore," Groth wrote, "he must go out and find another victim,
this time the 'right one.' His offenses become repetitive and compulsive,
and he may commit a whole series of rapes over a relatively short time."

It is a vicious circle.

While there hadn't been any reported rapes after the window-
peeping incident at the Whitehursts' apartment, someone with a remarkably similar MO to Escobedo's had pulled three burglaries
immediately south of Ski Mask's tried-and-true haunt in Woodbend.
The heists were professional, and concentrated on gold jewelry, not
bulky TVs and VCRs. The rip-offs hadn't been committed by geared-
up teenagers looking to barter for their next Baggie of crack. One burglary in particular, committed sometime on September 17 or 18, fit
Escobedo like one of his fine Italian suits.

After spending two days at her boyfriend's house, Traci McMillen,*
twenty-eight, a model, returned home to find the front door of her
condominium ajar. The deadbolt lock had been pried. It wasn't,
McMillen knew, the first time someone had attempted to get into her
house. Only a few days earlier, maintenance workers had replaced a
bedroom window that had been shattered. The broken window had
frightened her. It was why she had been staying at her boyfriend's place.

The burglar hauled off everything of value McMillen owned: a Rolex
watch, a string of pearls, a diamond solitaire, two gold rings, two pairs

of gold earrings, an ankle-length rabbit coat, a short fox coat, $500 in cash she had tucked beneath the mattress, even a box of frozen prime steaks.

But even more unnerving to the young model than the loss of $8,000 in property was discovering her lingerie, panties, and bras scattered over the floor of her bedroom.

Predictably, the burglar left no prints or any other evidence behind.

McMillen called burglary investigators back a week later. She had discovered yet another belonging missing, one that had absolutely no value among the fences who moved stolen property. Missing from the bottom drawer of a dresser was McMillen's modeling portfolio.

The pictures, probably along with some underwear that McMillen hadn't even missed, were "trophies," Touchton knew, not uncommon thefts for rapists. It didn't take a Ph.D. to figure how Escobedo would weave the items into the fantasy world in which he lived.

Watching Escobedo's auto detail shop from a parallel parking slot down the street and, occasionally, walking past the driveway to the parking garage, Touchton saw immense activity. The guy apparently had all the business he could handle. Early in the mornings the detective counted as many as seven men coming to work in the green T-shirts that advertised Ultimate Polishing on the left front.

At one point, Touchton saw an obviously ebullient Escobedo drive out in a Ferrari, returning maybe three hours later. At the end of the day, he drove home in it. Stakeout teams variously reported him in Porsches, BMWs, Jags, and other luxury imports. But Ferraris? Weren't they like $200,000?

One Sex Crimes detective, only recently reassigned from the auto theft detail, had been convinced Escobedo was dealing "chop shop" cars, stolen vehicles that were cut into pieces and parts, then reassembled with new Vehicle Identification Numbers, called VINs, to cover the thefts. Thieves customarily replace license plates, but the VIN numbers, located on the left-hand corner of the dash and visible through the windshield, are the real identification that officers use to track stolen cars. Unknown to most car owners and even to some car thieves, manufacturers replicate the VINs in hard-to-find places on the undercarriages of the vehicles. Locations of the concealed VINs depend on the manufacturer and the model.

Spotting Escobedo's newest set of flashy wheels one night as it was parked in his drive, the former auto theft detective chose to resolve the issue once and for all. If the VIN on the dash didn't match the concealed number beneath the car, then they'd at least take the bastard off the street for car theft. It was toward two A.M. and there were no lights on in Escobedo's apartment. The suspect, the officer assumed, had been tucked in all night.

Grabbing a flashlight, the detective lay on his back and used his feet to thrust himself beneath the low-slung sports car. Raising his head to follow the beam from the flashlight, the cop's forehead met with the gearbox, searing an evil red-and-black burn into his head above and between his eyes. The meeting of flesh and hot metal produced an anguished curse that shattered the silence of predawn. Escobedo had parked the sports car only minutes before the detective decided to test his VIN theory; the gearbox hadn't cooled.

The detective endured unmerciful kidding the next day, but he had been committed, even in the face of pain, to his mission. The VINs not only matched, but the number hadn't been reported stolen. Next time, the officer vowed, he would put his hand on the hood; if it was warm, he'd be damned if he'd crawl beneath it.

If Escobedo was driving detectives crazy with a multitude of cars, it was because he had access to as many as sixty vehicles at a time. In addition to having the keys to Republic Bank's repo pool, which was parked on the upper levels of the garage, he also had a lucrative new contract to detail sports cars for a major import dealer. Virtually every day he left in a different exotic car.

Touchton was right about Escobedo's business thriving. Angie Welburne had seen it firsthand. Escobedo was so stretched supervising all the jobs and new employees that he fell behind in statements and paying bills, jobs that had fallen to Angie on nights and some weekends. He actually was becoming a success story, Angie realized as she looked at his books and bank statements. He had taken on hard manual labor and parlayed it into a respectable middle-class existence.

Escobedo, it seemed to Angie, had immersed himself even more deeply into the business, particularly since that nuclear night in Nashville. She thought he was trying to impress her with his stability and dedication.

Stability. It was something Angie found herself craving. A year earlier, the trait wouldn't have made her top ten list of requirements for marriage. But a year of frequent disappointment in a whiplash relationship had redefined her goals. Handsomeness, luxurious gifts, Porsches, all that was nice, but superficial, too. What she wanted was a foundation. God forbid, she wasn't asking for boredom by any means, but stability, *responsibility*. She longed for it. Her husband, she now knew, would have to trust her enough for her to know *everything* about him. And those things would be volunteered, not trickled out in remorse or coercion. She had to have someone she could depend on, a man she knew intimately enough to predict. She needed maturity.

No, Escobedo needed to demonstrate change. By his actions, he needed to make amends. He had made a complete ass of himself in front of her mother. As he later explained, he had walked to a motel near Patricia Welburne's house and spent the night. The next morning he took a flight back to Dallas. Like he always had, he apologized profusely to Angie for his jealousy and temper, even calling her mother in an attempt to repair her frayed feelings.

There wasn't any single catalyst that Angie could point to—not Escobedo's asinine temper tantrum at her mother's or even the night the cops hauled him off for questioning—but she had a vague, dull feeling about their relationship that made her weary. Their life together had evolved into a nonconfrontational, undeviating flat line with few peaks and valleys, the way Angie feared their marriage would be.

She cared about him, but he didn't make her feel inspired. The basic barometers by which she gauged her relationship—spontaneity, the caring and unplanned touching when they were within arm's length, and sex—were no longer priorities. It wasn't just him; it was her, too. She realized that.

From the beginning, their sex life had been adequate, if not all that intriguing. Escobedo, from Angie's perspective, was "Mr. Missionary Man," so reluctant to depart from the conventional sex position that he never suggested anything else. Sex, she confided to a friend, was "wham, bam, it's over," whether in actuality she wanted it to be over or not. She didn't regard him as a particularly selfish lover. It was more, she suspected, a manifestation of the same unimaginative conservatism that he had shown the day she first met him at her apartment.

Earlier on, particularly in the aftermath of minor spats or when she feared the relationship was ebbing, Angie would become the resourceful and provocative instigator, initiating sex to repair damage or to break the monotony. Gilbert never dodged the opportunities. Still, Angie generally was left feeling that she had given more than she had received.

Now, she knew, she was watching the distance between them grow greater, but she couldn't muster the energy or will to stop it. Gilbert, she sensed, realized it, too. But he relied, as he always had, on his lavish gifts to break the fall. She might have been dazzled early on by his materialism—a possibility too painful for Angie to contemplate—but his gifts of gold watches and earrings no longer moved her.

The gifts only added to the deep questions she had about her relationship with this paradoxical man so alien to her imagined ideal for a husband.

November 17, 1987

The scene, as Gina Venzuela* later described it to her sister, was like something out of *Psycho*. It's 9:20 P.M. and she's lying on the couch in the living room with the television on; some guy in a black ski mask leans through the drapes with a pistol, saying, "Don't scream or I'll shoot you."

He crawls on through the window, saying, "Put your hands over your face. I don't want to have to shoot you."

Hands over her eyes, Venzuela asks him what he wants.

"You're either going to let me look at you or I'm going to kill you."

"Well, you're full of shit, buddy."

He brought the pistol down hard across the left side of her face.

"Shut the fuck up," he said. "You're either going to let me look at you and feel you up or you're gonna get hurt real bad."

"I'm having my period," Venzuela said, feeling the throbbing in her face. "I don't want you to touch me."

"Look, you'd better shut the fuck—"

In a flash, Venzuela was angered beyond any concern for her safety.

"You want a look, you bastard," she said, ripping open her blouse and exposing her breasts, "go ahead! Take a *good* look!"

He grabbed her, shoving the gun in her face.

"You don't shut the fuck up, I'll shoot you. Just shut up."

He dropped his pants and forced her hand onto his penis. He could not get an erection. He masturbated. He forced her to take off her pants and underwear.

"I don't want to hurt you," he said, forcing her to the floor and placing her pants over her head. "I just want to get off."

He forced open her legs and fondled her genitals. He forced her to sit up, still with the pants over her head. He moved behind her, moving his penis onto her shoulder, then masturbated. Finally, he ejaculated onto her back. He moved her to the couch, forcing her to lie facedown, and fondled her buttocks. Then he became quiet, and she couldn't feel his hands on her.

Thinking he had slipped back through the window, Venzuela reached, ever so tentatively, for the pants that covered her head.

"What the fuck do you think you're doing?" he yelled, slamming her again with the butt of the pistol.

"Look, I just want you to leave," she pleaded. Her head and face pulsated with pain. "I promise. I won't call the police."

"I know you," he said. "I've been following you for weeks. I live in this complex, and I watch every move you make."

Then he left.

Gina Venzuela was a twenty-seven-year-old airline employee who taught flight attendants. Several times over the previous three months, she told Marshall Touchton, she had received obscene phone calls. The male voice was so specific in his description of her body that it chilled her and made her scan the windows to see if she was being watched. Who *was* this person who knew her body so intimately? Was he guessing, or did he really know? How? The last call, she said, came at 2:15 A.M. the day she was assaulted.

The only thing missing after the attack, Venzuela said, was a student portfolio that had been lying on the coffee table. The portfolio contained the photos and backgrounds of flight attendant candidates.

December 6, 1987

The Texas Board of Pardons and Paroles, having determined that Gilbert Escobedo had satisfactorily completed the terms of his mandatory supervision, released him from parole. It was a perfunctory paper trans-action with no hearing and no notification to police. Based not on Es-cobedo's ability to conform to the law but solely on the calendar, the administrative paper was generated from a tickler file in some bureau-crat's office.

December 9, 1987

Detective Corporal Evelyn Crowder was jubilant. For the first time in more than two and a half years, Dallas was down to only two major serial rapists—the M Street Rapist and the ever clever Ski Mask.

Like Gilbert Escobedo's, Gregory Darnell Bradford's name was well known among rape investigators. Bradford had become a suspect in 1984 when Dallas officers had arrested him on an outstanding warrant from Louisiana.

Rape victims in Dallas as young as fourteen and as old as fifty-eight had described an assailant who fit the same general description as Bradford, an independent moving contractor. Sex Crimes detectives questioned him at the time, but had no evidence.

Rapists generally lapse into an MO, operating within perimeters in which they feel safe and comfortable. If the approach works for them over time, some even become superstitious, fearing that if they deviate from their plan, they'll get caught.

It explained Ski Mask's primary concentration in Woodbend, detec-tives believed, and it also explained why he nearly always surprised his victims as they slept, neutralizing them before they could fight back.

Bradford hadn't been nearly as geographically predictable as Ski Mask, choosing his victims instead from throughout the city. He did, however, have a frequent MO when it came to discouraging resistance. Wielding a knife, he frequently told his victims that he had just been released from prison.

"I've already killed six women," he'd say. "One more isn't going to make any difference." The threat was chillingly effective, and virtually none of his victims resisted.

A year after detectives first questioned Bradford, a rape victim, whose head had been covered during the attack, believed her assailant's voice resembled that of a man who had moved her furniture. Checking the moving company's records, detectives discovered that the move had been subcontracted to Gregory Darnell Bradford. The attacker had worn gloves, and the witness couldn't identify him. Periodic surveillance on Bradford over the next two years was fruitless.

In all the rapes police attributed to Bradford, his victims said he wore gloves during the attacks. But on September 8, the mover departed from his MO, leaving one of his fingerprints at a rape scene.

Media reports attributed Bradford's arrest to the fingerprint, a not altogether accurate scenario that police didn't rush to correct. Because the rapist had covered the victim's face, she couldn't identify him. With one latent print and no witness, detectives didn't have nearly enough to get the district attorney to accept the case. They needed to catch him inside an apartment with the intent to rape.

Sex Crimes improvised. They recruited "plants," female officers who arranged to be moved by the same company. Bradford had drawn one of the moves. Just as detectives had hoped, he returned to the woman's house within nights, crawling through a window and right into their hands.

In interviews after his arrest, the deferential Bradford belied the public's stereotype of rapists, a fact that came as no surprise to Crowder.

In characterizing the suspect for the media, one detective said: "He's very quiet-spoken. He speaks very good English and rarely uses profanity. He doesn't yell and he doesn't scream. He said he knew it was wrong."

Bradford's lawyer pushed a plea bargain, one that officers and prosecutors reluctantly accepted. They still had no rape victims who could identify Bradford as a rapist. Without his cooperation, they had a case of breaking and entering, *maybe* with intent to rape.

Part of the agreement, which Sergeant Larry Lewis insisted on, was that Bradford admit to every rape he had committed, a figure officers estimated at somewhere between twenty to twenty-five. In return, the twenty-nine-year-old rapist would plead guilty to two concurrent fifty-year sentences, which could make him eligible for parole in twelve and a half years.

Knowing all too well the public's skepticism of plea bargains, Assistant District Attorney Mike Gillett took special pains when he talked to the media, pointing out that officers never would be able to resolve all of Bradford's rapes without his own help.

"It provided an avenue to be able to at least help those victims know that the person who did it was in the penitentiary," the prosecutor said.

The negotiated confessions with Bradford took longer than detectives imagined. Since 1981, the serial rapist acknowledged, he had raped fifty-one women in Dallas. The figure shocked officers, particularly Crowder. The number of his victims would have been higher, Bradford confided, but he had gotten married a year earlier and spent more time at home.

Detectives underestimated the number of rapes attributed to Bradford by at least fifty percent because he changed his MO, something the Ski Mask Rapist seldom did. Some of Bradford's victims were women whose households he had moved, others he chose at random. They spanned Dallas. They ranged in age from young to old. Some were attractive, others weren't.

And while his "I killed six women" ploy was his most effective, he didn't use it every time. (Detectives determined, to the best of their ability, that Bradford had never killed anyone.) In the absence of evidence and witnesses, the changes in MO, Crowder knew, made it virtually impossible for detectives to detect patterns.

In part, Bradford confirmed one of the most ominous realities in investigating stranger-on-stranger rapes: If a rapist was careful enough to conceal his identity, if he was disciplined enough to leave no physical evidence, and if he was creative enough to change his MO, he could continue to rape with virtual impunity.

Those precautions, however, depend on dispassionate, rigid adherence to detail by an emotionally stable, detached, and rational person. Rapists fall at the extreme opposite of the spectrum, steered by erratic fantasy, anger, sadism, and obsession stronger than their own self-discipline.

Understanding the difference was the only modicum of hope in the netherworld of a Sex Crimes detective.

17

Early January 1988

"Gilbert, I need to tell you some things," Angie Welburne said tentatively. She had rehearsed the speech a hundred times while she was in Nashville with her family over Christmas and New Year's. Now, delivering it in person as he sat on the couch with wrinkled brow wasn't easy.

Her decision was, however, so obvious that she couldn't believe she had overlooked it for so long. So with the reassurance that she was taking the right fork in the road, Angie moved on.

"Angie, let me—" Gilbert Escobedo interrupted.

"No," she said, pulling him up short. "Let me finish this. Things aren't working out real well for us. The distance is growing between us. You've been getting on my nerves, I've been getting on your nerves."

She didn't want to hear alternatives or promises from him. That would only prolong the pain. Her thoughts had to appear unequivocal, and they had to be heard:

"I'm just not sure I love you anymore. And I'm not sure I ever truly loved you the way I should for two people to be talking about getting married."

The truth sounded harsher than her intent. She hadn't wanted to hurt him. She was well past anger. Desperately, though, she had to change her course, to put a major mistake behind her. She studied his face for reaction. Finding no anger, she finished what was on her heart.

"I'm moving back to Nashville. I've already made plans. It's really where I want to be, with my family and friends. I miss them. You've got some wonderful qualities, Gilbert, and you deserve to be happy, too. I know you will be."

She was surprised and relieved at his reaction. Yes, he had felt the distance and had questioned their future, too. He would miss her, he said, and while marriage apparently wasn't to be, he didn't intend to lose her friendship. He made her promise they'd continue to be friends. Dutifully and painlessly, Escobedo went out immediately and found himself a new one-bedroom apartment on McCallum Boulevard, farther north in Dallas.

Two weeks later, after a pair of Angie's friends came down from Nashville to help her load her rental truck, the three of them stopped off at Escobedo's on the way out of town. He fixed sandwiches and drinks for everyone, and they chatted like old friends. He hugged Angie tightly before she climbed into the truck and drove off.

August 25, 1988

Rapists, Evelyn Crowder once said, are where you find them, without regard for appearance, criminal history, or stature in the community. Rule out any suspect for those reasons, she frequently told young rape detectives, and you set yourself up for a fall.

Reporter David Jackson's article in the *Dallas Morning News* only added validation to Crowder's theory of rape investigation:

> A Southern Baptist minister pleaded guilty Wednesday to a series of rapes in North Dallas and was sentenced to 10 concurrent life terms.
>
> Gregory Charles Goben, 28, minister of the Outreach Baptist Church in Garland, pleaded guilty to five counts of burglary of a habitation and five counts of aggravated sexual assault, all first-degree felonies.
>
> As part of the plea agreement, Assistant District Attorney Mike

Gillett said he interviewed Goben about other offenses and Goben admitted to six additional sexual assaults, five in Dallas County and the other in Denton County. . . .

A sobbing Goben, questioned during the hearing, said viewing pornographic films and magazines contributed to his behavior. . . .

The hearing included testimony from a victim who said a man broke into her bedroom early one morning in September.

"He told me that we were going to make my face all up and that he was going to shave me and that he had brought a movie for us to watch and we were going to do all of those things," the woman said. "And that if I did everything he wanted me to do, he wouldn't kill me."

The victim, a widow who said she lived away from her home for a month and sought counseling after the incident, said she had a special reason for wanting to testify against Goben.

"I wanted him to have to sit there and listen to what I had to say and how it made me feel when he did all of that to me," the woman said.

November 7, 1988

Even as Claire Miller* awaited police in her apartment on the northwest corner of Preston and Arapaho roads, Ski Mask was stealing through the unlocked front door of Jenny Lynn Baxley's* heavily alarmed, half-million-dollar house three blocks northeast of the same intersection.

Ski Mask had to be as precise as NASA in his planning or the impervious exploiter of extraordinary happenstance. His window of opportunity to rape Jenny Baxley hinged on his being able to see her husband leave through the front door for his morning jog at exactly 5:32 A.M.

It was the only way to ensure that Jerry Baxley was, in fact, no longer in the house and that he had disarmed the couple's state-of-the-art security system. And even then, Ski Mask had to be undeterred by the real possibility that police units would be saturating neighborhoods adjacent to the scene of Claire Miller's apartment, where he had raped her only minutes earlier.

Or that Jerry Baxley could, say, twist an ankle, or for some other unforeseen reason return home from his jog earlier than usual. Perhaps the rapist considered both, accounting for the fact that he raped Baxley and slipped back into the predawn darkness in seven minutes.

The second of the two rapes to occur in two hours and forty minutes was so bizarre that it challenged the descriptive abilities of the uniformed officer who wrote the report. Amazingly, not until after the attack was over did Jenny Lynn Baxley fully comprehend that she had been raped.

It was not unusual for her husband to crawl out of bed after 5 A.M. to jog, and over time Jenny Baxley apparently had learned to ignore the predictable movement of the bed and rustle of covers. At 5:32 A.M., according to the digital clock on the bedstand, she felt the weight of someone, separated only by the covers, on top of her. Momentarily, she felt the covers being pulled off and realized she was being penetrated. "During the assault," Officer Mark King wrote,

> complainant shut her eyes and was thinking that it was her husband and that he had gone crazy. Complainant stated that her husband has never done anything kinky or strange sexually. . . .
>
> Complainant's 13-year-old daughter and 8-year-old son were in the house sleeping and suspect did not disturb them. When the suspect finished, he got up without saying any words, pulled his pants up and left through the front door. At this time, complainant realized that it was definitely not her husband and she hid underneath the table near her bed. . . .
>
> Complainant stated this happened during a dead sleep and that is why she did not recognize this as being a rape.

Baxley had seen so little of her attacker in the groggy darkness that the rape couldn't have been attributed to Ski Mask were it not for his attack earlier the same morning three blocks west across Preston Road.

Claire Miller lived directly across the street from Preston Greens, in a luxury apartment complex that sloped its way down to McKamey Branch, a picturesque creek that wound its way through Prestonwood Country Club. Except for the fact that at age forty-nine she was the oldest of Ski Mask's known victims, Claire Miller was the stereotypical target who triggered the rapist's fantasies. She was blond, her body was well toned, and she had the finely chiseled, high cheekbones of a cosmetics model, all of which belied her age by a good fifteen years.

Miller, a divorcée who lived alone, was asleep at three A.M. in her ground-floor apartment when she was awakened by the barrel of a gun pressed against the left side of her head. The sexual attack lasted an hour and a half, during which time, Miller told officers, the rapist was very apologetic. She gathered from snippets of his conversation that he may have been in her apartment for some time before he awoke her and assaulted her.

Strangely enough, he didn't appear in a hurry to flee after the rape. For a half hour afterward, the rapist and his victim, he in a blue ski mask, she with a towel wrapped around her face, "talked casually," as the officer noted in his report. The rapist acknowledged during the curious conversation that he had been watching her well before the rape. Further, he confided, he was very attracted to her.

The initial rape investigation would not be the last time police would hear from Claire Miller. And when her name would resurface months later, even veteran detectives would proclaim the scenario one of the weirdest twists in their investigative careers.

The two rapes in the same morning occurred almost exactly a year after Gina Venzuela was assaulted in her apartment a half mile to the south. They were not, however, an indication that Ski Mask had been silent for a year.

On June 1, he had assaulted a forty-one-year-old woman who lived at Preston Greens, and on July 12, he broke into a twenty-five-year-old woman's apartment in the same area. In both attacks, he had trouble maintaining an erection and wasn't able to rape the women. In each instance, he ended up fondling them and forcing them to perform oral sex, finally resorting to masturbation.

There was one other common thread in both attacks. Each occurred, as had several of Ski Mask's previous assaults, during steady rainstorms, a quirky little footnote probably too obscure and too irrelevant to mean anything to investigators.

More tangible to detectives was Gilbert Escobedo's arrest October 3. Officers William B. Smith and Marlon K. Waters, responding to reports of a prowler, stopped Escobedo about nine P.M. in the midst of a sprawling apartment community on Preston Oaks Road, two miles south of his own apartment on McCallum Boulevard.

Unable to satisfactorily answer the officers' questions about his presence in the apartment complex, Escobedo reluctantly led them to his car, a beautifully restored, off-white classic 1955 Chevrolet Bel-Aire. Beneath the driver's seat officers discovered an eighteen-inch club and arrested him for unlawfully carrying a weapon.

After spending about four hours in jail, he posted a $200 bond and was released. In his prosecution file, under the section for prior offenses, a prosecutor listed eleven priors before he ran out of room on the form.

But for the first time in eighteen years, Escobedo was not on parole. Sex Crimes detectives, without enough physical evidence to prove probable cause for even a search warrant in the felony rapes, didn't attempt to intercede on the misdemeanor weapons charge. It would have been futile. Further, there was no parole to revoke.

The scenario frustrated Marshall Touchton. Escobedo obviously was window-peeping, masturbating outside some woman's window and probably scouting a new rape target. Waiting for proof, even as he *knew* Escobedo was the Ski Mask Rapist, was the most debilitating part of his profession. He accepted the burden of proof, one that seemed more impossible with every court decision that favored a defendant. What the veteran detective couldn't accept was that more and more women were becoming needless victims while that proof eluded him.

At arraignment on the weapons charge, Escobedo pleaded innocent to the charges. He would request continuance after continuance, delaying adjudication of the misdemeanor charges for more than a year and remaining free on bond.

December 22, 1988

Two and a half months after Gilbert Escobedo was arrested prowling through the apartment complex and only three blocks south down Preston Road, Margaret Michaelson* and her fourteen-year-old daughter, Chris,* were up late. School was out for the holidays, Christmas was three days away, and rules had been suspended in honor of the occasion.

Half an hour past midnight, Michaelson, a single parent and an administrative assistant at a downtown real estate firm, announced she was turning in. Chris was still up and the television was on as her mother headed upstairs to her bedroom.

Between three and three-thirty A.M., the condominium was darkened and quiet. Inexplicably awakening from a heavy sleep, Michaelson surmised that Chris must have turned off the TV and gone to bed. Ominously, she also sensed someone standing over her bed. As she attempted to raise up in bed, a man put his hand over her face and pushed her back into the pillow. In the darkness, she could make out a gun.

"Big gun, huh?" he said.

Michaelson struggled as the intruder held his hand over her mouth.

"Shut up," he said, "you're making too much noise. I'm not going to hurt you, just don't scream. I'm going to let you go. Just relax."

He forced Michaelson to commit oral sex before he raped her. In the midst of the attack, as Michaelson was lying facedown with her head shoved into the pillow, there was a noise outside the bedroom.

"It's my daughter," Michaelson said, swept by a new wave of fear. She had hoped he would leave without knowing Chris was asleep in her room just a few feet away.

"She's just ten," Michaelson lied. "If she saw this, she wouldn't understand."

The mother heard the assailant walk to Chris' room. Michaelson was petrified, lying in total darkness and straining to hear. In the dark and with Chris beneath the covers, the rapist apparently didn't question Michaelson's lie about her daughter's age. He returned and calmly resumed his assault, ejaculating outside her vagina.

He went to the bathroom and returned with a wet towel, which he gently used to wipe off his victim.

"Do you prey on all the women in the complex?" Michaelson asked.

"No," he said, "this is the first time."

"Well," she said, "why didn't you just ask me out instead of doing it this way?"

The question appeared to genuinely intrigue the stranger.

"Don't you have a boyfriend?"

"Yes, but I have other friends, too."

He warned her repeatedly against calling police, claiming he, too, lived in the complex and that he'd know if she reported the rape. He went downstairs, took her cordless telephone, punched a few numbers into the dial, wrapped it in a towel, and deposited it on the back patio. Then he walked through the house to the front door and left.

"Excuse me. I hate to bother you, but would you have change for a dollar? I'd sure appreciate it."

Claire Miller glanced quickly over her shoulder, but finished removing her mail. Only when she relocked the mailbox and withdrew her key did she look fully in the direction of the voice.

The man was holding a one-dollar bill and nodding toward the soft drink machine on the other side of the walk from the row of tenant mailboxes. He was short, maybe no more than five-foot-six, but muscular, dark-complexioned, and dressed in crisply laundered jeans and shirt. He smiled cordially.

There was still a lot of sun left in the sky, and the mailboxes and drink machine were located in a common area in the midst of the apartment complex, sheltered with a roof, but open on either end. This was the kind of inconsequential encounter that Miller knew she would have to become accustomed to if she were ever going to fully recover from the rape. Not all men, she had to remind herself, were rapists.

She returned his smile and obligingly groped through her purse. She didn't have enough change for a dollar, but she gave him two quarters for the machine.

"I hate to take your money," he said even as he accepted the quarters. "That's really nice of you. I was over here visiting a friend, just leaving. Seems like I never have the right change when I need it."

He rambled on, turning to drop the coins into the machine, and she couldn't hear everything he said. Drink in hand, he thanked her again. At the end of the walk, he turned quickly to steal a glance at the uncommonly attractive woman who had helped him. Realizing she was still watching him, he waved a hand in the air, shouting, "Thanks a lot." He disappeared down the steps and into the parking lot.

A week or so later, as Claire Miller was pitching two more quarters into the toll basket on the Dallas North Tollway, a grinning man in a glistening old car honked at her from the next toll lane, pointing his finger at a parking area just beyond the tollbooth. She was perturbed until she recognized him as the pleasant stranger to whom she had given drink money. She veered to the right into the widened parking area and watched in the rearview mirror as he pulled the classic old Chevrolet up behind her and opened the door.

"You remember me?" he asked with a grin.

"Yes, I think I bought you a Coke a while back."

"You sure did, and I wasn't very polite. I forgot to introduce myself," he said as he handed a business card through the window. He didn't withdraw his hand, but opened the palm for a handshake.

"I'm Gilbert Escobedo. The least I could do after you buying me a drink is to repay you. If you'll call me or bring this card to my shop, I'll put the best shine on this car you've ever seen. You'll think it's new. It won't cost you a penny. It's the least I could do."

Miller scanned the card. Gilbert Escobedo, it said, was owner of Ultimate Polishing Enterprises, located someplace downtown. She thanked him for his card and his offer.

"Call me," he said, stepping back and waving.

Escobedo was charming and unusually outgoing. His over-the-shoulder glance from a week earlier might be subject to interpretation, but there was no mistaking his motive in the happenstance meeting at the toll plaza. He was interested in her. Beyond a doubt. You could see it in his eyes.

Claire Miller was deeply burdened by the rape. Maybe it was because she needed a reprieve, or just a diversion, but she found herself dialing the number on the card.

18

In the almost two years she had been Escobedo's girlfriend and, ultimately, his fiancée, Angie Welburne had been a family favorite, particularly with the patriarch, Robert Escobedo. But in early 1989, a different woman began appearing with Gilbert Escobedo at the impromptu weekend gatherings at his father's house.

"What can I tell you, Pop?" the younger Escobedo had said of his breakup with Angie. "Things just didn't work out. But we're still good friends, and I talk to her all the time on the phone. You'll probably be seeing her around."

He offered the explanation to his family with the same aplomb as he had most other topics he hadn't wanted to discuss; the news was delivered with a carefree, easy-come, easy-go attitude that belied any deep feelings. Offered with his ubiquitous grin and frequent shrug, his reaction was fully compatible with his family's perception of the free-wheeling bachelor with a checkered background. He was a man who appreciated the finer things in life and who surrounded himself with high-dollar sports cars and beautiful women. The image was one that left some male members of the Escobedo family, particularly the younger ones, smiling and shaking their heads with envy.

The woman on whom Escobedo now focused his charm and energy

was a studied contrast to his erstwhile fiancée. Most obvious was that he had gone from spending time with a woman thirteen years his junior to one who was twelve years his senior. Angie Welburne's beauty, indeed her charm, was irrepressible even in a ponytail, jeans, sweatshirt, and tennis shoes. She was natural, unpretentious, and down-to-earth. Claire Miller, whom Escobedo told his father he "just bumped into one day," was studied chic, sophisticated, well-dressed, and, by inference, monied. The initial image was one of cool detachment.

Over time, the Escobedos appeared to accept Claire as openly as they had Angie Welburne. She became a regular at family gatherings. And when cameras inevitably were brought out, Claire, her highlighted hair meticulously in place and her eyes shadowed in just the right shade, appeared prominently in the snapshots that would be pasted for posterity in family albums.

Angie remained a favorite, though, with Escobedo's oldest daughter, seventeen-year-old Rebecca, who still kept in regular touch by phone. One of Angie's major regrets was leaving behind Becky and Martie, to whom she had become a big sister during her engagement to their father.

On weekends, the girls routinely had stayed over at their apartment and a ritual evolved that necessitated Angie and the girls spending major portions of Saturdays at the mall while Escobedo worked. Angie's relationship with the young Escobedo sisters remained solid in the aftermath of the breakup, and the girls were planning to visit Angie in Nashville during the summer.

Escobedo had been earnest in his claims about wanting to remain friends with Angie. In that regard, he hadn't hesitated in telling his former fiancée that he was dating a woman named Claire Miller, whom he described as a "classy woman."

As the long-distance phone conversations with Angie evolved, Escobedo confided that his relationship with Claire had turned serious. They were not only spending virtually all their spare time together, he said, but Claire also was investing in his business, which hopefully would be expanding.

Because Claire Miller would decline to discuss the specifics of her relationship with Escobedo, much of what is known emerges through their conversations with others and events that would become a part of the public record.

As he had intimated to Angie in one of his phone conversations, Escobedo and Miller did become business partners. On April 7, 1989, they filed documents in Dallas County that identified themselves as owners in a general partnership called Ultimate Polishing Enterprises, which did business at 318 North Akard, Escobedo's current downtown location. At the same time, Escobedo and Miller listed themselves as partners in a second business, Ultimate Polishing Enterprises II, apparently an expansion location planned for a site on the northeast edge of downtown Dallas in the midst of several of the city's largest law firms.

There were indications, however, that at least their personal relationship had become stormy early on. In May, a month after Escobedo and Miller filed their joint business ownership in the courthouse, Angie Welburne received a phone call in Nashville that both surprised and irritated her. It was from Claire Miller.

"She and Gilbert obviously had had an argument," Welburne would recall. "I didn't know what it was about. I was busy. It was my second week on a new job. I told her I really couldn't talk to her just then."

The conversation, she recounted, went like this:

"I just want to ask you one question," Miller said.

"What is it?"

"What was Gilbert like with you? I mean, did he treat you good?"

"Yes, we had our arguments, but basically, Gilbert and I had a normal relationship. He got on my nerves; I got on his. We had good times; we had bad times."

"Well," Miller said, "he and I were talking, and I was telling him he was too picky and too peculiar and too possessive. And he said, 'I know how I am. If you want to know how I am, call Angie and she'll tell you what I'm like.' "

Welburne was irritated that Escobedo and Miller were using her as a counselor, particularly during working hours. Decorum notwithstanding, the timing was horrible. She was admittedly curt with the woman she had never met.

"I can tell you this, Claire. I left him. If you guys have problems, *you* work it out. I can't help you with your problems. Good luck and good-bye."

Welburne never heard from Claire Miller again, but she certainly heard about her several months later during a telephone conversation with an obviously steamed Escobedo. God only knew what the real facts were, Welburne thought, but Escobedo's scenario had him and Miller arguing, each apparently claiming rights to a large amount of money.

According to his story, Miller had stuck the disputed funds in her purse. He apparently grabbed her purse, jumped in his car, and drove down the street to remove the money, which he claimed was his, from her purse. When he returned to the detail shop, he said, Miller had summoned police.

Officers arrested Escobedo for stealing Miller's purse, and booked him for simple assault. In fact, a charge of assault, a misdemeanor, was logged on his lengthy rap sheet on October 5. There was no disposition for the charge listed in official court records, indicating it probably was dropped.

But Claire Miller's conversation with police about Gilbert Escobedo would not be her last. In ensuing months, Miller became acquainted with Detective Corporal Roberta "Bobbie" King, who only recently had been assigned to Sex Crimes. King, married to Sergeant Jerry King, the former head of the Sex Crimes Squad, had a reputation as a tough, efficient cop who tended to be a loner.

If King ever wrote supplemental reports on any intelligence she collected from Miller, they were not seen by key detectives assigned to the squad, nor would any reports appear in the official investigative file that contained the reams of information pooled by other detectives on the Ski Mask Rapist.

The fact that one of Ski Mask's victims not only was in business with, but *sleeping with the key suspect* in the serial rapes was not even known at the time by Marshall Touchton, Evelyn Crowder, or Steve Hatchel, the three detectives who had dogged the case for more than three years.

"If their conversations produced anything that helped us on Escobedo," said one detective, "I never knew what it was. Whatever the deal was, it wasn't passed around to the rest of us. Apparently they became kind of friends. But even the fact they were talking wasn't common knowledge."

The realization that an officer had developed a rapport with a woman uniquely positioned to provide intelligence on the wily suspect—a revelation that came too late to matter—left some detectives frustrated.

"Escobedo was hard to watch, paranoid, and always looking over his shoulder," said another detective. "We decided that about the only way we'd ever catch him was to get him in the act. For that reason, it would have been great to have some information on when he came and went. Maybe we did, and maybe the information just didn't work out. I don't know. Or maybe Bobbie didn't get enough information to even write a supplement. But it sure as hell wasn't common knowledge that she [Miller] was talking to one of our detectives."

Through the years in CAPERS, as it probably was in many police departments, there were two general types of detectives. There were those who brought their pieces of the investigative puzzle to the table, pooled that information with their colleagues', and tried to complete the bigger picture. Others, however, kept their pieces to themselves. Only when their piece completed the investigation or became a "key" development in the investigation did they offer it up.

Sometimes it was to advance careers and grab headlines. Other times it was the innocent failure to recognize the significance or potential of a piece of information or a source.

Pieced together from the recollections of several detectives, the scenario is that Claire Miller apparently first phoned Sex Crimes to inquire about the progress of the investigation into her case. Ending up with Roberta King, Miller ultimately voiced her own growing suspicions about the man with whom she had gone into business and was dating.

Apparently there were several conversations between Miller and King over weeks, though both women later would refuse to discuss them. (Miller, speaking through her attorney, said she did not want her relationship with Escobedo to be exploited or publicized. King, later promoted to sergeant and transferred to the department's Uniformed Patrol Division, said discussing the case would be a violation of Dallas Police Department policy.)

Whatever happened in the Claire Miller incident, the casual pooling of information on which the small division had relied so heavily apparently had been short-circuited, as had the task force itself. The Ski Mask Rapist had become less prolific in his assaults—from eight in the last seven months of 1985 to five in all of 1988—and, as a result, surveillance of Escobedo had been difficult to justify.

Investigators hadn't wavered in their belief that Escobedo was the elusive Ski Mask Rapist, but they had been diverted not only by the daily barrage of new rapes, but by the labor-intensive investigations into the so-called Moving Man Rapist and the "Preacher Rapist." The Ski Mask Task Force, while it still existed in concept, had lost momentum, with its members being assigned to new sexual assault cases even as the normal transfers had detectives moving into and out of Sex Crimes.

19

In daylight hours, people of dubious motive and criminal predisposition move inconspicuously among the masses, their presence covered by the majority who work hard for a living, who obey society's major rules, and who return to their homes in the evenings to begin the process anew the next morning.

As these good and decent people sleep, an old Dallas prosecutor was fond of saying in virtually every closing argument, it leaves the darkened streets almost exclusively to those who would want to exploit society's law-abiding members.

"Darkness," he would say, "is the criminal's tool, as important to what he does as the Bible is to the minister, the wrench to the mechanic. The thief and rapist are so despicable to humanity that their actions can't stand the light of day."

Lest the import of his message be lost on the jury, the old gentleman would point a weathered finger at the defendant and assume the inflection of a Southern Baptist preacher.

"Good people," he said, "*decent* people, don't prowl around in the middle of the night. There's no good to come from it."

The prosecutor's simple premise, rooted in forty years of convicting criminals, is a commonsense rule of thumb practiced by every cop who works deep nights. Incidents that might go unnoticed on the day or evening watches create suspicion for cops on the eleven P.M. to seven A.M. shift.

And so it was at 3:45 A.M. when Officer Bradley Jordan saw the off-white, classic Chevrolet ease south off Bentwood Trail onto Preston Road. Jordan and his partner, Officer Lorelei Tanney, were out of their car, issuing a minor traffic ticket beside Preston Road. The old Chevrolet crept past them well under the speed limit, slow enough that Jordan noted the personalized license plate: *1955*.

Jordan knew the car and its driver, Gilbert Escobedo, even before seeing the plate. And knowing Escobedo as he did, the ex-con's presence in the middle of the night was sufficiently questionable that Jordan would have followed him had it not been for the squelchy message moving across the two-way radio attached to his belt.

"Six One Five," the dispatcher said. "Investigate a rape." The address was four blocks down Bentwood Trail, from whence the old Chevrolet had just come.

An appropriate time for a rape is unimaginable, but the attack on Rene Williams* came in the grip of one of the most depressing and agonizing times in her thirty-one years. For the bulk of the previous six months, her boyfriend had virtually lived with her at her condominium. It had been a serious relationship, at least from Williams' point of view, until he abruptly announced at the end of June that he was leaving.

Williams, a mid-level executive with a Dallas-based Fortune 500 company, had gone away over the Fourth of July, hoping that distance would salve the pain.

It hadn't. A night earlier, in need of companionship, she had cooked dinner for a good friend from work, and they had had a few beers. Sundays were particularly brutal because they were lazy days that she and her former boyfriend almost always had spent together.

At one-thirty A.M., well after her guest had departed, Williams was still awake, tossing and turning, a recent habit she wondered if she would ever shake. As she lay nude on her stomach, the way she always slept, a man jumped from the darkness onto her back, jamming a metal object into the back of her head.

"Stay where you are," he said. "I've got a gun. Do what I say and I won't hurt you."

Rene Williams clung to her composure by trying to remember details about her attacker even as he defiled her. She felt jeans on her legs. He must have kept his pants on. He appeared fully outstretched in her bed. She had a footboard, so he had to be short.

The psychological challenge helped her through. Until her mind seized on a thought from nowhere: *Rene, what if you don't live to tell anyone?*

Detective Roberta King questioned Williams later in the day at police headquarters. In a lengthy supplemental report, King wrote: "This detective feels strongly that Escobedo is the suspect on this case. However, almost all leads have come to a dead end."

In fact, they had. Latent fingerprints had been discovered by physical evidence officers, but the partial prints lifted from the back stairway railing belonged to Williams. The latents off the inside patio door handle belonged to Officer Jordan.

"He follows patterns, sure," Evelyn Crowder told Captain John Holt, "but the patterns don't leave any presentable evidence." Presentable, she meant, as in terms of presenting the case to a grand jury for charges.

Officer Jordan filed his own supplemental report to the Williams rape case. It, too, identified Gilbert Escobedo as a suspect in the case and listed intricate detail that didn't customarily appear on rap sheets or any other police record.

The report noted Escobedo's home telephone, for example, his business address and phone number, his Social Security number, his parents' address, his previous addresses on Arapaho Road and Woodbend Lane, a physical description of his car (which Jordan noted was in "mint condition"), the personalized plate "1955," the fact that Escobedo was divorced "and has two children, ages 15 years and 17 years that do not live with him."

In the last paragraph, Jordan revealed how he had discovered all the information:

"This reporting officer is employed as the night manager in an off-duty capacity at suspect's listed residence. On previous occasions, both on and off duty, the management of the complex has related to reporting officer numerous complaints and concerns about listed suspect's aggressive behavior towards female residents in this complex."

The Ski Mask rapes were among the most maddening and frustrating cases to pass through Sex Crimes in years, if for no other reason than that virtually everyone *knew* Gilbert Escobedo was the rapist. And *he* knew they knew.

Except for maybe his shoe size, they knew him like they had known no other suspects. Intimately, in fact: that he was uncircumsized, that he had thick body hair at the base of his back, that he periodically was sexually dysfunctional, even that he was insecure about the size of his penis. Now there were two officers who had seen him leaving a rape scene.

And while it apparently wasn't widely known even in the Sex Crimes Division, Detective Roberta King had phoned Claire Miller after the Rene Williams rape.

"Was Escobedo with you last night? No? I didn't think so."

King presumably also had called Miller two months earlier, after Kelly Todd* was raped on May 15 in the same MO, and again on August 20 when Heather Gates,* a twenty-six-year-old aerobics instructor, would be raped, again by apparently the same rapist.

Because of her reluctance to discuss her relationship with Escobedo, it is unclear what sparked Miller's original suspicions about her business partner and lover. But whatever the catalyst, those suspicions had to be heightened by the detective's repeated calls in the aftermath of the ongoing rapes.

One night after he had dozed off to sleep, Escobedo would recall, Claire Miller flicked on the bedside lamp and pulled his head nose-to-nose with hers. Studying his eyes with a penetrating stare, she asked:

"Gilbert, I've got to know. Are you the man who raped me?"

"Are you crazy?" he replied. His tone was incredulous. "I think you're losing it," he said, rolling onto his side away from her.

November 3, 1989

Even before Holly Adams and Claire Miller were raped in their apartments, Bitsy Wesner was a vigilant, hands-on apartment manager, the kind that management companies coveted. The thirty-two-year-old resident manager not only maintained one hundred percent occupancy—admittedly not a difficult chore in the fashionable, convenient far North Dallas neighborhood—but she also made it a point to know virtually every tenant who lived in the sprawling complex.

Wesner not only was aware of the two rapes at Woodhaven, she also had heard about the rapes across the street at Preston Greens. Wesner had altered her busy routine to accommodate sporadic walking tours of her complex, particularly late at night. Nor did she confine her sporadic tours to the well-lit parking lots. Wesner's nighttime tours of the property, particularly with a serial rapist on the loose, would have been considered risky by most people; to Wesner, who prided herself on the apartment complex, it was simply part of what she was paid to do.

At ten minutes after nine on this Friday night, Wesner was walking alone between the rear of the apartments and the heavily wooded creek that separated the complex from the golf course at the adjoining Prestonwood Country Club. As she neared the rear of Leigh Ann Drumman's* apartment, Wesner saw a man crawl from the window of her utility room. When his feet hit the grass, the apartment manager noticed the man was carrying a long screwdriver; clearly, he had seen Wesner.

"You look like you could use some help," Wesner said cordially, careful not to appear confrontational.

The man said his name was Gilbert Garcia and that he lived in apartment 1601. Wesner knew he wasn't a tenant. Drumman, the twenty-five-year-old woman who lived in the apartment, was single and lived alone.

"Will you call the police?" he asked. "There is a black man locked in the bathroom inside and I can't get him out."

Apparently sensing that Wesner wasn't buying his story, the man turned and ran along the creek. Wesner ran behind him, hoping to stay close enough to get a description of a car, but she lost him in the darkness and heavy underbrush along the creek.

Drumman wasn't home when the man broke into her apartment. Curiously, nothing had been taken, she later told police. The only indication that someone had been in her apartment was the fact that her bicycle had been moved.

The intruder, Wesner told officers, was a Hispanic man, short, maybe five-foot-five, with a stocky build, around 160 pounds, who had a square jaw, a mustache, and hair cut short on the sides.

"You find him," Wesner said, "and I'll be able to identify him."

It would be five months before Bitsy Wesner would get the opportunity. It would come in her own apartment complex under strikingly similar circumstances. She wouldn't waver.

March 10, 1990

Across a parking lot, up a small set of cement steps, and across a terraced and landscaped greenbelt from where Gilbert Escobedo once lived with his fiancée, the Ski Mask Rapist found his last known victim in Dallas. He found her even as she and her friends moved her belongings into the small apartment at Preston Greens.

Like previous victims who were attacked in the midst of bitter divorces, devastating breakups with boyfriends, and impending loss of jobs, Meagan Finley,* barely twenty-two, alone, secretary at a temporary service, was not enjoying one of life's upswings.

That Finley was raped three hours after she moved into the apartment, assaulted amid the clutter and disarray of belongings yet to be put away, and on a bed yet to be fully assembled, was a coldly ironic twist to a string of bitter luck: She had moved because she no longer felt safe in her old apartment.

Only two weeks earlier, Finley had come home to her East Dallas apartment after work to find her front door smashed in and her VCR and jewelry gone. The burglary, the only one in her apartment complex, made her paranoid. She feared the entire neighborhood, a heavily apartment-based transitional area where the rate of burglaries and drug deals was beginning to rise dramatically.

Moreover, the break-in plunged her into depression. Immediately preceding the burglary, she had broken up with her boyfriend, a UPS deliveryman whom she still saw virtually every day as he made his rounds, an event that only prolonged and deepened the pain. She had changed jobs and still was barely able to make ends meet. She had major arguments with two of her dearest friends, and her cat had to be euthanatized by the veterinarian.

Meagan Finley had no idea how she would pay for the more expensive apartment in North Dallas. It wasn't an act of youthful impetuousness; it was, from her point of view, a necessity. There was no crime in far North Dallas, she believed. The apartment complex, she was told, was inhabited by young professionals. Better yet, Preston Greens had a high fence around all four sides, and she had been impressed by the guard booths at its major entrances. And maybe, Finley hoped, a change of scenery and friends would help her get her life back on track.

To save money, she implemented the time-honored moving method used by virtually all young apartment dwellers. In return for a couple of cases of cold beer, five friends, one of whom owned a pickup truck, volunteered to help in the move after work on Friday afternoon.

It was after six P.M. when everyone arrived at Finley's old apartment, and there were several trips across town. It was midnight before the last of Finley's belongings were plopped down in the middle of the floor of her new apartment. The friends sat around and drank beer for about an hour before drifting out.

Apartment 5-C had been vacant for several weeks before Finley moved in, and the front door had been left open most of the night to accommodate the move. Even in March, the air conditioner hadn't been able to beat the heat out of the apartment. Finley peeled out of her clothes, wearing only a pair of purple panties as she roamed through the apartment depositing boxes in the appropriate rooms and tidying up her belongings as she went.

The day had been long and finally she lay on her couch, picked up her phone, and chatted with a friend for an hour. She was oblivious to the pair of eyes staring through her living room window, close enough that, had it not been for the window with a faulty lock, the man could have touched her shoulder.

The Ski Mask Rapist would wait in the dark until Meagan Finley had been asleep for two hours before he would jar her awake, threaten her life, and brutally defile her. The young victim, who had told her parents long-distance that she moved to better herself, had walked blindly into the circumstances she had fought so desperately to escape.

It was the first and only night she would spend in Apartment 5-C at Preston Greens; immediately, she would pack her belongings and move to her parents' in the Northeast.

20

April 24, 1990

The Tuesday night Men's Bible Study Class at Prestonwood Baptist Church was about to lose one of its most enthusiastic members. An excited Gilbert Escobedo arrived at the church a good half hour early for class, reserving ample time to pass out pictures he had taken during his month-long vacation to southern California.

There were typical tourist shots of Los Angeles, with magnificent white stucco buildings with red Spanish tile roofs, lush palms, and towering, mirrored skylines. More particularly, there were also shots of a sleek black BMW and panoramic views of Rodeo Drive in Beverly Hills, replete with a flawlessly dressed man with sunglasses and a conspicuous Rolex on his wrist as he stood outside one of Rodeo Drive's swank jewelry shops.

The unidentified man in the photo, Escobedo explained to classmates at church, was a jewelry broker, an old friend from Dallas who soon would be his new boss. The old acquaintance, Escobedo bragged, had offered him a deal he couldn't turn down. Not only would he be making a hefty salary even by southern California standards, but the employment package also included the use of the BMW and a luxurious company-owned condominium, also depicted in the pictures, that came with a doorman and a valet.

Soon, Escobedo boasted, he would be wining and dining some of LA's wealthiest and most influential residents—maybe, he pointed out with a shrewd grin, even a few movie stars—and selling them Rolexes. He had returned from California only long enough to tie up some loose ends, work out the transition of his detailing business to his partner, and pack his belongings for the move. He would be heading to southern California by week's end. Several of his classmates hung around after class to congratulate their friend on his newfound good fortune.

Among the loose ends that apparently needed to be tied was Escobedo's burgeoning relationship with Lynn Stratford,* a divorcée and member of Prestonwood whom he had been dating for the last few months. Though there had been no formal declaration ending their relationship, Claire Miller and Gilbert Escobedo had quietly begun spending time with other people, making their business hours at the downtown Dallas detail shop even more tense.

Miller, Escobedo knew, had begun seeing an advertising executive who had been an occasional customer. As for himself, Escobedo had become infatuated with Lynn Stratford after meeting her at church. The relationship had won the blessing of Escobedo's classmates in Bible study, one of whom had characterized the union as "wonderful things happening to wonderful people." Stratford, a few years Escobedo's senior, lived within a mile of Prestonwood in a comfortable, upper-middle-class house she had won in a divorce from her business executive husband a few years prior.

The relationship with Stratford had been serious enough that Escobedo, during one of his frequent and lengthy phone calls to Angie Welburne in Tennessee, had confided to his former fiancée that he was thinking about asking Stratford to marry him. Angie wished him well.

"You don't care?" Escobedo teased. "You don't want to run back down here and marry me before Lynn gets a chance? I may not be on the market much longer."

"No, Gilbert," Welburne reassured him. "I hope you're happy."

What Escobedo didn't confide in his conversation was that Lynn Stratford had volunteered—insisted, in fact—to write him a personal check for more than $3,000 to bail him out of a delinquent tax case with the Internal Revenue Service.

"Are you sure this is enough?" she had asked before she filled in the amount. "If it's not, we can take care of it. I don't want you to be under a lot of stress about this."

The lure of the job offer in California, however, had become more attractive than a future with Lynn Stratford. On this cool Tuesday night, Escobedo gave Stratford a ride home after Bible study, presumably explaining his impending move to California.

It was early, not yet nine P.M., when he left Stratford's house. Escobedo, ebullient at his good fortune and optimistic about his new career, was an excited man with time on his hands.

As apartment complexes go, Apartment 408 at the Woodlands is secluded. Located on the second floor of the building and opposite the parking lot, its balcony entranceway is surrounded by trees and overlooks the pool, which almost always is vacant on nine o'clock Tuesday nights in April.

Inside Apartment 408, Melanie Winston,* a twenty-one-year-old college student, was lying in her nightgown on the bed studying when she heard a noise at the front door. Initially, she dismissed the interruption as a gust of wind. But focusing her thought on the noise, she determined it was the sound of someone trying to turn the locked doorknob. Then the startled student heard what unmistakably was someone throwing his weight against the front door.

While she was huddled in the closet and on the phone with the police operator, Winston heard the footsteps move to her bedroom window. Peeking through the closet door, she saw a man standing on the landing outside.

Gilbert Escobedo was still standing outside Winston's window when two uniformed police officers spotted him. Apparently unsure if he had been seen by the officers below, Escobedo moved stealthily down the staircase opposite the officers; they were waiting for him at the bottom of the stairs.

Earnest and cool, Escobedo told a story similar to one a Hispanic intruder at Woodhaven had told manager Bitsy Wesner five months earlier. In the current scenario, too, the purported culprit was a black man.

He had been driving down Arapaho Road, Escobedo said, when he spotted a black man on the landing outside the apartment, peeking through a window. He made a U-turn, Escobedo told officers, and returned to the apartment to investigate. He was glad officers arrived so quickly, he said, because he saw the direction the intruder went. If they hurried, the officers might still catch him; Escobedo pointed helpfully toward the adjacent row of apartments.

Melanie Winston, however, told a different story. From her safe haven in the closet, she had watched Escobedo's feet through the bottom of the blinds. They hadn't moved from the time he first appeared outside the landing until officers arrived. There was absolutely no doubt in the college student's mind. The man now standing between the two officers was the same man who first had tried to enter her apartment, then stood peeking through her blinds.

Whatever was left of Escobedo's credibility soon unraveled like polyester on barbed wire. As officers continued to question him in the parking lot, a car pulled into a space and a woman emerged. Scanning the situation, the woman motioned one of the officers to her car.

"I'm Bitsy Wesner, the manager here," she said. "I don't know what he's done *this* time, but that man you're talking to is the guy I saw coming out of a tenant's apartment last November. He'd broken into it while the woman was gone. That's him. No question."

Wesner's on-site account, coupled with the radio's confirmation of Escobedo's sex offender card from the Allison Whitehurst window-peeping incident in August 1987 and his own voluminous rap sheet, left the suspect no latitude for negotiation.

Sergeant Louis Merritt and Michael Miller, undercover members of a deployment team that coincidentally was working in the area and who also answered the burglary-in-progress call, advised Escobedo he was being arrested for attempted burglary. They read him his Miranda warning, asked him if he understood his constitutional rights as they had explained them, and led him to a police car with his hands cuffed behind his back.

The arrest transpired not two hundred feet across the parking lot from where Claire Miller, his business partner and erstwhile lover, had been raped seventeen months earlier.

Criminal investigations almost never unwind the way movies and television depict them: A single detective, or maybe a pair, works around the clock, doggedly pursuing one case exclusively, overcoming seemingly insurmountable odds, then masterfully tidying up the loose ends into an irreversibly conclusive case for which there is no conceivable defense.

On the real mean streets where crime occurs as often as McDonald's sells Big Macs, few detectives have the luxury of working a single case. Since their assignment to the team, each member of the Ski Mask Rapist Task Force had investigated an average of 150 rapes a year in addition to almost as many cases of indecent exposure. Some had been transferred to other divisions.

The detectives were scattered over three shifts, just like their colleagues in uniform. Overtime was reserved for only the hottest of leads, and even then it had to be approved by supervisors who always eyed the bottom line in a stretched budget. Unless a detective was on call for a particular case, he wasn't called in when leads developed off his shift.

Detective Corporals Marshall Touchton and Evelyn Crowder, the pair of detectives who had worked more consistently on the Ski Mask rapes than any of their colleagues, were both off duty at the time patrol officers brought a surprisingly confident Escobedo to Main and Harwood headquarters at about ten P.M.

Sweating Escobedo would fall to Detective Steve Hatchel, Touchton's old partner, and Detective Bob Rommel, both of whom had worked on previous Ski Mask rapes, including the Constance McIntyre case in November 1985. Notwithstanding the fact that the McIntyre case was four and a half years old, it was an easy one to remember: It was the only case in which Hatchel had ever found a Dallas Police Department baseball cap at a crime scene.

Even as Hatchel prepared to question Sex Crimes' most elusive rapist in the tiny interview room on the third floor of headquarters, Rommel and other officers were collecting and feeding him information, all of which the veteran detective tried to digest as quickly as possible.

The more time Escobedo had by himself, the more intricate, detailed, and steadfast his denial would become; Hatchel wanted to hit
him before the shock and depression of the arrest wore off. It was a
delicate psychological game and the first few hours were critical to cops.

The good news was the vulnerability, and therefore leverage, afforded by Escobedo's history. Because he already had been convicted
of at least three felonies, all burglaries, he was a candidate for a life
sentence under the Texas Habitual Criminal Statute, even if detectives
could prove no more than the burglary five months earlier at Leigh
Ann Drumman's Woodlands apartment.

Too, his rap sheet showed his propensities for deviate sexual behavior: the 1981 indecent exposure at the Sears store in Town East Mall;
his bizarre fixation a year later with the two sisters in Oak Lawn, one
of whom he stabbed trying to climb through their bedroom window;
locating his fiancée's car only blocks from where Suellyn Teal was raped
in April 1987; and the window-peeping incident only four months later
at Allison Whitehurst's house.

By 11:20 P.M., a patrol officer had shown Bitsy Wesner a photo
lineup that contained six pictures of Hispanic men. Unflinchingly, the
apartment manager picked Gilbert Escobedo, reaffirming her identification from earlier in the night.

There was, however, more than enough bad news to offset the good:
A quick review of the Ski Mask files showed that none of the victims
could identify her attacker. And among the assault cases that spanned
five years, there still was not a single conclusive pubic hair, head hair,
semen stain, or latent fingerprint to put Gilbert Escobedo at a rape
scene.

Hatchel would go into the interview with Escobedo long on rhetoric
and short on substance, like a poker player holding a pair of deuces.
The success of the bluff would depend on how aggressively he controlled the game.

If Escobedo expected to be rousted and intimidated, he already was
taken off guard by the detective who entered the stark interrogation
room. Well under six feet, bespectacled, and with the demeanor of the
Baptist deacon he was, Steve Hatchel appeared more bank loan officer
than rape detective. He introduced himself, moved quickly to the

straight-backed chair on the other side of the table, pulled it around the table close beside Escobedo's, and sat down next to him.

For most of the next several hours, Hatchel's voice would occupy the majority of the conversation in the small room. It was Hatchel's trademark: "I never shut up until the suspect starts talking. Never." Likewise, the detective's voice would never rise, nor would it invoke a single curse word.

"Gilbert," Hatchel began, "I don't have to tell you, you've got a major problem here. I'm here to help you work it out. You were caught tonight trying to break into a woman's apartment. You know what you were going to do, and we know what you were going to do. We also know about all the rapes you've committed over the last five years.

"You've gone down before. You know the law as well as I do. You're looking at the habitual. That's life in TDC [Texas Department of Corrections]. You've done time as a burglar; we're talking a life sentence as a rapist."

Momentarily, the veteran detective gave the ex-con time to acknowledge the distinction and appreciate the stakes. TDC was filled with garden-variety burglars, and their commonality allowed them to blend in inconspicuously and unmolested inside the walls, like four-door Fords in mall parking lots.

Rapists, the well-traveled Escobedo would know, were moving targets behind bars. The theory is that even hard-core cons have strong attachments to mothers, sisters, and daughters. Hatchel wanted Escobedo scared.

"My partner, the big guy with the mustache, is over getting a warrant right now," said the detective, not missing a beat. "That will allow us to take your body specimens—blood and hair—and match them with evidence from the rapes."

Hatchel was heavy into the bluff now.

"Using this new thing called DNA, this scientific process, we'll be able to put you at the rape scenes with 99.9 percent probability. DNA doesn't lie, and no jury in Dallas County has ever acquitted on DNA evidence."

Hatchel never slowed down, never allowed Escobedo a second to question evidence, of which there was none. The detective delivered the soliloquy with authority, as if he had a desk full of physical evidence in the next room. Beneath the detective's cool exterior, he was frantic to make his pair of deuces good.

Escobedo later would acknowledge he had never heard of DNA testing. The import of what he was hearing, though, scared the hell out of him. He saw scientists in white coats examining his ear wax and telling him what he had eaten for dinner last Thursday.

"So here's what we're prepared to do, Gilbert," Hatchel plunged on. "After midnight, we're going to go out to the forensics lab at Parkland with our warrant and draw some blood. We'll match it with evidence from a rape, and we'll file the case. Then we'll match it with another one, and we'll file that one. Then we'll file some more. And we'll keep on filing them. If we have to search them out with our own diligent effort, we'll file them all. You know how many that is. But now if you want to cooperate with us on this, we might not file every last one of them."

The veteran interviewer paused only briefly to allow the threats to take effect. Comfortable with the reaction he had elicited from Escobedo, Hatchel plunged in a different direction.

"You told the officers who arrested you that you had been to Bible study tonight. That right? You a Christian?"

"I'd never do something like that because I *am* a Christian," Escobedo replied. "I was on my way back from Prestonwood Baptist Church."

Hatchel detected the defiance, maybe even smugness, in Escobedo's voice. He had hit a weak spot. He would probe some more.

"Well, I'm a Christian, too. So's Detective Rommel. You familiar with that passage in the Bible, 'By their fruits, you will know them'? If you truly are a Christian, Gilbert, what you've been doing has got to weigh heavy on your soul. You need to get rid of it, turn it over to the Lord and ask for forgiveness."

At 12:36 A.M. on April 25, three hours after his arrest, Escobedo, in his own meticulous, draftsmanlike printing, wrote out a statement. He prefaced his admissions by noting: "After talking to Detective Rommel and Detective Hatchel, I voluntarily want to clean up my business, since I am a Christian and I do have a conscience."

The ex-con admitted to the November break-in of Leigh Ann Drumman's apartment and to window-peeping at Winston's apartment, where he had been arrested the night before. Additionally, he admitted to a burglary two years earlier "about five blocks from my apartment . . . address unknown at this time."

Escobedo's statement, Hatchel knew, was garbage. The suspect was admitting to two offenses that he knew police already could prove with eyewitnesses, and he threw in a phantom burglary—date, complainant, and place unknown—that he knew police never could prove enough to even get charges. Rape apparently was not going to be part of Escobedo's vocabulary.

If the self-righteous Escobedo wanted to play games, Hatchel was more than willing to raise the ante after reading his statement. The detective glanced coldly from the handwritten statement toward Escobedo.

"Let's get the car, Bob," Hatchel said to Rommel, his eyes never leaving Escobedo. "Gilbert's not being honest with us. He wants us to do it the hard way. We're taking Gilbert out to forensics to get his blood for the DNA."

Escobedo appeared genuinely shocked that his statement hadn't been warmly received, but he said nothing. Truth be known, neither Hatchel nor Rommel was even certain there was a lab technician at Southwest Institute of Forensic Science at that time of night.

From Hatchel's viewpoint, it didn't matter. He was dealing with a smug, experienced ex-con who had persevered in a full day of questioning in April 1989 after the Teal rape. Already he was playing games. He had to understand the detectives were serious.

Rommel drove. Hatchel sat in the backseat with the handcuffed prisoner. The nearer the unmarked car got to Parkland Memorial Hospital, the more Hatchel could sense Escobedo's uneasiness.

Casually, as if the suspect weren't in the car, Hatchel discussed with his colleague the scientific miracle called DNA, how the process had virtually revolutionized police work, and how heretofore unsolvable cases were ending up with convictions. Escobedo heard everything; he said nothing.

As the unmarked cruiser stopped in the darkened alley that led to

SWIFS, Rommel got out and made his way to the front door, hoping with every step that he could even get into the building in the middle of the night.

Before the detective got to the door, Escobedo turned to the detective beside him.

"I'm not saying I did any of these sexual attacks you're talking about," Escobedo said, backing in to the conversation, "but *if* I did, I mean, what would happen?"

"If we go back to the office," Hatchel warned, "you're going to have to talk and not give us the runaround. Then we'll see what happens. Maybe we wouldn't file all of them. We'd have to talk to the prosecutor. But it all depends on you, and whether you're willing to be honest."

Hatchel was back in the game with his deuces; Escobedo, the savvy ex-con with the five-page rap sheet, was about to fold without calling the cop's pitiful hand. The slightly built prisoner used the return trip to headquarters to negotiate his best deal.

"Say I did talk about some of these things you're asking about," he said coyly. "You think you could take me to my girlfriend's house and let me talk to her and my daughters, you know, tell them some things? See 'em before I have to leave?"

"I think we could work that out," Hatchel said. "But again, Gilbert, it's really all up to you. It won't work if we get the runaround. And you can't see them until you clean up all your business."

It was going to be a long night and following day. The cruiser pulled into the dimly lit parking lot of an all-night café where its three occupants had breakfast and fortified themselves with black coffee. The few patrons at that hour never would have figured Gilbert Escobedo for a man about to sign his life away.

Curiously, the man who had threatened, brutalized, demeaned, and raped women for five years appeared to be unfazed by the thought of explaining those perversions to the three women left in his life.

When truth is discovered by someone else, it loses something of its attractiveness.

—Alexander Solzhenitsyn

21

April 25, 1990

At 5:16 A.M., Gilbert Escobedo was handed a pen and a sheet of legal-size paper that had VOLUNTARY STATEMENT printed at the top, with the Miranda warning written beneath it. The bottom two-thirds was blank except for signature blocks for the suspect and witnesses. Hatchel and Rommel sat at the table with a stack of offenses a foot tall that, over the last five years, the task force had attributed to the Ski Mask Rapist.

They would tell Escobedo only a minimal amount about each case, generally no more than the date and the location of each offense. It would be up to the suspect to acknowledge whether he had committed the crime.

The drill was gauged not only to get his admission and signature on a chargeable offense—something detectives hadn't been able to do in five years—but also to test his honesty. If the suspect balked or shirked an obvious offense, there would be plenty of time to lead him back through the stack *if* they could get at least a single admission to a rape, something they could use to take him off the street.

The detectives began with the rape only a month earlier of Meagan Finley. Escobedo's memory should be fresh. It would be a good reality check.

Escobedo took the pen in hand and began a brief narrative. He was painstakingly detailed in his printing, paying special attention to the A's, each of which had an exaggerated left descender that dipped well into the line beneath it. He labored over his printing, apparently taking as much pride in its appearance as he obviously did in his heavily starched sports shirt and creased trousers. The brief statement contained grammatical errors and misspellings:

> March 10, 1990 I Gilbert H. Escobedo entered resident 5990 Arapaho #5C through a window and that was opened about 10 inches prior to entrance. I jumped on the female as she lied on her stomach in bed and covered her mouth with my left hand placed a towel over her head. I then told her that I had a pistol which I didn't and would take action if she didn't coraporate. I told to feel me (my penis) at this same time I felt of her all over. I even used a vibrater (her's) on her. Following that I made love to her. Previous, to all above I picked her out as a victim by window peeking the same night. She was disrobed with only her panties on

The one-paragraph statement had taken Escobedo more than half an hour. Given the stack of pending offenses and the amount of time it had taken Escobedo to meticulously print his account, Rommel and Hatchel realized the process could take days.

Minutes before six A.M., the detectives, relieved at having at least one signed rape confession they could present to a grand jury, switched to a tape recorder to expedite the questioning. The burden of writing lifted, Escobedo appeared more relaxed.

The ensuing interview would span more than three hours and account for eighteen pages of transcription that chronicled one of the longest and strangest sieges of rapes in Dallas history. That the admissions were coming from the docile-appearing, polite man who at five-foot-five and 160 pounds was hardly bigger than some of his victims was all the more incongruous. Gilbert Escobedo would not have been the actor sent from central casting to play a rapist who committed at least thirty-four rapes, maybe as many as a hundred.

Escobedo's first recorded comments would typify the rest of his statement; they would be spoken with apparent sincerity, but beneath the aura of honesty, his words would mitigate, rationalize, and minimize his acts:

> Well, basically, this first started back in 1984 when I was released from TDC. That's where it started. A number of rapes that I have committed right now is countless—I'm figuring probably 12 to 15 that I can think of right now, there may be less, there may be more —but I just want to be up front about it and honest about it. I've been going to church previously the last three years and I had one foot in church and one foot out of church and so I've had a problem all these years concerning this weakness for females, and it just started when I was a little boy and it led up to this. . . .

Not only did Escobedo dramatically underestimate the number of his victims, but not once in three hours of conversation did he ever use the word *rape*. Consistently he relied on euphemisms like *seduced, made love to, intercourse*, and even *injected* to describe the rapes.

While most of his recollections flowed fluidly and without interruption, the slightly built ex-con appeared hesitant in describing the actual sexual assaults. The hesitations came in sentences in which *rape* clearly would be the most accurate and honest word to depict what he had done.

In admitting to the April 1987 rape of Suellyn Teal, he calmly described how he broke into Teal's parents' house, discussed the layout of the bedrooms, and even admitted carrying a nickel-plated derringer. But he stumbled and groped for the words, ultimately ending up with his euphemisms, to describe what he did when he finally crawled through the window:

> [I] felt of her and had her feel of me and, uh, I believe she was on her stomach, if I recall, she was on her stomach when I approached her. And, uh, I did inject her physically, I think she was on her stomach, so I injected her from the, uh, you know, as she was lying, I injected her, in other words, I made love to her, you know. . . .

For a high school dropout with obvious problems with grammar, Escobedo's statement reflected a recurring awareness of semantics. While he admitted, for example, to raping Wendy Spense in 1985, he didn't recall hitting her repeatedly in the face. In his recollection, he simply "struggled," as if the rape victim were the aggressor and he merely was trying to fend off her unwarranted attack. Spence, in Escobedo's account, "fought"; by context and inference, she hadn't played by the rules:

> She gave me some problems, she kind of fought me, fought with me and we struggled around the bed and then we ended up on the floor and I was still struggling because she was fighting. She was fighting with me, and I can't recall striking her or anything like that because I never did get violent as far as hitting somebody . . . like I said, we just struggled, but there were no physically harming as far as hitting her or anything like that. I didn't do anything like that. I never did that.

Escobedo likewise admitted to raping Gina Venzuela, but he never mentioned pistol-whipping the airline flight attendant instructor. Similarly, he didn't deny sexually assaulting and robbing Kelly Todd, but he made no mention in his statement of hitting her repeatedly in her stomach.

Though his steadfast denial of physical violence in the rapes obviously was an important distinction to Escobedo, it was a moot point in the law. The fact that he carried a pistol in many of the attacks elevated the charge from sexual assault to aggravated sexual assault, which under Texas law meant he would have to serve additional time before qualifying for parole.

As his confession droned on, Escobedo's accounts became increasingly perfunctory. But even as he casually acknowledged some of his more twisted encounters, he nonetheless couldn't bring himself to use the word *rape*. Yes, he knew that a couple lived upstairs in Camellia Michaels' condo on Woodbend when he broke in in July 1985, but the couple's presence hadn't been significant enough to even explain in his confession.

I masturbated a few times in front of her. Of course, she couldn't see anything, she had the pillowcase over her head. Then I asked her to put her shoes on, which is high heels that I had got from the closet area. She put them on and I, you know, I did some perverted sexual acts there as far as cunt licking at her and masturbating, and anyway, I did have oral sex with her and I did have physical contact with her. In other words, I did sexually assault her. In other words, have sexual intercourse with her, is what I'm trying to say.

Over time, the diminutive thirty-eight-year-old suspect painted a daunting self-portrait of a cunningly obsessive stalker and voyeur so committed to the perfection of his crimes that he sometimes broke into targets' houses, knowing they weren't there, simply to prepare himself for the ultimate attack.

The MO was unprecedented in Hatchel's career as a sex crimes investigator. While Escobedo's peculiar scouting missions ostensibly doubled his risk of being apprehended—he almost had been caught four months earlier as he emerged from Leigh Ann Drumman's apartment at Woodhaven—Hatchel also knew it was this fanatical attention to detail that had allowed Escobedo to rape with virtual impunity for five years.

Quietly, matter-of-factly, Escobedo made parenthetical references to the dry-run break-ins in which he memorized floor plans, noted the presence of roommates and the bedrooms in which they slept, prowled women's closets for the presence of men's clothing, checked for burglar alarms, and searched nightstands for pistols and knives. It explained why he had never been surprised in the commission of a rape and why he sometimes never turned on the lights. Likewise, it helped answer the question of why he never was careless enough to leave evidence behind.

Having cased the women's apartments and routinely peeked through their windows, Escobedo had familiarized himself with their routines; he assured himself of a comfortable margin of time in which he could wipe away semen, pluck his pubic hair from the sheets, and wipe his prints from furniture and windows before leaving.

Escobedo's chilling confession also bore out Marshall Touchton's twofer theory, that while the suspect's primary motivation for breaking in was subject to change—sometimes rape was the catalyst, other times burglary—neither goal was mutually exclusive.

In recounting the events that led to the rape of Wendy Spense, for example, Escobedo said:

What happened there is that I was window-peeping and I saw the individual and I wasn't looking at her diamond at the time. I was looking at her. She was physically in shape, heavy top, and anyway, she fell asleep and everything. . . . Anyway, she had a big diamond ring on and I noticed that when I grabbed her by the mouth and told her to keep quiet. I noticed the diamond ring on so I asked her for it, and she said she swallowed it. And what happened was, she laid it by the foot of the bed or the foot of the table in the bedroom and I told her, "Hey, well, it's not worth your life, not no ring." So she went for that and she gave it to me.

Escobedo's original motivation had been different, he acknowledged, when he broke into Constance McIntyre's luxurious North Dallas house in November 1985. The suspect also provided an answer that had vexed Hatchel and the rest of Sex Crimes for more than four years.

It happened on a Friday morning, and I'd been in the residence previous and I've window-peeked there before, so basically at that time I was after a diamond ring that she had on. It was about four carats, single round diamond, that caught my eye. I wasn't after her as a victim as far as sexually assaulting her.

But I called that morning and I asked for her husband because I knew he was an M.D. from the previous business card that I picked up there when I was in their residence. Anyway, the wife indicated that her husband wasn't in. So then and there I knew that she was home alone. I went over there. I had a Dallas Police Department baseball cap that was given to me from an officer friend and he wasn't aware of my previous record and so, anyway, I left the baseball cap in a waste basket there, in a trash can, or I could have dropped it on the driveway there because I didn't want to go into the residence with it on.

Escobedo recalled hearing the maid's vacuum cleaner, but accurately gambled that she wouldn't see or hear him as he made his way to the rear of the McIntyre house.

I entered her bedroom and then I noticed she was taking a shower, so I wait 'til she finished taking her shower and I believe I had a small pistol with me . . . and I pointed it at her, told her that if she made any noise that I would take action. So she didn't, she didn't make any noise, she just drying herself and then she dropped the towel and I told her to lie down and she lied down and then that's when I seduced her. And then I asked her for her diamond ring and she gave it to me. . . .

I went back to the waste basket to . . . pick up the Dallas Police Department cap and it wasn't there so I would assume that something was wrong, somebody had saw me, so I kind of panicked then and basically that's what happened in that situation.

One of the hallmarks of being an effective police interrogator is the ability to remain poker-faced even in the midst of grotesque and sick admissions of guilt. The slightest hint of repulsion, anger, or judgment on a cop's face shuts down the suspect like a clogged sewer.

Gilbert Escobedo's confession was loaded with bizarre and perverted twists and turns. But just when the two veteran sex crimes investigators were lulled into believing the interview had leveled into a traditional rape interrogation, Escobedo would have them glancing curiously at each other again.

Nothing in Escobedo's admissions—or, for that matter, in Hatchel's and Rommel's police careers—was more dramatic or freakish than his rape, seduction, and exploitation of Claire Miller, the woman who unwittingly would become his victim, lover, and business partner.

I'd seen her previously before by window-peeping . . . and that kind of got to me as far as picking her out as a victim.

So I came back. . . . She had her bedroom window open, oh, about a foot or so, and she fell asleep and I left and I came back in about an hour later, assuming she was sound asleep by then. That's when

I took the screen off quietly and I raised the window up quietly. I entered the residence and . . . I covered her mouth and told her, you know, if she made any kind of noise . . . that I have a pistol at Claire's head, which I can't remember if I had one or not. 'Cause sometimes I would say I had one, and then didn't have one. I just used my finger up to, you know, an individual's head and they could feel it solid so it felt like a pistol. . . . So she was assuming, again, that I had a pistol, and she cooperated.

You know, I felt her and she felt me and then I seduced Claire and then we just did it in different positions. She kind of volunteered different positions because, more or less, she was scared so she just kind of volunteered the different positions that we did.

So I lied there afterwards with Claire and talked to her for a while. And we were just lying there talking and she just said, "I can't believe that you are doing something like this. You seem like a nice guy and you sound like a nice guy and you're just so nonviolent."

But anyway, about a month or two after this, I followed up. I met Claire in the mailroom and I introduced myself as far as I was looking for some change for a Coke. And, uh, she gave me some change. I saw Claire about a month after that on the Tollway. Anyway, it ended up when I gave her one of my business cards, she called me up and it ended up with a relationship with Claire and I. We went about a year, and we're still friends now. She's my business partner. But Claire—

"Did anything happen when you left Claire's house?" Hatchel interrupted. As fascinating as Escobedo's relationship with Claire Miller was, the detective's primary purpose was to lock the suspect into as many rapes as he would acknowledge. "Yes," Escobedo said obligingly.

When I left Claire's residence, I was on my way to get my vehicle, which is a '55 Chevrolet I was driving at the time, which was parked about three blocks away, and I noticed a resident coming out of his front door. At that time, it was about 5:30 in the morning, 5 in the morning. . . .

He came out of his residence and went jogging and I had been to this certain residence and noticing, and I knew that there was a lady there. She was up around my age 'cause I window-peeped that window before. But anyway, I was assuming that he left the front door open, which he did. I entered his residence and basically did the same thing, sexually assaulted her in the same pattern as previous with Claire Miller. But just about five minutes max with this resident because I knew her husband was out jogging.

By eight-thirty A.M., it had been ten hours since the uniformed officers had turned over Escobedo to Detectives Hatchel and Rommel. Except for the trip to SWIFS, breakfast, and a few breaks to use the bathroom and grab a soft drink or coffee, the process had been continuous.

In the interim, Escobedo had confessed to ten rapes: Meagan Finley, Constance McIntyre, Wendy Spense, Claire Miller, Jenny Lynn Baxley, Kimberly Baker, Suellyn Teal, Camellia Michaels, Miriam Maloney, and Merilee Watson. The detectives and the rapist were ragged, and the weariness was beginning to show in Escobedo's answers:

HATCHEL: Gilbert, here is an offense that we're looking at on May 1, 1986. Happened out on Hillview.
ESCOBEDO: Okay, I still have little doubts on this case here on Hillview. Uh, the residence sounds familiar, the offense sounds familiar, and everything, but I'm still not sure on it, so I have no comment on this one. You know, I don't want to say that it was me when it wasn't so. . . .
HATCHEL: Okay, Gilbert. We don't want you to take something that doesn't belong to you. All right, Gilbert, I've got another stack of offenses, and I'm just going to go down through them one at a time, and I want you to make comments, "Yes," or "No," "I think that's mine," "It sounds like me," or whatever the comment might be. Uh, here's one on July 19, a white female about 19 years old that lived on Woodbend.
ESCOBEDO: No sir, I don't believe that's mine.
HATCHEL: All right, we'll look at another one here. April 23, 1986,

about 2 in the afternoon, almost 3 in the afternoon on Abrams Road?

ESCOBEDO: No. I know that wasn't me because I never did anything during the day.

HATCHEL: Okay. All right, Gilbert. Here's one the twenty—

ESCOBEDO: I mean, I did one offense during the day. I can remember. That was . . .

HATCHEL: What was that one, Gilbert?

ESCOBEDO: That was the one I, at the beginning of the tape, I told you about. The very first one.

And so it went. As the detectives thumbed through the stack of rape reports, the answers became "No sir," or "Doesn't ring a bell," or "I just can't recall."

"Okay," Hatchel said finally, leaning back from the remaining stack. "Some of these could be yours, but you just don't recall them all, is that right, Gilbert?"

"Yes sir."

Hatchel called a brief break. When he and Rommel returned, they brought with them a civilian clerk. With the tape recorder running, the senior detective read into the record Escobedo's three previous handwritten statements, the two burglaries, and the rape of Meagan Finley. Escobedo confirmed the authenticity of the statements, and they were witnessed by the clerk, Vickie Harrison.

After eliciting Escobedo's confirmation that he hadn't been forced or coerced into making the statements, Hatchel asked Escobedo if he had any requests before ending the interview.

"No sir," the rapist said. "I just, all I've got to say is, you know, I feel better that I got this off my back and I know, you know, there's a lot that I have to face in the future, and you all have been real cooperative, and I feel that I've been cooperative, and we're just handling the complaints in the best way possible."

There was relief in Escobedo's voice, as if he had just survived fifty miles through broken glass. His trip was not over. He would not merely walk away from the stack of rape reports with a simple denial or flaw in his memory. He would be given rest. But his trip was just beginning.

Sergeant Larry Lewis wore a disbelieving look and silently shook his head. Detectives who executed the search warrant at Gilbert Escobedo's apartment found no mask, no gloves, or any other evidence to link him to the Ski Mask rapes.

They did discover, however, an answering machine loaded with messages from women.

The street that transects Lynn Stratford's upper-middle-class neighborhood in North Dallas is lined with landscaped and manicured lawns and four-bedroom brick houses with discreet rear-entry garages. Half, maybe, have custom-designed swimming pools in the backyards, accounting for the fact that on any given summer day the customers leaving the Albertson's a half mile away will be toting canisters of chlorine and algae-killers.

Residents of the quiet neighborhood, located midpoint in the affluent Preston-Hillcrest rectangle of the North Dallas Corridor, had left for their offices a good two hours before the unmarked police car pulled to the curb of the beige brick house on Echo Bluff. Had anyone seen the two plainclothes officers escort the prisoner from the Chevrolet Caprice into the front door, it surely would have created speculation and concern among the CPAs, dentists, and business executives who were Lynn Stratford's neighbors.

Before leaving police headquarters downtown, Detectives Steve Hatchel and Bob Rommel, true to the agreement negotiated in the backseat of the cruiser a day earlier, allowed Gilbert Escobedo to set up the meeting at his girlfriend's house. From the Crimes Against Persons office, Escobedo had been allowed to call Stratford and his two daughters. The prisoner had been cryptic about the rendezvous over the phone, preferring to break the shocking news in person where maybe he could at least help cushion the blow for his daughters and the woman he had once talked of marrying.

In return for his agreement to discuss the sexual assaults, Escobedo also had been granted other phone calls. One he placed to his stepbrother and stepsister-in-law. During that phone conversation, he re-counted a visit to their house weeks earlier. When his sister-in-law had excused herself that night to take a shower and get ready for bed, Es-cobedo had quickly said good-bye, put his coat on, and left.

In actuality, he now admitted in the call from police headquarters, he had driven a block from their house, parked his car, crept back down the alley, and watched through the bathroom window as his stepsister-in-law showered and dried herself off.

He was doing the Christian thing, Escobedo explained, in confessing a transgression against the couple. He sought their forgiveness, a pos-sibility his incensed stepbrother couldn't contemplate. Convinced he was doing God's will, Escobedo appeared unfazed by the rejection.

Detectives also allowed him to phone Claire Miller. Escobedo's and Miller's personal relationship had long since passed, but they still were partners in the downtown auto detailing business. He owed her the truth, Escobedo told her.

"You were right about me, Claire," an emotional Escobedo said, referring to the night she had confronted him about the rape. "I realize now what I had been doing. I *am* the guy who raped you. I'm sorry."

Escobedo appeared tearful and emotionally frayed when he hung up the phone after talking to Miller. His recovery was remarkable. A short time later, during the trip to Lynn Stratford's house in North Dallas, Escobedo appeared composed, even confident. Was there some knob, Hatchel wondered, that Escobedo turned to shift emotions?

Now Detectives Hatchel and Rommel watched Escobedo sit in Lynn Stratford's den with his girlfriend and daughters, Rebecca and Martie, acknowledging that he had raped untold women over the last five years. While he spared them the horrific detail, he was forthright in admitting his was the face behind the Ski Mask.

The scene was bad soap opera. Escobedo, the star, had sufficiently shocked the supporting cast with his bizarre confession. Lynn Stratford, the trusting divorcée from church, was too stunned to talk; the teenage girls, certainly pretty enough for TV, were slumped speechless in their chairs.

The silence was a cue for several minutes of uninterrupted monologue from the remorseful but persevering main character who had lost, but now found, his way. He had disappointed himself, those he loved, and, most importantly, Escobedo said, God.

He was going to prison for many years, he told them, which was precisely where he deserved to be. He would use those years, he said, to rededicate himself to God and "make something of myself for whatever time I have left."

Hatchel and Rommel shot glances at each other; they were the only ones in the room who weren't sobbing. It was apparent from Escobedo's lines that his confession clearly had been guided by God's hand, not a mere detective's threat a night earlier to bring the toughest statutes in the Texas criminal justice system down on him. Nor did he mention, as he explained God's grand plan for him, that his decision to do the right thing came only minutes before he was about to be tested for DNA.

The scene was strong enough for a Friday afternoon tease, one guaranteed to bring back viewers on Monday to see how the devastated lover and the daughters dealt with the evil revelations of the heretofore trusted companion and father. There was, however, yet another scene to be played out.

In the aftermath of the confession, Lynn Stratford's doorbell rang. She opened the door to a distraught Claire Miller, who insisted on seeing Escobedo one last time before he was hauled away to prison.

The tension between Escobedo's current and erstwhile lovers was obvious, but before Stratford dispatched Miller, the officers heard both women tell Gilbert Escobedo they loved him.

"I have never seen a rapist," Hatchel would tell Rommel later, "who had that kind of control over women. Never."

22

The ten rapes Gilbert Escobedo acknowledged in the marathon tape-recorded interview session were, by Evelyn Crowder's assessment, merely the first few drops that splatter the windshield before the bottom falls out of the clouds. There were another thirty or so cases that carried precisely the same MO and another handful, including that of teenager Vickie Wells and Bonnie Wyatt, that could go either way. The dearth of evidence in all of them, however, meant that they would go uncleared without Escobedo admitting to them.

He had appeared more than cooperative during the early hours of the interview with Detectives Hatchel and Rommel, not only admitting to the ten rapes, but adding enough detail about each assault that detectives were able to match his recollections with some piece of information in the reports that confirmed him as the attacker.

Then the suspect shut down, shaking off every rape about which he was asked. He may have been tired, certainly not an implausible scenario considering he had been in detectives' custody for ten hours. Too, the rapes spanned five years with an as yet untold number of victims; he easily could have forgotten the locations. Or, detectives knew, the savvy ex-con simply may have admitted to all he intended to admit.

His admission to the rapes, most of which were committed with a firearm, already was enough to put Escobedo away for a minimum of twenty years. Texas law allowed him to be charged as a habitual criminal, which carries a mandatory life sentence. A life sentence, though, with its massive reductions for so-called good time, in reality means the convict is eligible for parole in barely more than twelve years.

However, because Escobedo carried a firearm during the commission of the sexual assaults, the law also made it mandatory that he serve "flat" time, meaning that he wouldn't be eligible even to be considered for parole until he had served twenty calendar years.

In a curious twist, Escobedo retained a lawyer *after* he admitted to the ten rapes. Pat Robertson, an experienced and well-respected defense attorney, negotiated with Assistant District Attorney Howard Wilson to allow his client to plead guilty to nine counts of aggravated sexual assault and one case of burglary, the break-in of Leigh Ann Drumman's apartment at Woodhaven. Though each case would carry a life sentence, the plea bargain called for the sentences to be served concurrently.

The fear to defendants like Escobedo, accused of multiple crimes, is that their sentences are "stacked," that is, one sentence doesn't begin until the preceding sentence is completed. At age thirty-eight, three life sentences stacked—tabulated at a minimum of thirty-six years, with good time—would make him seventy-four by the time he was eligible for parole, which literally could be a life sentence.

As part of the agreement, Escobedo would cooperate in resolving other rapes and burglaries he committed, a provision police insisted upon. His confessions to other rapes were moot from a legal perspective. In all likelihood, any additional cases probably wouldn't have netted any more time behind bars than he would receive for the ten cases to which he already had confessed. With all the cases served at the same time, the way most Texas courts dispense sentences, ten life sentences actually meant no more actual time behind bars than twenty or thirty life sentences.

Eliciting Escobedo's help in clearing up his remaining rapes, however, could be important in restoring peace of mind to his victims, providing them with the security, maybe even satisfaction, of knowing that the man who raped them not only didn't pose a continuing threat, but was in fact being punished for what he did to them.

Tying up the loose ends in the Ski Mask Rapes would fall to two of Sex Crimes' most senior detectives, Steve Hatchel and Marshall Touchton, neither of whom was known for his tolerance for loose ends. Hatchel had spent hours with Escobedo since his arrest, while Touchton, along with Evelyn Crowder, knew the Ski Mask Rapist's MOs and history better than anyone on the squad.

On this already warm April morning, the detectives checked a handcuffed Gilbert Escobedo out of the Lew Sterrett Criminal Justice Center, a windowless fortress on the city's near western fringe, and headed against the rush-hour glut to Escobedo's old haunts in North Dallas.

The process would be tedious. Touchton drove the four-door sedan slowly through the neighborhoods while Hatchel, seated in the back beside Escobedo, asked the suspect a series of questions.

"Okay, Gilbert," Hatchel would say, "we're back in September of '85 here in this neighborhood. There was a rape out here. A woman with two children in the house. Woman about thirty-six. Anything look familiar? Can you show me a house?"

"Well, could be," the suspect would say. "I window-peeked over here before."

Occasionally, Escobedo would ask Touchton to drive through the alley.

"Let's see this house from the back. I think it has a pool. If there's a pool . . ."

Touchton and Hatchel were amazed at Escobedo's recall. Periodically, he would remember small, innocuous landmarks, maybe a bush or a gate, which would trigger his memory.

"Yeah," he would say. "I think this is mine. I remember that dog next door." Then he would add a detail from the assault that matched a reference in the offense report.

Escobedo was being cooperative. At points during the tour, he would give Touchton directions from the backseat: "Turn in here and go to the corner. I want to show you something." At the corner, he'd point to another apartment, unsolicitedly acknowledging another rape.

Equally amazing to the two veteran cops was Escobedo's method of entry. Time and again throughout the day, Escobedo, in answer to the detectives' questions, said simply: "The window was unlocked."

At some point, Escobedo asked if he could call Lynn Stratford at work. Based on his cooperation, the detectives accommodated his request and pulled to an outdoor pay phone. Still holding the receiver, the prisoner asked if they'd allow him to meet his girlfriend briefly in a parking lot near her office. The request created a difference of opinion among the two partners, not a common occurrence.

"I don't like it, Steve," Touchton said. "Hell, it's out in the open. The guy's got family, friends, we don't know. It could be a setup. It's a needless risk."

"Naw," Hatchel said. "He's resolved to going to prison. He just wants to see his girlfriend. He's done a good job today. We'll just give him fifteen minutes. It won't be a big deal."

Reluctantly, Touchton gave in. The meeting in the parking lot was tearful between rapist and girlfriend, but uneventful. Still, Touchton's eyes didn't stop scanning the parking lot until he and Hatchel had the prisoner back in the car.

By day's end, Escobedo had admitted to twenty-six more rapes. Five of the assaults—two of which occurred on the same day, June 10, 1985—came as surprises to detectives; at least two hadn't been reported, and they hadn't figured Escobedo for the other three. Sex Crimes detectives know not all victims report rapes. That phenomenon, coupled with the fact that Escobedo admitted to some for which they hadn't figured him, made detectives question the actual number of rapes the cunning ex-con had committed over half a decade.

They would never know, and they doubted that Escobedo himself remembered. In the squad room, educated guesses ranged from seventy-five to one hundred.

The earnest-appearing prisoner also made references to rapes he committed in suburban Richardson, Houston, and southern California, while he was on vacation. The vagueness may have been because Escobedo's plea bargain was with Dallas and didn't extend to other jurisdictions.

The detectives notified Richardson Police. Touchton called the rape squad in Houston. And while he explained to a Houston detective that he had a suspect in custody who might be good for rapes in his jurisdiction, no one returned his calls. He tried again before he gave up.

"I guess they had so many suspects on the street that they weren't going to take the time to go back and clear old ones," Touchton said.

With his attorney as a witness, Gilbert Escobedo signed two documents entitled "Defendant's Admission of Unadjudicated Offenses." While he would plead guilty only to the nine aggravated sexual assaults and one burglary, the two documents bore official testimony to other crimes he admitted, but for which he would not be charged. The first sheet listed the names of seventeen Dallas residents and the dates they were burglarized; the second bore the names of twenty-six women and the dates that they were raped.

The documents would be introduced during the guilty plea to show Escobedo's cooperation. The last line of each page said: "Wherefore, Defendant prays that the Court consider these matters in determining punishment in this cause."

April 28, 1990

This definitely was not what Angie Welburne had envisioned for her Saturday morning. The clock on the nightstand verified it was not yet eight A.M., and already the phone was ringing?

"Come on," she muttered. "Gimme a break."

The voice belonged to Mona Huntington* and it came long-distance from Dallas. Mona had worked with Angie at the computer software company in Dallas and, coincidentally, lived three doors from Gilbert Escobedo in the apartment complex on McCallum. Mona was excited.

"Did you hear about Gilbert?"

Angie groped for some context. She had talked to Escobedo on the phone; he was gushing about marrying Lynn Stratford. This was, Angie thought, a stupid discussion this early on a Saturday morning.

"Yeah," Angie said finally. "I talked to him."

"Oh, you did?"

"Yeah."

"When?"

"About a week ago."

"So you already knew about all this?"

"Yeah, I know. He told me he was getting married. I don't care. It's his life. Uh, do you know what time it is?"

Mona's voice took an ominous tone. "Angie, I don't think you know what I'm talking about."

Angie's eyes moved to her boyfriend in bed beside her. She had been seeing him since her return to Nashville more than two years earlier. They were going to get married. Discussing an old boyfriend with him in bed beside her didn't seem right.

"Mona," Angie said, "can we talk later?"

"Yeah, but would you *please* call me?"

Angie Welburne threw on some clothes and headed for a nearby friend's house, her mind considering the range of possibilities that could involve her former fiancé. My God, had Gilbert been killed in a car wreck? She used her friend's phone to call Mona back.

Escobedo had been arrested, Mona said, and the story was on the front page of the *Dallas Morning News* under two lines of type that said: MAN CONFESSES TO RAPES; HE TELLS DALLAS POLICE OF AS MANY AS 30 ATTACKS.

"Angie," Mona said, "this says that *Gilbert* is the Ski Mask Rapist."

Angie slumped speechless into a chair. Her mind was deluged by diverging questions and feelings, so many that she was incapable of following any of them to a logical conclusion.

In minutes, the fog lifted and Angie's mind seized on one thought that left her feeling cold, angry, and betrayed:

He knew the whole time he was with me what he was doing. He knew that he was raping women and then crawling back in bed with me. If in his own strange little way his heart was capable of feeling anything—if he really did love me in any sense—then why did he hang on to me when he knew?

May 1, 1990

The legal documents that chronicle births, deaths, marriages, divorces, real estate transfers, even rapes and murders, owe their existence to archaic and aloof wording that bears no similarity to, and sometimes isn't even understood by, the people whose names are mentioned in them.

The sterile documents, written by lawyers generally for the understanding only of other lawyers, are arcane, obscure tributes to legalese that minimize, if not exclude, the human beings whose lives they touch.

There is no place in the official measurements and exact time in a birth certificate, say, for mention of a boy child "with a cute, sideways grin," or in probate for a word about how the deceased may have sold his most prized possessions to accumulate the wealth about to be divided among his children. Nor does the inevitable "irreconcilable differences" boilerplate cited in divorce petitions come close to describing the trauma and fear of a woman thrown into a wall by a drunken husband.

For all their noble attempts at specificity and absolute interpretation, many official documents give little window to the actual events as they occurred, and certainly not as they were felt by the human beings involved.

The first of the ten indictments to which Escobedo would plead guilty was that of Meagan Finley:

> One, Gilbert H. Escobedo hereinafter styled Defendant, on or about the 10th day of March in the year of our Lord One Thousand Nine Hundred and 90 in the County of Dallas and State of Texas did unlawfully then and there knowingly and intentionally cause penetration of the female sexual organ of Meagan Finley, hereinafter called the complainant, without the consent of the complainant by means of an object, to-wit: the sexual organ of Gilbert H. Escobedo, and, in the course of this same criminal episode, used and exhibited a deadly weapon, to-wit: a firearm, against the peace and dignity of the State of Texas.

For all its loftiness and specificity, the document hardly did justice to the sordid "episode" that left a twenty-two-year-old woman sobbing childlike in a corner, nude and alone, and as vulnerable and dependent as the day she was birthed.

Gilbert Escobedo was issued Texas Department of Criminal Justice Inmate No. 551949, his fifth such number in twenty-one years. After a series of diagnostic intelligence and psychological tests, he was assigned to the Ellis I Unit near Huntsville, a maximum-security penitentiary that houses Death Row and Texas' hard-timers, lifers, and escape risks.

His first opportunity at parole is April 25, 2010.

III. The Prey

23

"My God, the thing I think about most?

"What is the population of Dallas? Dallas–Fort Worth is, what, maybe three million people? And out of three million people, I chose *him?*"

Three years after a phone call shattered the tranquillity of a Saturday morning and her new life in Nashville, Angela Welburne has moved her life forward. Married to a man she met after her aborted engagement to Gilbert Escobedo, the mother of a little girl, and a working mother with a career, Angie tries not to allow her mind to wander back to the two years in Dallas she spent with Escobedo.

"It's a part of my life that I'm not proud of and that I'd just as soon put behind me. Especially now that I have a child. It's not something that I ever want to dwell on or care for her or any other family member to ever know about.

"I couldn't believe it," she said, recalling the phone call from her friend in Dallas. "I was really hurt and shocked and angry. Every emotion you could possibly think of, I felt it. I never felt sorry for him. Not at all. I still don't. I don't care if you hate your mama. I don't care what happened. I think that mainly I'm mad at him for wasting my time. . . .

"I guess I was just a good cover for him. As long as he was living with someone, or engaged to someone, then maybe he was a little less of a suspect. It's the only thing I'm still mad at him about, that he wasted nearly two years of my life."

Events she didn't understand at the time they occurred came into harrowing focus after Escobedo was arrested, particularly the knock on her apartment door in Dallas on April 3, 1987. It was the night her fiancé raped Suellyn Teal, an assault to which he would plead guilty three years later.

Angie had defended Escobedo to the officers. "No way he could have raped somebody," she steadfastly had told them, unaware that as she slept, he had used her car to drive to Teal's parents' house. "He was right here in bed with me. He has been since *Knots Landing* came on."

"I just adamantly took his side of it and stood up for him until the end, really believing what I was telling them," Angie recalled years later.

There were other random events that took on clarity after Escobedo's confessions:

"He went out once to take the garbage to the Dumpster and he was gone for a while. I walked outside to the pool and walked around. I saw him. He wasn't window-peeking, but he was walking around between the buildings looking around.

"I said, 'What are you doing?' He said, 'Oh, I'm just taking a walk.' It just seemed strange to me that he wasn't walking on the sidewalk, but on the grass and the hills behind the apartments. I thought it was stupid, but I say, 'So what, it's Gilbert. He's different.' "

And: "One time he had a great big scratch on his back, and I noticed it when he was getting into the shower. And I asked him about it. I sort of was just teasing around with him, and said, 'One of your girlfriends clawed your back up or something.'

"He got real defensive, and said, 'Well, no, I was up under one of the cars, and something tore my shirt and scratched my back.' Those things didn't mean anything then, but now I know it was probably from somebody fighting him."

The discovery that her former fiancé was a serial rapist left Angie Welburne shaken in her own judgment, a trait in which she previously had prided herself.

"I just don't understand," she said. "I am one of the most logical,

reasonable, level-headed people that I know, and I say that with all
sincerity. I'm such a realist. I'm not a very spontaneous person, to have
jumped in headfirst. In this case I did, with him. It didn't pan out, work
out, and I'm just really glad that I moved and came on back and got
on with my life before any of that went down.

"I'm glad I wasn't married to him or bore any of his children. I'm
just glad I wasn't there."

Just as Angie Welburne was immersed in dealing with the most unimaginable betrayal of her young life, yet another phone call, unavoid-
able considering the circumstances, added humiliation.

"When he was arrested and admitted to the rapes, the Dallas Police
Department contacted me, asking questions. Basically, if I knew of anything going on. Well, of course not. Do you think I'm going to live
with someone if I know he's raping women?

"But they started asking about a fur coat and jewelry. I turned over
some jewelry to the Nashville Police Department who, I guess, was
going to get it to Dallas. One bracelet I kept because I was with Gilbert
when he bought that. I even paid for a third of it myself. The fur coat
I sold and paid off credit cards and bought a washer and dryer. I sold
it for two thousand dollars when I moved back here to Nashville. I
didn't need it or want it."

Escobedo called, too.

"He called Becky [his eldest daughter] from the Dallas County Jail.
Becky put him on a three-way call and sent it to Nashville to my mother's house because she knew I was there. It wasn't a very long conversation at all, and at that time he hadn't even been in jail a week yet.

"I was still very angry and bitter. I said what I had to say, got it off
my mind, off my chest, cursed him, yelled at him, told him I hated him
for what he did. . . .

"Right after the arrest, I thought of him daily. But as time went on,
it got better. Now I regard him as a sad human being. It's very sad that
someone who has the potential that Gilbert had, as a father, as a human.
I mean, he was a good person. That sounds really strange to say that a
rapist was a good person. He was. He was good to his family. He was
thoughtful, cheerful, and would have had a lot to offer someone had he
not screwed himself and ended up in prison. . . .

"He wore a wonderful mask. Everyone who knew him liked him.

Even my father liked him. My father used to tell me all the time, 'You just need to go back to Dallas.' I think that was just because he thought Gilbert was taking care of his little girl. Of course, he felt different when he heard the news.

"I was very hurt, bitter, and angry, and I went to a counselor and discussed it right after it happened. I felt so bad.

"I felt guilty because I didn't see any of it. Why couldn't I have seen what was going on? Why couldn't I have stopped it? I felt so bad for the other women, but at the same time, when I first found out, I was thinking at least he only victimized them once. He broke into their homes and he raped them one time.

"He crawled in bed with me every time after each time he committed one of those crimes. I felt victimized over and over again."

24

I have been seeing [Meagan Finley] . . . since March 29, 1990, approximately three weeks after the rape occurred. To date, I have seen her eleven times. . . . Her diagnosis is 308.30, post traumatic stress disorder, acute. . . .

Like most rape victims, she was consumed with the question, "Why me?" She was experiencing panic attacks, acute anxiety, palpitations, dry mouth, upset stomach, and nightmares.

Our session on May 1 focused on her feelings about the rapist and his being caught. By that time she felt safe living with her father, although she continued having the nightmares. These nightmares continue now into July, haunting [Meagan] about her experience, and she still fears walking outdoors at night after dark.

—Letter from Meagan Finley's therapist

"In the beginning, he tried to make me give him oral sex, and I said, 'No way.' I said, 'I'll choke. I'll die, I can't breathe.' Luckily, he just forgot. I would rather somebody shoot me in the head than go through that.

"He had a stale breath. I could hear it in my ear, like a forced, raspy kind of voice. Just kind of unclean, kind of stale.

"I could turn my head a little without him flipping out. I always had a towel over my head, even when he turned the light on. I didn't have the guts to take the towel off, but for some reason I thought he had long hair. I didn't know who I was with. He just seemed like really, really gross. Gross and dirty with a very stale breath.

"I mean, you just try to visualize who you're with, and I picture what you see on TV, like one of those convicts with scraggly long hair. He wasn't circumcized, which really grossed me out. I knew he wasn't black. I had no idea he was a Mexican. I didn't know how old he was.

"The scary thing was lying there hearing the zipper and rummaging through things. He came prepared. He wiped me up. I didn't realize until later on that he had his own bag of tricks. He had his own towel. He had a bag and that's what I was hearing. I kept waiting for him to stab me or something. . . .

"Then he turned on the lights and made me lie there in the position he wanted me in while he masturbated. Then he lay down beside me and masturbated himself. I mean, it took him a long time. That was probably the most humiliating, having to lie there in the light like that with a towel over my head. It was so humiliating.

"The thing that scared me the most was, he said, 'If you say anything, I'll kill you. I have a silencer, and no one will know you're dead.'

"And that really upset me to think that I'm in this new apartment, I'd just broken up with my boyfriend, and my parents are not here, and I could be dead in this place for a month and nobody will know."

Unlike virtually all of Gilbert Escobedo's victims, Meagan Finley, barely twenty-two at the time, had not been stalked, nor had she been the target of his late-night window-peeking sprees until the night she was raped. He had stumbled on her precisely as she and her friends were moving her belongings into an apartment at Preston Greens. Then he waited until her friends trickled out, leaving her alone in her new apartment.

Peering through the blinds of a window not four feet from her, Escobedo later acknowledged, he knew he would give her an hour or so to fall asleep, then come back. In the interim, he watched Meagan as she roamed the cluttered apartment clad only in a pair of purple panties, unpacking boxes and hanging clothes. He saw her finally give up in frustration when she wasn't able to reassemble the frame that held her mattress.

And he stared at her as she collapsed onto the couch and dialed a friend on the phone. Only the window kept her from hearing his breath.

Preying on Meagan Finley would be a dangerous departure in his MO, Escobedo knew that. No time to monitor her habits, no time to build a comfort factor. But he was obsessed with the woman beyond the blinds.

"I never saw a woman built like her," he would say later. "She was a 'ten.' She was beautiful and very heavy in the chest. I told myself, 'I'll risk a life sentence for this.' "

Rape and its aftermath, as tortuous by nature as they are, also amplify and distort the preexisting sensitivities, fears, and considerations of their victims. For Meagan Finley, that sensitivity was, in fact, her build.

"He talked about my chest and said, 'You must love all the attention you get. The boys must like it.' I hated that. Because stupid, ignorant boys would always say, 'Hey, nice tits.' They stare you into the ground, particularly Mexicans. When I was working at Chili's [a chain of restaurants] as a hostess, you'd hear the *'grande chi chi's'* as you walked past. That used to really make me mad. I knew what the jerks were saying.

"It's that kind of attitude. I'd always gotten that. He tried to get me to admit that I liked comments like that. It was demeaning and humiliating."

Two and a half years after her ordeal, after moving from Dallas to the Northeast, after countless hours of counseling, and after marrying a supportive, even doting husband, Meagan Finley is never far from fear.

She recounted her experience as she sat in the den of her comfortable apartment on the sixth floor of a high-security apartment complex, replete with closed-circuit monitors and twenty-four-hour security guards on the premises.

Across the room, her husband, Vincent, a friendly, soft-spoken carpenter, periodically winced and stared at the carpeting as she explained the fear and bitterness that, while diminished with time, still are real enough to haunt her now.

Ironically, the same fear that forced her move from Dallas to her parents' home in the Northeast reappeared immediately after the move. She walked into her parents' house shortly after it had been burglarized.

"Things were amiss," Meagan recalled. "I called my stepmother at her work. She screamed for me to get out of the house and call police. 'The same thing could happen to you again,' she said. I was petrified.

"That's my biggest fear now. That I'll be raped again and next time I won't get off as lucky. That I'll be killed."

Meagan met the man she would marry two months after she was raped, and after she had moved to her parents' home. She and a girl-friend stopped off for a drink after work, and she met Vincent in the crowded bar. They went out a few days later.

"He apparently just brushed against my chest," Meagan said. "I got pretty upset with him, because he had been such a nice guy, and I didn't want this guy to be a sleaze. Everything just came back. He was a little defensive and said it was just an accident. The night was a little shaky."

The couple nonetheless went out a week later, and she felt comfortable enough to tell him about the rape.

"I wanted to tell him because I knew I was pretty much a basket case, scared of the dark, scared to be alone, scared of everything."

The courtship wasn't easy for either of them. Once, wrestling on the couch, Vincent playfully put a pillow over Meagan's head, realizing too late the implication it had for his girlfriend.

"Going to movies, there'd be some really intense scene, an action scene, and she'd get very tense and stiff," Vincent recalled. "One time, even during *Home Alone*, she hyperventilated. We didn't make it through the movie.

"I learned to avoid some things. Like flipping through the TV channels, it might be some talk show about rape victims. I avoided things like that. I didn't want to upset her.

"The other day we saw *A Few Good Men* with Tom Cruise. The very first scene of the movie was some guys jumping on another one in bed and taping him up. She got very upset."

"It's that fear of lying in your bed and being jumped like that," Meagan said. "It's like the guy in the movie is lying there sleeping and all of a sudden he's attacked, just like I was jolted awake with a gun at my head."

Innocent, even loving incidents become unpredictably twisted into horror-filled flashbacks that take Meagan Finley back to two hours in April 1990.

"There was a time when Vincent came in after working outside all day," she said. "Of course his breath was stale and he hadn't showered, and the smell of his breath and his voice in my ear made me start crying. It felt like I was with this guy again."

The occasional nights when Vincent works late are agonizing, worse even than the trips on the packed mass transit train or the trips through the tunnel, parts of Meagan's daily life that still create anxiety.

Even six floors up in a high-security apartment with an intercom isn't enough to take the edge off the irrational fear that a shadow on a wall creates; the shadow always is Gilbert Escobedo.

And when she consciously fights the recall of the rape, Meagan's mind involuntarily returns to that night in the small, cluttered apartment in Dallas.

"The worst thing that happened to him was that he couldn't keep an erection, and it was damaging to his ego," Meagan said. "It was about ego and sex because he kept making me tell him how good it was and how great it was and 'put your hands on my ass and squeeze,' and he made me do all these things. I think that's ego.

"He said, 'I'm going to turn the light on. I want you to spread your legs and I'm going to masturbate.' It just makes me sick. He knew he was making me feel awful. He just didn't care."

It is not unusual, Vincent allows, for nightmares to awaken Meagan, screaming and crying in the middle of the night. "She's almost always trapped and trying to get to a door. I've got to grab her. She's screaming, 'Help me, I'm trapped! I'm trapped!' "

"He took away my independence," Meagan said. "I had lived on my own for four years. I'm terrified to do that. It scares me that you can't even trust anybody. You think you're safe, but you're not. I resent that it happened to me."

Meagan Finley's bitterness runs as deep as her fear. In her most desperate times, she doubts if she'll ever feel truly safe or be able to stop the hatred.

"I'm very upset," she said. "He'll be eligible for parole in twenty years. He's been doing it longer, I'll bet you; he's been raping for twenty years. The guy doesn't even suffer. I read that they go to school, even learn computers. How dare they even be able to read a book.

"This is a prison," Meagan Finley said, her eyes scanning her apartment. "I lost my privileges, the right to feel safe and whole. He doesn't seem to be losing his.

"What's a fair sentence for what he did to me?" she asked quietly. "Hard labor. And I want him raped once a day for every day he's in prison."

25

So the officers and I went back upstairs, and they wanted me to go through every single gory detail, minute by minute, from the time I woke up. They took all the bedding off the bed. They had me take my nightgown off. They had me put some clothes on. They told me not to take a shower, they were going to have to take me down to Parkland [Memorial Hospital] to do some tests.

I sat there about an hour, going through all their questions and details. They wanted to know who said what. And they asked me kind of personal questions about him and me. After about an hour of that, they said let's take her down to the hospital.

I was sitting in the back of the cruiser and I remember going down the Tollway. There was a black officer and a white officer, and the black officer was driving. I was just sitting there crying. I couldn't stop crying. The white officer said something to the black officer and kind of chuckled. It was something having to do with me. I don't remember exactly what it was. I heard it, but it was something under his breath. It only made me feel worse. It hurt my feelings. It was just very insensitive. I started crying harder.

And the black officer turned around and patted my hand and said, "You're going to be okay." He was the consoling one. I thought that was really unusual, a black officer consoling a white woman versus the white officer.

And then they turned around at one point and gave me a little piece of paper about the rape hotline or a group that I could call. They said I didn't have to, but if I felt like I needed to talk to somebody, call these people.

Parkland was just a madhouse. I had to sit in this waiting room. They have a certain code for what happens, like everything else, and they said, "Well, she's a Code Something." I'm sitting there and there's this hustle and bustle going on. I'm just a mess, shaking. Nobody from my family had come with me because they didn't know where we were going, so I was by myself. I sat there about forty-five minutes in this waiting room and, finally, they let me go into another room and had me change. They said, "Somebody will be with you in a little bit."

Well, I sat there for over an hour with my little garb on. They said a doctor would be with me in a little while. That was another twenty minutes. Altogether, I spent probably twenty minutes having all the tests done, just going through the usual stuff they have to do, and about four hours of waiting. Then somebody from the hospital . . . said they'd call a cruiser to pick me up. And I had to wait another thirty minutes for the cruiser to come. It's like five hours for twenty minutes of tests that I had to take.

It was very ordinary, like, "Here's another one." They had a code for she's been raped. You feel like a number. Everything's just very insensitive. And there was nobody there trying to console you. I just basically cried the whole time. I cried and I shook the whole time.

Part of the problem was that I felt like there was nobody there who cared. It's like, "We need to check you out, we need to do this test, we need to do this blood work." Then it was, "All right, you can get dressed." They were just doing this for the police department. They were going through their routine tests for the police department and that was it.

When I went back to work, I was a little shaken up and a little out of it for quite some time, withdrawn from people, and I didn't want to talk to people and couldn't really concentrate on my work.

People said, "What's going on?" I had just said somebody had broken into my house. I said they had a gun, but that I had scared them away, that it had scared me and shook me up. That's all I said. So when the detective came to question me, I just said he needed to ask me some more questions about the break-in. I never told them more than that.

But there was a situation in which a black girl was working in our office and she was dating a black officer on the force and she decided to pry into what had happened. She told him my name, and he got the police report and told her I had been raped. And the word spread through the office. We were kind of friends, too.

Later on, about a year later when I was at the office, she told me, "Oh, by the way, I checked with my boyfriend and he got the police report and you didn't have a break-in. You were raped." She accused me of being a liar.

I knew that she had spread the word, because she was that type. You know: "Guess what happened? [Margaret] didn't really have a break-in. Somebody raped her." There were all kinds of vicious stories going around about how it could have happened, and why it happened.

I didn't know how to handle it. There was nothing I could have done. It just hurt more. Everybody knew, and my privacy had been invaded once again.

That happened in December and in June of 1989, I was released from my job. It's like a lot of people took an attitude toward me. I knew there was something going on, but I didn't know that everybody in the office knew. Everybody was getting transferred and moving to New York to go with another company. Everybody kept asking, "Are you going to be a team player and work with us?" I said, "Yeah, sure." They kept on making promises about what they were going to do for me at the office and two weeks later, they let me go with no explanation.

It hurt my feelings. I had a daughter to support. I didn't have any other opportunities on the horizon. I'd only been in Dallas a year.

Almost five years after she was raped as her fourteen-year-old daughter slept in an adjacent bedroom of their luxury North Dallas condominium, Margaret Michaelson agreed to relive the most tragic night of her life. Remarried since the attack and living at the time in a small town in the Deep South, Michaelson still was looking for answers to the one hour and forty-two minutes on December 22, 1988, that forever altered her life.

Tall, blond, sophisticated, and strikingly attractive, the stereotypical target of Gilbert Escobedo, Michaelson sat by her husband, Richard, in the booth of a crowded coffee shop in Addison, a northern upscale suburb of Dallas.

The last year had been good for her, she said, probably the only decent year she had had since the rape. Until she remarried and moved from Dallas, she had lived four years in the same condominium. Unlike the majority of Escobedo's victims who lived in leased apartments and many of whom moved immediately after the attack, Michaelson owned her condo and, for financial reasons, relocating wasn't an alternative.

Her attacker told her that he lived in the same cluster of condominiums—a lie, as it turned out—and that he watched who came and went. For four years, Michaelson said, she lived in her condo, overpowered by memories of the rape and dreading nightfall when anxiety always would lay waste to whatever feelings of security she felt during the day. She slept like a child, initially with the ceiling lights on, then "graduating," as she put it, to a night-light.

As harrowing as the actual rape had been, parts of her recovery had been just as searing to her soul. Forced penetration, she learned, was only the immediate manifestation of rape, merely the terrifying catalyst for the dread and fear that would linger long afterward. Unconsciously, her life revolved around coping with the fallout and trying to fit the pieces back together.

Not knowing if her attacker still was at large only heightened her anxiety. He found her once; would he find her again? Over time, Michaelson doubted that he actually lived in her condos, but she had learned not to take anything for granted.

Her last contact with police was when the detective interviewed her at her office shortly after the rape. He had left his business card, saying, "If there's anything else you need or have any questions, call me."

"But the thing is, I never heard any more about it," Michaelson said. "I was never updated. Just nothing. I saw the story about the arrest and his picture in the newspaper. Richard had asked me, and I said, 'Richard, I want to say yes, but I'm not sure.'

"I pictured him as being different than that. But I said I really didn't know. I'd like to believe it was him. But I can't say for sure because I never saw his face."

Not until she was contacted for an interview for this book did Michaelson know that Escobedo had, in fact, confessed to raping her. She wanted to see Escobedo's picture.

"Are you sure?"

"I do," she said without hesitation. "This has been going on five years. I've pretty much put it behind me and dealt with it, particularly in this last year. I think this is part of it. I want to see his picture."

She held the police mug shot with her thumb and forefinger, staring silently for several moments at the dark-haired man in prison whites who stared blankly into the camera. Michaelson's husband studied her face for a reaction.

"I would swear the guy had a mustache," she said quietly. "But this guy has the same build."

Michaelson's instincts were good. Beyond the darkness, beyond the covering over his face, the man who raped her, indeed, had a mustache. Escobedo had shaved it before he was arrested.

Seeing the picture, knowing with certainty for the first time she was looking at the man who raped her, appeared to focus Michaelson's recollections.

It also resurrected one of the most painful experiences of her ordeal: her relationship with her daughter.

"He had heard somebody moving around," Michaelson recalled, "and he asked if I had a roommate. I said, 'I have a daughter.' And he said, 'How old is she?' She was fourteen, almost fifteen at the time, would have been fifteen in March. The first thing that occurred to me was, 'He's with me now. He'll go to her next.' So I said, 'She's ten.'

"So then he went into her bedroom because he wanted to make sure she's sleeping. He told me to stay right there and stay away from the telephone, and he walked to her room. He came back and closed the door and said, 'She's still sleeping.'

"I was worried because I just had this feeling that she'd wake up and get up in the night. Then he said, 'If she gets up and comes in here, I'll leave. I promise you. I don't want to scare her, I'll leave.' There was a door going out to my patio off the bedroom, and he said he'd go out that door and leave. And then I was hoping she would get up. But she slept through the whole thing.

"He left at four or five, I don't remember anymore. But after he left, I went downstairs. I waited about twenty minutes. It was quiet and I figured he had left. I turned on the lights. That's when I noticed the two doors were open. I closed and bolted them.

"And I just paced downstairs, the whole length of downstairs, and I just paced until the sun came up. I was shaking and I didn't want to wake Chris up. And all I did was, I was reliving the whole thing, and I was just a mess. I had no phone. I went to get the phone downstairs and I realized he had taken it. The others wouldn't work.

"I didn't want to go outside, go to a neighbor's house, until the sun came up. So I paced. It must have been about three hours. I was just beside myself. Finally, about eight o'clock, I felt safe enough to go outside and went out the back kitchen door.

"I found the phone lying by some bushes by the carport with the channel open. That's why I couldn't dial out; he'd opened the channel on the remote phone. So I found the phone and that's when I called. But it was a long three or four hours waiting to go outside.

"I didn't really know how to handle telling Chris what had happened. I thought she was old enough that she'd understand what had happened. Basically, I just told her that somebody had broken in and had raped me. I don't think she really understood what happened.

"Chris didn't take it very well. There were some repercussions. She was angry, and I almost felt because it all happened to me, that she blamed me. She didn't understand that I was victimized. It was, 'How could you let this happen to you?' She blamed it on me. There was a lot of tension between us, and she did not handle it well at all.

"I don't know if it was the way I told her or the circumstances. I don't know if there was a *right* way to handle it. I was trying to deal with it as my problem. She knew about it, and it's like she put it in the back of her mind. It didn't happen to her and she didn't have to deal with it.

"I went through a very bad time with her a couple of months after that. She ran away for three days and was very rebellious. *Extremely* rebellious. She didn't want to live at the house with me. It was real tough. We had a really terrible Christmas. Probably all the way through March, I had an unbelievably hard time with her. She was rebellious and didn't care what I said. It was part of what had happened, the emotions, getting it out as best she could.

"We went for some counseling, and the counselor just said your daughter's going through a very bad time. I broke down during some of the sessions. I said I couldn't take it anymore. And I told the counselor I had just been raped in December and the counselor said, 'What you need to do is take care of you and get yourself together because you're no good to her until you get yourself together.'"

Like most advice, it was easier to give than to take.

"I was such a basket case," Michaelson recalled. "It took me about a year to stop having the nightmares. I had stayed in the condo, but I slept downstairs on the couch for months with all the lights on. I wouldn't sleep in my bedroom and not in my bed. I slept with every light on in the house.

"Right after this happened, I took a butcher knife and I put it under the pillow on the couch. He told me that if I said anything, he would come back. If he comes back, I'm ready for him.

"Then I graduated from not having the light on because Richard couldn't sleep with the light on. We had met about a year after this happened. I slept with a night-light, which still bothered him. But I said, 'I'm sorry, but I can't sleep without a light.' Where I can actually *see* the room. Because that night, it was dark in my room. I was afraid of the dark. I could not sleep in a dark room. . . . I just have these visions of someone breaking into my house and robbing me and raping me. I have this phobia of being alone in a house, especially at night.

"It's just something I don't think I'll ever get over. If I'm at home and Richard isn't there, I sleep with the lights on. And I make sure every door is bolted. I won't sleep in the bedroom. I'll sleep on the couch in the family room."

Alone at night, the solitude and darkness become an ominous emotional mixture that equates to abject fear. Inevitably, the angst of a defenseless night in Dallas surfaces.

"He was so cool, calm, and collected through the whole thing," Michaelson said of her rapist. "He was cocky about his gun. He thought he was cool with the gun. The police called him a 'gentleman rapist' because he was not violent with me. But in essence, the whole act was violent."

She tried to reason with a man whose face or actions she couldn't fathom.

"Why are you doing this?" she had asked him. "Don't you have a girlfriend?"

"It's none of your business."

"Why don't you ask somebody out on a date? Why do you have to go to this length to be with a woman?"

"I told you. It's none of your business."

The attacker refused to talk about himself and was growing edgy under her questions.

"He wouldn't tell me anything. I was trying to find out where he was coming from, I mean, like why he was doing this to me. And he didn't want to talk about it. He was very defensive. I tried to talk to him because it made me feel calmer to talk. I felt like I needed to talk to him so that I wouldn't be there just for that one reason. It did calm me down for some reason, until he told me to shut up. He made that clear."

For months after the rape, Michaelson caught herself studying men around her. She wasn't looking at their faces. She hadn't seen *his* face. She was looking at the way the men were built, wondering if she could identify her attacker by his physique. It was a hideous mind game that left her leery of virtually all men.

"I was particularly suspicious of a lot of men in our condo complex," Michaelson said. "That summer, I was sitting out by the pool some and I was suspicious, and I'd wonder, Does *he* fit the description? Could it have been *him?*"

She saw him everywhere, yet she found him nowhere.

"I was just so suspicious of everybody that I didn't trust anybody," she said.

Shortly before she was raped, Michaelson had begun dating a man who commuted between California and Dallas. Their relationship had settled into a comfortable and pleasant arrangement.

"We had just finished dinner and we were talking," she said. "I'll never forget his reaction when I told him I had been raped. He said, 'How disgusting!'

"He acted like he was going to be sick. We went from having a nice relationship to zip. That was it. It was like I was damaged goods or spoiled material. He didn't want anything to do with me after that. It really made me feel terrible. It was like it turned his stomach. And then I wondered, maybe I shouldn't have told him anything like that."

The man's reaction struck Michaelson to her core. For more than a year, she avoided relationships with men. One man had stuck a gun to her head as she slept and forced her to have sex; another, one she thought she knew, had scorned her because of it.

Then Richard—tall, lean, and athletic—came along.

"It was totally different," Michaelson said. "He lived somewhere else. He never fit the description [of her attacker]. And we had mutual friends.

"I had seen Richard back and forth," she said, "and we started dating. I still had all my strange idiosyncrasies. I had some delayed things, like sleeping with the lights on. There were certain things that I would pull back, like déjà vu kinds of things. I would pull back. I didn't want him to think, well, she's really weird. I really liked him.

"And finally, I said, 'Richard, there's something I really need to tell you.'

"But he understood. There was no problem. He was very supportive, extremely supportive. He said, 'Well, I'm here and I'll protect you and I'll take care of you.' "

Michaelson took pride in her self-sufficiency before the rape. Over the years, she had survived divorce, had the courage to relocate from southern Florida, and was a single parent who worked hard at her career. Rape shattered that independence.

"I went for counseling and I got out all my feelings and I cried a lot. But the traumatization—of not being able to sleep, and when the sun would go down my anxiety level would go up—that lasted probably two to three years. It's just now, that we've moved away, that I don't think about it. My daughter's away at college now. Richard and I got married last year, and knowing that I have a husband to protect me, I think all that has pretty much helped me a lot.

"The actual crime, I've dealt with that. I can see a fourteen-year-old being traumatized by a sexual attack. But a woman in her thirties, it's not like you've never experienced it, at least the sex part of it.

"The trauma comes from having the gun, the violence that I had to deal with. That was the hard part to get over. Of not jumping out of bed, just reliving the hand over the face and pushing me down and the gun. That was the traumatization I had to deal with.

"I can't say that I'm traumatized anymore. It's an experience that I'll never forget. I can go about my daily life now, but it took four years to do it, and getting married and having a man in my life to feel secure.

"But I think until the day I die, I'll always be afraid to be in the house by myself with the lights off."

26

Every profession has its axioms, the simple, cautionary rules of thumb that have been predicated over years of trial and error. Among lawyers, the most popular of these fundamental laws is: A lawyer who represents himself has a fool for a client. With pilots, the basic principle is: There are old pilots and there are bold pilots, but there aren't any old, bold pilots. Among nonfiction writers, the saying goes thusly: When in doubt, leave it out. And, borrowing from the Hippocratic oath, rookie doctors always are reminded: First, do no harm.

Among veteran rape detectives like Marshall Touchton and Evelyn Crowder, whose arrests have netted business executives, ministers, movers, mechanics, and everything in between, the axiom well could be: Spend your time looking for a slobbering man in a trenchcoat and you've wasted your time.

The caution, obviously, is against buying into stereotypes. And to that end, there could be a corollary for dealing with rape victims: Barring clairvoyance, predicting how a victim will react emotionally to forcible sex is akin to predicting the weather.

In nearly thirty years of wearing a badge, Touchton has investigated cases in which average, middle-class women have been emotionally detached, even disinterested in finding their attackers.

"That's not necessarily because they're afraid or embarrassed about testifying," Touchton said. "In a few cases, they really just don't care about finding the guy. They talk about it like they would a car wreck, like it was just a bad day, and they want to go on with their lives."

Touchton has seen the opposite, pitiful end of the spectrum, too. "You really wonder whether some of these women will ever live a normal life again," he said. "They're paranoid, too scared to go to work, too scared to go to the grocery store. Some of them are too afraid to even leave their house to go to counseling."

To his knowledge, none of the victims on whose cases Touchton has worked has committed suicide, though some undoubtedly have contemplated it. One young woman, however, was institutionalized in a mental hospital after being raped.

"There was some indication she had had some mental problems in the past even before she was raped," Touchton said. "There's really no way of knowing if she would have ended up in the institution even if she hadn't been raped. But I'll tell you this: She was sure in a pitiful mess after the rape.

"It's impossible to predict the reaction. Sometimes you think you can, but you can't. Human nature, I'm telling you, it's a strange deal. One time I investigated a sexual assault against a prostitute, and I'm convinced she was genuinely totally devastated by the assault."

I don't hate him by any stretch of the imagination. I think being a woman of the eighties—not the nineties, but the eighties, I mean being single in the eighties—I've almost had dates that were worse than this.

That's probably an odd thing to say. You probably think, "What's wrong with this woman?" He didn't hurt me. I thought, obviously, he's got some kind of mental problems if this is what he does for entertainment.

That's why there's a part of me that wonders, "Does somebody like this belong in jail or where does he really belong?" I don't know if we need something else. It's obviously some kind of sickness. It's not a hobby, it's a sickness.

So I don't hate him; I was curious about him.

I was pretty shocked when I found out how harsh the sentence was. Not that I want him out. I guess there's also a part of me that says he's not going

to find me again, and it's not something he's going to do. But sticking him in
prison for concurrent life sentences? Wow.

Like I said, I've had worse dates.

Rene Williams, a systems engineer for a global computer company, was
thirty-one, single, "an incredible left-winger," and emotionally frayed
over a recent breakup with her boyfriend when Gilbert Escobedo came
through an unlocked patio door and raped her before daylight on
July 10, 1989.

Four years later, barefoot and wearing a faded T-shirt and baggy
shorts, Williams was seated cross-legged on a couch in her den, being
interviewed for this book. Having just allowed that the rape was no
worse than some dates she had had, Williams paused briefly, contemplating her comment.

"I realize this isn't what you may have expected to hear," she said
matter-of-factly. "I know that my viewpoint may be unconventional.
I'll be interested to see what you do with this. Some women are going
to think I'm crazy."

Hardly. Rene Williams, disarmingly honest and at ease with herself,
makes no apology for her lack of convention. Self-reliant and intelligent
by nature and analytical by profession, she has, apparently, over years
directed those traits inward, inventorying and assessing her own
strengths and weaknesses.

The extraordinary result is a guileless insight and knowledge of herself that allows her not to personalize, rationalize, or justify. Even as
she describes her own rape, she speaks dispassionately, as if she were a
radiologist discussing a stranger's dubious X rays.

She spoke with the realization that her views bore the possibility, if
not probability, of misinterpretation, particularly among some feminists
who would characterize her, erroneously, as being in denial.

Williams inferred, for example, that she bore some culpability for
her fate: "My theory is that I was in the wrong place at the wrong time.
He may have been watching before, but I'm pretty sure I left the door
unlocked. I made it easy for him."

On the clumsiness and indifference of the doctor who examined her at Parkland following the rape: "It was fine that it was kind of cold. I'm not the kind of person who likes people to come up and be real sympathetic or hold my hand or anything like that."

On rape counseling: "I never really went to any counseling; I never felt like I needed to."

About the role of women in rape: "In this day and age, the way rape is thought of, now with all the date rape and that stuff—and this is going to sound horrible—but maybe I think of women having more control over themselves and being more aware of their situations. I just think women—I don't want to say are brighter—but I just think they're more aware of what's going on around them.

"And when they get themselves into situations that end up in date rape, for example, I wonder a lot of times. It's such a hard call, particularly in the eighties. In the eighties, sex was rampant."

And in a truly unorthodox reaction, the intensity of the rape and its aftermath afforded Williams a reprieve of sorts:

"This is weird, but my whole frame of mind was that I had been so miserable for the whole week before that all I could think about was this guy I had broken up with, and now I have something else to think about. . . . I wanted to help.

"I wanted to catch him [the rapist]. It was a new goal, and I think because of that, I was pumped. It was a strange reaction. I really wanted to help. I wanted to remember something, to find something, some evidence. I was very productive. I was very busy."

Even her 911 phone call, Williams acknowledges, would have appeared "very odd" to someone monitoring the emergency radio frequency that night:

"Somebody," she told the dispatcher, *"has broken in here. I've been raped. But there's no emergency."*

"There was a part of me that worried they would come with the sirens going," she recalled. "I mean, he already was long gone."

Analytical dispassion notwithstanding, Rene Williams did not escape the rape without her own very real trauma. During the rape, she seized on how transitory her life was. After the rape and before the lab tests proved negative, Williams fixated on contracting venereal disease or HIV.

"It's interesting to see yourself in a situation like that, like the rape," she said. "I was kind of glad to see myself react the way I did because you never know what your mind's going to do."

Like an uncommon number of Escobedo's victims, Rene Williams already was in emotional chaos when she found herself having to cope with rape.

She hadn't slept in a week, not since she and her longtime boyfriend had broken up. It also was the first week in more than six months that Williams had been alone in the condo.

"I had had the pressure of the breakup to think about," Williams said, "and now I had this different pressure. I was just mentally concentrating. I was trying to think, 'Could I identify this man?' So my mind was cranking the whole time. I was trying to remember as much as I could. Since I couldn't see him—I had a pillowcase over my head the whole time—I thought, 'What's he wearing? Where are his hands?' I think I'm weird."

She focused her senses and strained for any information she could process. He was short, she could tell that from the fact that he appeared fully stretched on her bed. She had a footboard, and a tall man wouldn't have been able to stretch out. Did he have a mustache, or did she just imagine her hand touching one? No, there definitely was a mustache. There was no cologne, she was relatively certain of that, just a scrubbed, clean smell. He was uncommonly soft-spoken, but was it distinctive enough for her to pick him from a lineup?

"My big thing was trying to keep track of where his hands were," she said. "I figured if I knew where both his hands were, I didn't have to worry about the gun, because I think he put it down. I was very conscious of where his hands were.

"Then I said, 'Rene, you're remembering all this stuff and you may not have a chance to tell anybody about it.' And that thought truly shook me for a couple of minutes."

In the clear light of day, Williams had suffered no bruises or wounds, there had been no latent fingerprints, no footprints outside, no disarray to suggest violence, and, of course, no third-party witnesses to verify that a crime had even occurred.

Inside the condominium where Williams was raped, everything

looked almost precisely as it had before the attack. The orderliness confused Williams; over time, it made her question her sanity.

"The next morning when I'm trying to piece this all together, I'm looking around," she said. "First off, this stress from the boyfriend thing, and my mind's going: 'Is there some evidence that the rapist was here?' And there really wasn't.

"The only thing was a clothes hanger on the couch. And I had been laying on the couch before I went to bed, and I knew the hanger hadn't been there. So I don't know why he had a hanger. It wasn't unwound or anything like that. There's part of me that wonders if that was what he was pushing against my head instead of a gun. I don't know where it came from. I know he had to have picked it up and moved it there. I wouldn't have been laying on the couch on top of the hanger.

"When I had gone to bed, I had taken off all my clothes and I had a tank top. And I'm sure that he used that to clean up or something. And he took that with him.

"I began to think maybe I really did put that hanger there. And I didn't know where the T-shirt was. Maybe it would show up. There was part of me actually thinking maybe I made the whole thing up. That was the eeriest part. That shook me. That made me start to wonder about my mental state.

"The only thing I was hanging on to was that hanger. It was the only thing that I could find that made me think he had been there."

The doubt spread like ink on a paper towel. If she had been raped, where was the evidence? Had she even been raped?

"I thought I was really losing it. I was so distraught from this breakup that maybe I *had* concocted the whole thing. I thought, 'Maybe I did make it up.' Then, 'Well, maybe I did.'

"Then when they caught him, I thought, 'I really didn't make it up. It really *did* happen.'"

Curiously enough, Williams only added to her own agony when she tried to warn her neighbors that a rapist had struck in the condominiums.

"I felt obligated to go over to the condo manager and let her know about the rape," Williams recalled. "I lived in a condo complex that had a lot of women. I told the manager it might be good to warn people.

She said she would, but that she wouldn't use my name. She put up a note that there had been a break-in, that a rape had occurred, and to be wary, keep your doors locked and blinds closed, things like that.

"As soon as the note was up, everyone came in and asked who it was. And the manager told them she wasn't going to reveal the person's identity. Well, what happened is that one of these women who kept badgering her went to a policeman who lived across the street. She went over and asked him who it was, and he found out for her. I was outraged at that, and then, of course, it was common knowledge.

"Why do people care? The thing that made me so mad was that the woman went back to the condo manager and said, 'I know who it is.' Then the woman next door to me says, 'Oh, I don't know what I would have done. How'd you survive that? I'm not sure that I could go through that.'

" 'Well then,' I told her, 'you'd just have been shot, okay?' It was just sheer nosiness. What good did it do for that woman to find out?

"I thought I was doing those guys a favor by even telling the manager, just so they could be a little more aware. I couldn't believe they went out of their way to find out. I couldn't believe how easy it was to find out. I was so outraged, but I was told it was legal, that it was the officer's right to know."

Under Texas law, Williams' identity, in fact, could have been concealed, even from a police officer with access to the records computer. The so-called Pseudonym Law, versions of which exist in only a few other states, allows victims of sex crimes the option of using fictitious names on all public records. The law allows sex crime victims anonymity, from the original crime report throughout the criminal justice process, including their testimony in open court.

The legislative intent of the law was to reduce the public stigma of rape and to encourage victims to report and prosecute the crimes. Ostensibly, the law allowed officers and prosecutors to guarantee sex crimes victims that their names wouldn't appear in the media, another inducement to get their cooperation in testifying against rape defendants. In actuality, virtually no newspapers, television, or radio stations ever report the name of rape victims without their consent.

The Pseudonym Law, in reality, was moot. Dallas police seldom, if ever, informed rape victims of their right to a "Jane Doe" alias on reports, nor was there a standardized departmental procedure that required them to. Detectives informed neither Williams nor Ski Mask victims Margaret Michaelson and Meagan Finley of their right to use pseudonyms on police reports. Indeed, the names of all thirty-five women that Escobedo confessed to raping appeared not only on original police offense reports, but also in public prosecution records on file in the Dallas County Courthouse.

Not until 1994 did Dallas police implement a consent form for sex crimes victims that not only offers them the option of anonymity, but also requires their signature acknowledging that they were informed of their right to a fictitious name on official reports.

And ironically, it was uniformed police officers who had no official interest in the cases who prowled the files for Williams' and Michaelson's names and passed them on to friends who used the information to violate the victims' privacy.

Four years after the attack, Rene Williams, who married a colleague at work and moved to a middle-class Dallas suburb, doesn't dwell on the invasion of her privacy, fear of dying, or bitterness toward the man who raped her.

"There's a part of me that's sympathetic towards somebody in prison," she says, explaining her roots in a "liberally minded" family in the North. "But I don't have the sympathy for a lot of females. And that's something I find very odd, especially since all this happened to me.

"But also, I think I play the odds: What are the chances of this happening to me again?"

IV. The Predator

27

Shirley Escobedo remembers the shock of reading the front page of the *Dallas Morning News* that April morning in 1990. Had she not seen the police mug shot of Gilbert Escobedo that accompanied the article, she would have dismissed the account as that of another man with the same name. Nothing, absolutely nothing about the story of the capture of the Ski Mask Rapist was compatible with the man who had washed and waxed her car for three years and who, in the process, had become her friend.

But beneath the picture that unmistakably was that of her auto service man and friend was the caption in bold type: **"Gilbert Escobedo . . . being held on four charges of investigation of aggravated sexual assault, and burglary and attempted burglary charges."** Still the woman stared at the picture with disbelief.

"I was impressed with Gilbert because he was always dedicated to his work, he was fun to talk with, and he was one of the most polite men I had ever come in contact with," said the woman who, against all odds, would one day marry Escobedo. "When the publicity hit the newspapers and TV about his arrest, I was totally shocked, as were all of the people who knew him. He was successful in his business, was a very sharp dresser, had nice things, and all of this seemed completely contrary to his character."

Indeed, she had been so impressed with Escobedo that once, while retrieving her immaculately cleaned car from his garage on a Friday afternoon, she had casually asked him out for dinner and drinks.

"He was polite about it, but he turned me down," she recalled. "He told me he was seeing someone at the time, which didn't really surprise me. He was good-looking and one of the most charming men you'd ever meet. Anyway, he said he didn't think it would be right to go out with somebody else. Actually, that impressed me even more because some men wouldn't have hesitated to run around on their girlfriends."

During the time she had been one of Escobedo's customers, Shirley also met two of his brothers, Robert, Jr., and Al Escobedo, who periodically had helped out in the detail shop. Whenever she bumped into one of the brothers after Escobedo's arrest, Shirley always inquired about their brother.

"One day Al said it would be nice if I wrote to Gilbert and that he would enjoy hearing from me. It had been about a year since Gilbert had been incarcerated. So I sat down and wrote Gilbert a letter and asked how he was doing. I told him how confused I was by all that had happened with him and really didn't understand how not one soul had ever suspected him of this type of behavior."

The letter was typical of Shirley. Those who knew the attractive, divorced mother of two teenage daughters knew her for her loyalty, commitment, and perseverance. Among the lawyers for whom she worked at an old-line, prestigious law firm, she was the legal secretary they went to at five P.M. on a Friday, asking if she could work all weekend to help them prepare for trial on Monday. Seldom did Shirley ever disappoint them. She took pride in her job and she almost always could use the overtime.

Divorced for years from an abusive alcoholic, she was the sole support of her daughters, both of whom still lived with her in her comfortable suburban Dallas home with the impeccably kept lawn. She was a stranger neither to eighty-hour work weeks nor to being the strong disciplinarian and compassionate friend to her daughters.

Perhaps because Shirley had survived a wretched marriage from which she had safely extricated herself and her daughters, and maybe because she had relied singularly on herself through the ensuing years, she also developed a strong independence. Tempered with the compassion and empathy she learned through her own trauma, that independence and self-reliance seemingly made her invulnerable to the social pressures to which many succumb.

"People are going to think and say whatever they want to about you," she says with a shrug. "Much of the time those feelings aren't based on real facts anyway. So why be bound by it?"

Moreover, Shirley was not the kind to abandon a friend simply because he had been accused of committing a horrendous series of crimes.

"My experience has been that there's always more than meets the eye, and it can be good or bad," Shirley said.

Her letter to Gilbert Escobedo was an innocent one, an attempt to figure out how she could have been so misled by a friend, and to offer support.

"Gilbert wrote back to me and confirmed that he was guilty of the crimes he was charged with and that he was truly sorry for the pain he had caused everyone involved—his victims, his family, and his friends," Shirley recalled. "We wrote back and forth to each other for a while, and he placed me on his visitors' list.

"I'll never forget the first time I went to visit him in prison. It broke my heart to see him locked up like he was. We both laughed about some things, and we cried when he was telling me the story of how this had happened."

The story was sketchy, focusing not on detail, but on his own characterizations of the events and of himself. He had, as he would frequently explain, "one foot in church, and the other one out." The rapes were horribly wrong, he knew that, but he couldn't stop himself from committing the next. He didn't know why. He hoped to find out in prison counseling just as soon as his name came up on the waiting list. Remorse was the undercurrent of the conversation. That and, of course, his redemption through worshiping the Lord, Jesus Christ.

After a year of letters and almost weekly visits in which Shirley drove the six-hour round-trip from Dallas to prison near Huntsville, she and Escobedo were married in September 1992 in what Shirley acknowledges was "a pretty strange ceremony." Because the maximum-security prison wouldn't sanction a formal marriage ceremony, a lawyer for whom Shirley had once worked stood in as a proxy for Escobedo while a justice of the peace in Dallas performed the marriage vows.

Escobedo, in an interview a week after the marriage, appeared ecstatic. "Once again God has intervened in my life," he said. "He has given me a wife who loves me unconditionally despite the terrible things that I've done. That's God's hand. It's one of His miracles."

But except for a license on file in Dallas County, the marriage brought little substantive change in the relationship between the convict who will be imprisoned to at least the year 2010 and the woman who juggles weekend visits with her demanding work schedule.

The Texas prison system does not allow conjugal visits. The couple could meet in so-called contact visits, allowing them to talk without the restraints of the Plexiglas and wire screen between them, and to kiss and hug and hold hands under guards' constant scrutiny. "Inappropriate touching," however, is grounds for immediate expulsion for the visitor and, ultimately, permanent banishment from the inmate's authorized list of visitors.

Shirley Escobedo says she doesn't view her marriage to Escobedo through rose-colored glasses, and she knows people, particularly women, question her commitment to a man who raped scores of women. Among those who initially were suspicious were her own mother and two daughters.

"They were obviously shocked at first," Shirley explained, "but over time, they accepted and respected my decision."

Both daughters have accompanied her on visits to the prison, and the younger, seventeen, apparently has developed a strong bond with her new stepfather. If other members of her family haven't accepted her marriage, they've at least respected it, Shirley said.

The same apparently is not true of Escobedo's family. Except for the first Fourth of July celebration after their marriage, Shirley has not been a part of the frequent family gatherings at Robert Escobedo's house. The snub initially hurt Shirley and put Escobedo in an awkward balancing act between what he calls his "natural family" and his "new family."

In a visit with his father and stepmother, Escobedo said, he told them that he wanted them to accept his new wife. "Under God's eyes, we're one," he told his father and stepmother. "I want you to love her and her daughters like I do."

It was a message he said he passed on to his mother and brothers, too. But except for a few phone calls after his family's visits to prison, Shirley says she seldom hears from them.

The tentative relationship grew even more strained over time after Shirley attempted to coordinate weekend visits at the prison.

"I didn't want to drive six hours round-trip to visit him only to find out that he already had visitors, and vice versa," Shirley explained. "So I told his family that if they were planning to go on a particular weekend, to please let me know so that I wouldn't drive all that way and not get to see him."

What started out as merely an attempt to coordinate the logistics of prison visits, Shirley said, became an apparent affront to the Escobedo family.

"His mother said that she wasn't going to get clearance from me to visit her own son," Shirley said. "She said she was his *mother* and that should put her at the top of the list. Which is ironic since she hardly ever visits him anyway.

"Originally, I was surprised at their reaction. I figured they would be pleased that someone loved Gilbert enough that they would want to visit him. But they act like I'm trying to steal him or violate their family some way. They're clannish and I've got to admit I don't understand them.

"But God knows I'm a big girl and went into it with my eyes wide open."

And to some extent, she did. From his first letter to her, Escobedo acknowledged, if not detailed, the crimes he committed against women. For two years, Shirley went without details. But at one point, driving back to Dallas with me after a visit with Escobedo, Shirley asked to see the police reports that chronicled the attacks. She read through the reports, from which the victims' names had been deleted, for nearly an hour without saying anything. Periodically, she would wince and shake her head in apparent bewilderment and repulsion. She returned the reports to the file and rode several miles in silence.

"I feel absolutely horrible about what's happened to these women

[Escobedo's victims]," she finally said, "and I hope they've managed to pull their lives back together. I truly do. You can't minimize what he's done to these women. It's terrible.

"But I don't think people are all good or all bad. And by the same token, I don't think we should ever give up totally on anybody. I don't. Gilbert's getting counseling every week in prison, and it's a painful process for him to accept what he did. But I know he's trying. That's all any of us can really do."

Two years into the marriage, though, some of the same traits and character flaws that led Escobedo into trouble in the free world also were causing problems in the marriage.

Well before Shirley wrote or visited Escobedo in prison, for example, she had been writing to a young African-American man on Death Row, which also is housed at Ellis I, the prison where Escobedo is incarcerated. The prisoner is represented on appeal by Shirley's law firm. As a nineteen-year-old hitchhiker, he accepted a ride with a stranger, took enough drugs to make him semiconscious, and—according to his story, at least—was so whacked out he didn't remember the driver shooting a state trooper to death. The driver's version, however, put the murder weapon in his passenger's hand. The young black man's lawyer, a friend and colleague of Shirley's, had bemoaned the prisoner's lack of mail. Shirley periodically dropped him a line, a practice she continued after her marriage to Escobedo.

"It wasn't a big deal," Shirley said. "I felt sorry for the kid because he was on Death Row and didn't get mail and had no visitors. The letters were just casual chitchat, something he could open at mail call."

The occasional letters were not, however, casual to Escobedo. When he learned she had been writing the Death Row inmate and had visited him once, Escobedo demanded that his wife sever all contact with the condemned prisoner.

"How do you think that looks?" he yelled during a visit. "You're my *wife*, and I won't have you doing that!"

"Well, I'm an individual," Shirley replied, "and I won't have you dictating what I do with my life!"

When she refused to buckle under to his demand, Escobedo erupted in a jealous rage and stormed out of the visiting area. For the next few weeks, she received no letters from her husband, nor did she visit him.

As he had in his relationship with Angie Welburne, Escobedo apologized. He had been jealous, he admitted, and, thanks to God's intervention, he understood his error and asked for forgiveness.

The jealousy and control were not isolated, either in Escobedo's life on parole with Angie nor in prison. When Shirley acknowledged that prior to her visits and letters to him she had dated a man for five years, Escobedo sent a letter to me. He was aware that Shirley and I had had lunch together on several occasions, and he was forbidding the practice in the future.

"I didn't take this very well [that Shirley had dated a man for five years] especially knowing you and my wife stay close in touch and have lunch quiet [sic] often," Escobedo wrote. "I have decided that if you and I continue with the book, I *wish not* to allow Shirley to be in this book. I have my own reasons for this."

In a prison interview a few weeks later, Escobedo apologized profusely for his letter. "God has brought me back to my senses and made me realize my mistake," he told me. "I *want* Shirley to be a part of your book. She's part of my life. She's a gift from God. I was just overcome with jealousy. I'm making progress under His guidance. I didn't mean it. I don't know why I said it. Please forget it."

Just as Shirley Escobedo is unwilling to give up on Escobedo, she is mindful of his irrational and recurring character flaws. She is not an apologist. Sometimes, she admits, his allegations, suspicions, and unpredictable temperament push her limits and stamina.

"Mostly, I try to understand," she says. "Gilbert is a very complex person. He is one of the most affectionate and caring persons I have ever known, but there is a side to him that hurts me very much.

"He has had a love-hate relationship with several members of his family. He has never totally forgiven his mother for abandoning him as a child, and I believe this has brought on a lot of the problems he has had in his life. He has always wanted attention and love from those who are around him, and if he didn't get it the normal way, he did things to get this attention. He craves the love that he apparently never received as a child.

"I am not going to say that this has been a perfect marriage—far from it. We have had many problems because ours is not a normal, see-each-other-every-day kind of marriage. We had numerous problems over his jealousy of me and my friends, and we have had even more problems over his family. They have not been supportive of me or this marriage from day one and that has caused me much hurt and grief.

"But I know Gilbert is very remorseful for what he has done in the past and agonizes over the pain he caused so many," she said. "I saw a lot of good in Gilbert and knew that I was taking a great chance in marrying him.

"But I believe in him, and I think with the rehabilitation that he receives and with a lot of love, he will overcome his problems and live a normal life when he is released from prison."

28

Outside the Ellis I Unit of the Texas Department of Criminal Justice, a prison guard is savoring the last few drags off a Marlboro. When he finishes, he will wave up to the guard standing on the runaround of the tower. Electronically, the gates will open, allowing him controlled passage through two razor-wired fences about ten feet apart, and then into the cavernous red-brick prison on the other side.

Now, though, the guard enjoys his cigarette, periodically eyeing his wristwatch like a man who has somewhere to be and who doesn't want to get there early. Red-faced, clean-shaven, and heavy through his torso, he pushes the blue regulation ball cap back on his head and talks amiably with a stranger waiting outside the visitors' shack.

For the last seven years, the guard says, he has been assigned to Ellis I, arguably the toughest prison in the Texas correctional system. The red brick and razor-wire rises incongruously out of idyllic southeast Texas rolling hills and towering pines. It is this lush bottomland along the Trinity River that draws the dregs after the Houstons, Dallases, Fort Worths, and San Antonios purge their streets of their most violent and feared.

The penitentiary is home to more than three hundred men on Death Row; the two thousand men in its general population are lifers, escape risks, long-timers, and hard-timers who couldn't make it anywhere else in the system.

In a single bloody day in April 1981, the prison's warden, Wallace M. Pack, and guard Billy M. Moore were overpowered and slain by inmates. Almost four years later, in June 1985, Minnie R. Houston, another guard, met the same fate. The Texas Department of Criminal Justice calls Ellis I a maximum-security facility; the guard passing time at its main gate calls it the end of the road.

"Yeah, them's some hard ol' cases in there," the guard drawls, motioning with the Marlboro tucked between his thumb and forefinger at the fortress beyond the fence.

"Killers, rapists, all sorts of thieves, child molesters. You name it, we got it. Looks like onest would do it. But they slow to learn. Some of these ol' boys, you see 'em time and again. They get out and they come right back. Them's the dudes you see in the papers and on TV.

"I hear we're getting ol' Kenneth McDuff back tomorrow. That sonfabitch was already on Death Row onest. I remember him. You could look that sucker in the eyes and know he was a stone killer. Sure 'nuff, he got cut loose from here some way or another, went on the outside, and raped and murdered some more. Now he's coming home.

"They ain't no good 'uns, not onest they get to Ellis. This is big time. This here's the end of the line."

The guard tosses the cigarette and grinds the butt into the cement with the toe of his black Nocona roper and motions to the guard in the tower.

"Have a good 'un," he says as he heads for the first gate.

Thirty minutes later, Gilbert Escobedo is led from somewhere within the red brick maze into the visitors' room off the administration building. Two prison guards in gray uniforms are bookends to the diminutive white-uniformed prisoner between them, dwarfing Escobedo by a good six or eight inches.

Not until Escobedo is locked inside the tiny, individual steel-mesh cubicle does he extend his wrists back through the rectangular opening in the mesh where one of the guards unlocks and removes the cuffs.

He sits in a straight-backed chair on the other side of a half-inch Plexiglas shield, talking through a rectangular wire mesh screen.

"I'm glad I don't have to see all my visitors this way," Escobedo says apologetically. "When my family comes on weekends, I get contact visits without all this steel and glass."

Escobedo is clean-shaven and, despite prison barbers, his black hair is stylish and moderately long by prison standards. At forty-two, he has a perpetual boyish grin that flashes neon-white teeth and knocks a good ten years off his calendar. He's maybe fifteen pounds heavier now than when he was terrorizing women in Dallas, and the extra weight nags at him.

"I think I look fat," he says, "but my family says I look good."

His white uniform, stenciled with ESCOBEDO, G.H., 551949 on the left breast, is flawless and in conspicuous contrast with those of the prisoners who periodically are escorted through the runaround behind his cage. Ellis I is an agricultural and industrial prison, and most of its inmates wear Walker County dirt from the cotton fields and grease from the shops on their whites.

Escobedo is an inside trusty, an envied status that keeps him out of the 105-degree fields and un-air-conditioned shops where inmates repair and renovate buses for Texas' school districts. He is an orderly in the major's office, where he works side by side with ranking prison guards and even a handful of civilian women clerks and secretaries.

His schedule ("I don't work two hours a day," he says, grinning at his coup) allows him time to take courses in English grammar, a subject that continues to perplex him, and to work in the crafts shop where his favorite hobby is making air-brushed Bible covers from leather.

Through almost two years of periodic interviews, Escobedo consistently is charming, jovial, pious at times, and seemingly oblivious to the forced regimen around him. In the jargon of prison guards, Escobedo does "easy time," meaning that he adapts well, doesn't fight incarceration, follows the rules, and doesn't bother anybody.

He conscientiously avoids gangs like the Mexican Mafia, which always is at war with other racial gangs. He spends his time instead with what some prisoners derogatorily call the "God Squad," a group of self-professed, born-again Christians that Escobedo prefers to call the "Prayer Warriors." His trusty status allows him to bunk in a dormitory with other trusties instead of the barred, cramped cells where most of the maximum-security inmates are incarcerated.

"My biggest problem here is shutting out all the negative thoughts and attitudes," Escobedo says. "I don't want to be brought down by it. I try to avoid inmates with bad attitudes. When I can, though, I give them my testimony; I witness to them. I'm here to make progress. When I was on the outside, I had one foot in religion and the other foot out. I'm thankful God put me here. I've still got lessons to learn from Him. I want to work for His glory."

Gilbert Escobedo would become predictable in the two years of conversations and letters. Never, for example, would he use the word *rape*, relying as he had in his confession on euphemisms like "make love" or "assault" or "victimize" to describe the sexual attacks he committed. Similarly, he never uttered a curse word, and once complained about the "foul language" other inmates used.

And while he said he "wouldn't trade my father for a diamond mine," Escobedo spoke frequently of the "hollow feeling" he had for his mother, whose love he consistently questioned.

The thread woven into every conversation and letter, though, was religion: a Christian book he had read, a devotional video he had seen, the sermon at a recent chapel service, or a visit he had had from the prison ministry of his former church, Prestonwood Baptist in Dallas. When he discussed a specific rape, he ended the scenario by noting that God had forgiven him. Every interview ended with a prayer, during which he invoked God's hand in directing the story of the crimes he had committed.

Escobedo's cooperation in researching the book, however, became predictably unpredictable and, ultimately, on again, off again. In prison interviews, Escobedo was quick to please and accommodating, expressing his belief that telling the truth about his crimes not only would help his victims and maybe other sex offenders, but also be in accordance with "God's master plan" for him.

"I've thought many times about writing these women letters to apologize," he said in an interview in late 1992. "I want to help them for what I've done. Some may never forgive me, but I want to try. Maybe if I talk to you about what happened, the book would do that for them."

At one point, he agreed to write such a letter for the book.

"It'll be in my own words," he said, "but maybe you could proofread it for me and make some suggestions."

In October 1993, he wrote in a letter: "I truly believe that God has honored my decision, and that He will have His hand on this book, from the beginning to the end, and afterwards. I will view this future book as a helping tool to me, and to the others that read it."

Three months later, however, after a visit from his family, Escobedo wrote in another letter: "I'm giving second thoughts about the book. I wish to place a 'hold' on the process of the book, which means I'm confused and undecided about the book. I'm receiving pressure from my natural family being against the book, and on the other hand, Shirley is pressuring me to have the book written. . . .

"I dislike the fact that Shirley is siding with you and takes up for you when your name is announced."

To be sure, Escobedo's family pressured him to remain silent about his crimes. Even before I began research for the book, I met Shirley and Al Escobedo at a North Dallas coffee shop. Al, one of two brothers with whom Gilbert shared the condo on Woodbend Lane at the onset of the rapes, didn't hear me out before he announced he was against any further public disclosure of his brother's actions.

"I'll do whatever I can to stop it," he said.

Wasn't it conceivable, I asked, that Gilbert's recollections and views could help the women he had hurt, at least give them some kind of closure? Gilbert at least thought so.

"That's not our place," Al said. "Let somebody else do that. We don't want to read our name in public anymore. We've had enough of that. That's the bottom line."

Months later, when Al discovered Gilbert and I had had several discussions in prison, he convened a family meeting at their father's house in Irving. The decision, as delivered by Al, was that Gilbert would be ostracized by his family if he continued to interview for the book.

"It's Gilbert's decision," Al Escobedo said. "But if he talks for the book about the rapes, he does so at the expense of losing his family. It's that simple. Gilbert has put his family through hell for a lot of years. There's no need to bring this whole mess up again.

"Gilbert's not thinking of anyone but himself. That's the problem—he's never thought about anyone but himself. But we have to live in the real world. We have to pay the price for what he did. *Nobody* in this family is going to talk about what he's done. Don't even try."

Al Escobedo visited his younger brother in prison to deliver the family's ultimatum. Gilbert, middle-aged, married three times, the father of two daughters and a veteran of four trips to the penitentiary, still acquiesced to family wishes. There would be no more interviews for a while, he said.

Curiously, at one point, after a visit with his parents, Gilbert said his father and stepmother had changed their minds and agreed to be interviewed. At Gilbert's suggestion, I called a week later for his father, and got his stepmother. She politely told me Robert Escobedo would be returning my call when he got home from a walk. Within five minutes, the phone rang. It was an irate Al Escobedo. Not only did his parents not wish to talk about Gilbert, no one in the family would discuss him. Should there be any more phone calls, Al Escobedo said, the family would regard it as harassment and file a lawsuit.

Indeed, outside the family, its most notorious member was *not* discussed, not among friends, colleagues, or neighbors. Al Escobedo said he feared office co-workers at the company where he worked would find out his brother was the Ski Mask Rapist. The reaction, however, was schizophrenic, judging from the observations of Angie Welburne and, later, Shirley Escobedo.

Within the confines of the close-knit family, they said, Gilbert Escobedo still enjoyed the unqualified support of its most influential members. Gilbert, Shirley said, was spoken of sympathetically in the context of his being locked away in prison, not as a man who could have raped as many as seventy-five to one hundred women.

Among his staunchest supporters were Al and father Robert, both of whom had stood by Gilbert through his three previous trips to prison. Various other brothers and Gilbert's mother, Pauline Hernandez, visited him sporadically during those incarcerations, but the most frequent visitors always were Robert and Al Escobedo, the family's patriarch and most outspoken sibling. They not only visited regularly, according to prison visitor logs, but they also wrote and sent him money for use in the prison commissary. They appeared at parole hearings to vouch for Gilbert's rehabilitation and to say positive things about his future. Nothing the family's wayward member had done, including his recent convictions as being perhaps the most infamous rapist in the Southwest, apparently had diminished that support.

That same unconditional support was not necessarily shared by Escobedo's daughters. Rebecca, the eldest, wrote her father only a few times after his convictions for rape, and never visited him. Martie, who married and had a child, neither wrote nor visited. The last time they saw their father, in the den of Lynn Stratford's house, had left them devastated and confused, according to people close to the family.

In January 1994, three months after Al Escobedo personally delivered the family's ultimatum to him in prison, Gilbert Escobedo underwent yet another change of heart.

"I cried, and at altar call, I went up to the altar and requested prayer for my health, the jealous spirit which was instilled, and the lust of the flesh which resurfaces from time to time," he wrote me.

"I honestly accepted that God has delivered me from the above. I'm now relieved! Let's continue on and do this book. My target is to help people with the book, and tell people what Jesus has done and still is doing in my life!

"I'm taking a stand and if my natural family chooses to disown me . . . that's their choice. I will not place an ounce of judgment on them, but I will continue to pray for them and love them."

Sporadically over nearly two years and despite pressure from his family, Escobedo nonetheless talked for the record; the caveat was that the interviews be kept "between us," and that his family not be told. He would take care of that before publication.

A pattern quickly emerged in the interviews. The first hour was spent discussing prison regimen, his family, his wife, visits he had had, and, always, religion. Only after the preliminaries had been dispensed with did he turn to the crimes that had put him there.

And periodically in his recollections, the soft-spoken, self-professed born-again Christian reverted to the out-of-control career criminal who burglarized with precision and raped with obsession.

The fitful accounts sometimes emerged with pride, even arrogance, as he related how he targeted only "high-quality jewelry and Rolexes" and "beautiful, educated women" for his crimes, of how he used a fleet of repossessed cars to thwart police for five years even while he knew he was their prime suspect, and how a few women "got into the attacks," presumably enjoying the sex so much they didn't report the rapes.

Inevitably in his candid moments, Escobedo would stumble suddenly and hard on the realization that he was acknowledging events and acts that would appear publicly. Realizing the depth of his revelations—and undoubtedly how they would be interpreted—he abruptly would change the subject, almost always contrasting the recollection with his current life as the redemptive sinner seeking salvation. That was then, he seemed to say; this is now.

"I'm not that person anymore," he would say at the end of each revelation. "There were things I didn't learn when I was down here before. Through God's grace and mercy, I've moved beyond that. Bad as I was, God has given me eternal life. God has answered my prayers."

Six months after he was transferred to Ellis I to serve ten concurrent life sentences, Gilbert Escobedo's newfound, self-professed faith in God would be severely tested. He would come closer perhaps than ever to feeling the raw random violence of the sort he himself had inflicted on strangers.

October 6, 1990, a Saturday, began with excitement. At mail call, he received a thick envelope bearing daughter Rebecca Escobedo's return address. Even as he opened it, he was elated at the promise of renewing his splintered relationship with Becky. Maybe, he thought, she finally was beginning to forgive him. Inside was a lengthy letter and a photograph of a striking young Hispanic woman in a cap and gown. Becky, eighteen, had graduated from high school and, according to her letter, had become a dental hygienist.

His name and picture had appeared on the front pages of newspapers and on television after his arrest as the Ski Mask Rapist. In the working-class Oak Cliff neighborhood of Dallas where Rebecca and younger sister Martie lived with their mother and stepfather, it undoubtedly was common knowledge that the girls' father was a serial rapist. He hadn't heard from Martie, and he had worried that the humiliation and embarrassment he had dealt his daughters ultimately would end any hope for reconciliation.

In the predawn hours of Sunday, Escobedo was awakened by a guard who ominously escorted him through a succession of bars and steel doors to the chaplain's office.

"I have some bad news for you, Gilbert," he was told. "There's been a tragedy in your family. Your daughter, Rebecca, is dead."

Said an article the next morning in the *Dallas Morning News*:

An 18-year-old pregnant woman was killed in a drive-by shooting early Sunday at Mountain Creek Park, which is becoming increasingly known as a flashpoint for gang violence.

Rebecca Escobedo, who officials said was about five months pregnant, died after she was shot in the back as she stood in a group of about 30 young people at the lakeside park.

A second bullet struck another youth, Yolanda Rios, 15, in the upper leg, police reports showed. She was not seriously injured. . . .

Although witness accounts indicate gang members were present at the party and the park, Detective [Kevin] Navarro said there was no indication that either victim was intentionally shot.

"I don't believe the girls were targets," he said. "They were just bystanders."

Ms. Escobedo's relatives gathered Sunday at her home . . . where a wreath of red roses marked the front door. . . . A young man who identified himself as Ms. Escobedo's uncle said he thinks his niece may have been the innocent victim of a gang initiation.

Escobedo's attendance at his daughter's funeral, even accompanied by guards, was not a possibility. The inmate was issued a chit that allowed him to stay in his bunk throughout the following day and to visit the chaplain if he wanted.

On May 2, 1991, fifteen-year-old Prudencio Orellana, the youth who admitted firing a .45-caliber automatic from the window of a moving car at Mountain Creek Park, was sentenced to thirty years in prison for killing Rebecca Escobedo, a woman he had never met. By law, he would serve seven and a half years before being eligible for parole.

Gilbert Escobedo professed no ill will toward the teenager who killed his daughter. "Vengence, bitterness, that's not God's way," he said simply. "I pray for him."

———

The seven-year-old dark-haired boy with the engaging grin and pre-adolescent innocence stands out in the faded family snapshot. Mother and father, his four brothers, and his baby sister wear the awkward, forced smiles of people who realize they're being photographed for posterity. Little Gilbert, obviously unawed by the camera, is singularly conspicuous in his spontaneity.

The easy and persistent, often mischievous smile would become an endearing hallmark among those who would know Gilbert Hernandez Escobedo through subsequent years; his lack of innocence would be a matter of lengthy public record.

At face, the snapshot is a freeze-frame of hard-earned Hispanic success in Dallas in the late 1950s. The parents in the photograph, Robert and Pauline Escobedo, were themselves the progeny of families who spoke only Spanish and marginal "Tex-Mex," a mongrelization of Spanish and fractured, make-do English. The fifties were tough times for Hispanics in Dallas and throughout Texas.

They were derisively called *mes'kins* and *wetbacks*, a slur rooted in the fact that many Hispanics had swum illegally across the Rio Grande to get to Texas. Exploited by employers who paid them destitute wages, ignored by politicians, and ostracized by the white community, the bulk of Dallas' Hispanics were abandoned to themselves in the clapboard and plywood shanties in the rutted barrios of West Dallas.

Robert Escobedo, as a recently married young apprentice upholsterer, vowed his family wouldn't be relegated to the unpaved poverty of West Dallas. Long on independence and with an artisan's pride in a job well done, he went into business for himself, parlaying sixteen-hour days and seven-day weeks into respectability and a modicum of financial stability.

Indeed, the Escobedo family captured in the snapshot reflected the patriarch's commitment as a provider. To the person, its members were attractive, particularly the petite wife and mother Pauline, fashionably dressed and well groomed. And if Robert Escobedo wore a prideful look, it was with good reason.

He not only had managed to feed and clothe his large family, but he had bought a house on the other side of the Trinity River from the notoriously poor barrios. The modest and well-kept green frame house in the 2300 block of Wycliff Avenue lay in the noisy southern approach path to Love Field, but it was within walking distance of a park.

Years later, Interstate 35E and the Dallas North Tollway, with their six lanes of backed-up, bumper-to-bumper traffic, would squeeze the little neighborhood on both sides, but at that time in the 1950s it was a tranquil and safe haven for the Escobedo brothers, Robert, Armondo, Alfred, Reuben, and Gilbert.

There are, however, emotions, traumas, and transitions in every family that faces don't reflect and film doesn't capture. Shortly after the handsome snapshot was taken, Pauline Escobedo shattered everyone in the picture. Abruptly, she announced she was leaving; she had fallen in love with another man. Perhaps worse for the family, the other man was a cousin.

Her decision was extraordinary, particularly for a Hispanic woman in the late fifties. By tradition, Hispanic families were uncommonly close; by culture, Hispanic wives were docile and enduring and singularly devoted to their families. Pauline left the five boys with her husband, taking only her daughter, Yolanda, the youngest of the brood.

If there had been any signals of impending crisis in the green frame house on Wycliff Avenue, they had been lost on Gilbert. The little boy was shattered.

Thirty-five years later, locked in a wire mesh cage the size of a phone booth, Gilbert Escobedo's ever-present smile vanishes and he falls uncustomarily silent when the conversation turns to his mother's departure. He confides that he has trouble remembering what was fact and what has been colored by the years of denial, rationalization, bitterness, and, at times, even defensiveness.

"She never explained what she was doing or why," Escobedo finally said. "I was old enough to know. She didn't explain it, though. I don't think my behavior changed that much. I was always a happy kid. But I hurt inside. I felt like we were rejected. That feeling kind of followed me.

"At first, she would leave, then come back for a while. Then it'd start all over again. Then one day, she just left and stayed gone. She took Yolanda, and she left all us boys. That seemed strange, but that's what she did. Anyway, my father always worked hard, and he had to have help taking care of us. We spent a lot of time at our grandparents', who cared for us. They were good, decent people. There was always a lot of people around, my grandparents and my brothers, but I remember feeling lonely anyway. I had my father, my brothers, and my grandparents. But I felt rejected. I guess I must have missed her."

Clearly he did. Pauline Escobedo, her baby daughter, and her new lover moved to Fort Worth, about thirty-five miles west of Dallas. Escobedo remembered riding a Greyhound one weekend to surprise his mother on her birthday.

"I had bought her a little ceramic squirrel," he recalled. "I walked eight miles from the bus station to give it to her. I don't know why that particular day stands out, but it does."

Through the years, a family acquaintance said, Pauline "moved more times than a gypsy." She also, according to Escobedo, traveled through a succession of unsuccessful relationships and marriages with men who almost always were substantially younger.

"I couldn't really tell you how many," Escobedo would say, his voice trailing off. "I guess I don't know, really. I just know they always were real young guys. I never really knew what she was doing or why."

All the boys felt the pain of abandonment, Escobedo said.

"We didn't really talk about it all that much, I guess. Maybe it didn't affect the others like it did me. Maybe I'm too sensitive or something. But we kind of fended for ourselves, you know, watched out for each other. We were close."

It was at some point after his mother left that young Gilbert first got caught stealing.

"It was bubble gum from a store and I got caught," Escobedo said. "I remember I was scared to death."

It was an event familiar in the lives of a lot of little boys. Usually, the fear and humiliation of apprehension were sufficiently traumatic to become ingrained as lifelong reminders of the drawbacks to stealing. Unfortunately for Gilbert, the shoplifting incident would become only the first and most innocuous in a long and twisted path of increasingly serious crime.

"That's truly how I started out," he recalled. "I thought then that I'd never do anything else bad in my life. And I swore every time that I got in trouble that it would be the last. I know I meant it at the time. I *did*. But it didn't work out that way for me. For some reason I never learned what I needed to learn."

If ever he were capable of being scared straight, it should have occurred at age thirteen. When most boys were playing pony league baseball, fighting the embarrassment of pimples and reconsidering their opinion of girls, Gilbert, caught yet again for theft, was sent to the Dallas County Boys Shelter.

The stark, institutional red brick boys' shelter was isolated fifteen miles south of the city on a dead-end road in an undeveloped, rural part of the county. Society didn't tolerate bars on juvenile detention centers in 1964, but every steel door at the boys' shelter bore heavy key locks, and there were periodic head counts throughout the day to account for every boy's whereabouts. The youthful charges were force-fed discipline, academics, and religion. Likewise, their attendance was mandatory in the fields and livestock sheds in the back of the dormitories.

Robert Escobedo would establish a pattern that he would continue throughout his son's career as a habitual criminal. During the few months Gilbert was incarcerated at the boys' shelter, his father would visit him at every opportunity.

His father's seeing him locked in the institution embarrassed the teenager. He inquired about his brothers and wondered to himself why he, who shared the same mother, father, and fate, had been the only one of the boys to consistently run afoul of the rules. Clearly, he was different; he had no idea why.

"Dad has always been there for me, no matter what I had done," Escobedo said. "I know it was hard for him, but he was always there." His mother? "Well, she always wanted to. But she lived in Fort Worth then."

During his succession of incarcerations, his mother generally visited no more than twice a year, usually at Christmas and Mother's Day. So infrequent are her visits since Escobedo has been incarcerated for the rapes that he at one point took her name off his approved visitors' list.

The decision produced an outcry in his family, even among his brothers, who apparently regarded it as a symbolic slap in their mother's face. Under family pressure, Escobedo reinstated his mother's name to the list.

"She says she loves me," Escobedo says wistfully, "but I don't feel it. She says she's there, but I don't see her or hear from her. I want to forgive my mom for leaving us, because it had an impact. It did. And it still does."

The prisoner becomes pensive momentarily, then reemerges in the conversation with reddened, watery eyes.

"I'd appreciate it," he said barely audibly, "if you wouldn't write anything bad about my mother. I don't understand her, but she *is* my mother."

Escobedo's emotional request was consistent with a nugget of research contained in the reams of often conflicting psychological research on rape. Dr. Richard T. Rada, who has done extensive research on rape behavior, found that "Spanish-American males often have great difficulty reporting any negative features of their parents or early life at home even when other evidence indicates parental cruelty or deprivation."

Moreover, Rada's findings perhaps explain why Escobedo, despondent in his conversations with Angie Welburne about his mother's leaving him, nonetheless never confronted his mother with his anger and disappointment. Similarly, the unearned benefit of the doubt extended to Hispanic parents could account for Escobedo bowing to family pressure to reinstate his mother on his list of approved visitors in prison.

Back on the streets after his release from the boys' shelter in 1964, Escobedo made it through Gaston Junior High and stumbled disinterestedly through both Bryan Adams and North Dallas high schools. While he apparently was only a marginal student and uninvolved in extracurricular activities, Escobedo nonetheless enrolled in Army ROTC classes.

"The uniforms were really sharp," he explained. "I liked them."

In October 1968, Escobedo, then eighteen, was arrested by Dallas police for investigation of burglary. No charges were filed, but two months later, in December, Escobedo was arrested for burglarizing Susan Burman's apartment of nearly $9,000 in jewelry.

The incident, which occurred while the young Braniff flight attendant slept, was prophetic of Escobedo's future as a rapist. Buried in the police documents of the burglary was Escobedo's crude blueprint for what would become his favorite modus operandi as a serial rapist.

By the flight attendant's account, Escobedo was loitering outside her apartment complex and saw her as she came in shortly after midnight. As he would in the series of rapes he committed nearly fifteen years later, he gave her time to get to sleep before entering her apartment. He prowled through her jewelry, separating the gold from the costume, as she slept only a few feet away.

When Susan Burman was awakened, it wasn't from the sound of his leaving or a creaking door. She was awakened as the covers were being pulled slowly from her body. Had Burman not screamed, Escobedo had positioned himself to commit his first rape.

Less than a year later, Escobedo, a month shy of nineteen and free on bond for the Burman burglary, was arrested in a stolen car in Hope, Arkansas. Within a month, he would be given a three-year, probated sentence for burglarizing the flight attendant.

He was still two years short of being old enough to vote or buy liquor.

Although rapists may share certain common motivations, the concept of the "typical" rapist is a myth and each rapist must be understood in terms of his individual psychodynamics.
—Dr. Richard T. Rada, *Psychological Facts in Rapist Behavior*

29

Rape, most researchers agree, seldom is an irrepressible and spontaneous act. Indeed, Dr. Rada found, "The rapist will often expend more psychic energy building himself up for the rape than trying to control his desire."

Gilbert Escobedo, asked in the initial interview to characterize the women he raped, replied, not without noticeable pride: "They were centerfolds. They were young, and they were beautiful."

Escobedo methodically parlayed virtually every moment of his spare time toward identifying and isolating targets that fit his very precise standards. And in the elaborate and perverted ritual of surveillance that would follow, he obsessed about his prey, as he had that night in 1982 when he tried three times to break into a pair of sisters' duplex even knowing they already had seen his face and had called police.

Once he locked on to a potential victim, he could not or would not stop until he had raped her, even if it took weeks or months.

On the night before he happened onto Meagan Finley and raped her, an unprecedented departure from his tedious stalking ritual, he had seized on an attractive young schoolteacher. He had asked her out, taken her to an upscale restaurant, and lavished her with perfume from Neiman-Marcus, but he could tell she wasn't interested in him. He would lie in wait for a few weeks.

If he held true to form, he would fantasize about her, as he had others, while he watched pornographic films or read sexually explicit magazines. Only once in the interviews did he mention his use of pornography.

"Looking back, that [pornography] was a big part of the problem," he said. He was embarrassed by his admission and declined to discuss it again.

"I would have gotten to her one way or the other," Escobedo said of the schoolteacher. "I knew it. It was going to happen." Undoubtedly only his arrest kept the woman from becoming yet another of his victims.

Some of the women he found in malls on Saturday afternoons, others he saw driving down the street or walking along a crowded downtown sidewalk after work. A few he undoubtedly discovered at the busy swimming pool next to his condo on Woodbend Lane. More frequently, though, he found them randomly while window-peeking.

By Escobedo's own admission, he spent inordinate amounts of time lurking outside strangers' windows. Just as some people watch television, read, play video games, or go to movies, Escobedo's passionate pastime was watching people, particularly women, when they didn't know they were being watched.

Unwittingly, they shared their most secret and intimate moments with a man whose eyes followed their every move and committed them to his fantasies. Many times, he obsessed for days or weeks over what he saw through the blinds, returning to force those fantasies into realities.

"People think just because their blinds are drawn that no one can see inside," Escobedo explained. "They're wrong. You can see through the little slots in the blinds that the cords run through. You'd be surprised what you can see."

At the height of the Ski Mask rapes in 1985 and much of 1986, Escobedo located his prey effortlessly, like a hunter in a wildlife refuge.

Not coincidentally, Escobedo worked for a time at a grocery store in the midst of neighborhoods hit hardest by the series of sexual assaults. As he checked groceries and made friendly chitchat with attractive women who fit his criteria, he merely took their names, addresses, and phone numbers off their checks.

Days, even weeks later, he appeared outside their windows, watching in the dark as they undressed, showered, and readied for bed. He observed their routines, noting the times they normally went to bed, if boyfriends came over, and whether they had roommates. Occasionally, he broke into their apartments while they were gone to memorize floor plans so he could maneuver in the dark and to search for weapons.

That Miriam Maloney, Camellia Michaels, Wendy Spense, and other early victims of the Ski Mask Rapist shopped at the Tom Thumb Grocery Store at the intersection of Forest Lane and Abrams Road didn't elude Evelyn Crowder and her extensive victim questionnaires. Certainly, the pattern hadn't been conclusive; the store was the largest in the area and undoubtedly attracted the bulk of business from the surrounding neighborhoods.

Escobedo would be fired abruptly from the store in late 1986.

"There was some resentment," Escobedo recalled. "Here I was working in a grocery store and driving a brand-new Porsche. People noticed, and the managers were always saying, 'How can he do that?' I was restoring classic cars and selling them on the side. I was legitimately making good money. One day, the manager caught me outside talking to a guy about a car and he fired me. Really, I think they were just jealous."

In reality, Escobedo was fired almost immediately after Marshall Touchton began asking questions about the ex-con. Checking out the pattern from Crowder's victim questionnaires, Touchton happened on Escobedo's prison record. Touchton was a casual acquaintance of the grocery chain's security chief, himself a retired Dallas detective. Shortly after Touchton made what he thought was a discreet and preliminary inquiry about Escobedo, Escobedo was terminated.

"The security manager panicked," Touchton surmised. "I guess they looked for a reason to get rid of him fast."

Just as abruptly, the Ski Mask Rapist changed his territory, moving farther north and west.

Three years after his arrest, Escobedo would acknowledge another less obvious, but telling rationale for the women he chose as victims.

"They were attractive, yeah, but they were educated and upper-class women, and I thought I could never have a relationship with women like that," Escobedo said. "With women like that, I always felt uncomfortable."

The cash he made from fencing stolen jewelry and much of the legitimate income later in his successful auto detailing business, sometimes several thousand dollars in good weeks, went toward expensive clothes and Porsches. Always from his pilferage, he held out a Rolex, which he was painstakingly careful to exhibit on his wrist just beyond the cuff of his left sleeve.

He took to hanging out at Randy's, a trendy North Dallas club near the Tollway that was a mecca for the young, the beautiful, and the definitely upwardly mobile. He heard snatches from their conversations, about skiing in Vail, about extended vacations in Europe, and about the fabulous six-figure incomes that awaited them after their next big deal.

Immersed in the fast lane of beautiful people and wearing the guise of success, he imagined himself the equal of those around him, yet never believed it himself. He was the little boy with a brand-new bat and top-of-the-line glove who feared even standing at the plate.

During a prison interview in which he boasted of excelling at his years-long cat-and-mouse chase with police, Escobedo was asked if police could have done anything to catch him earlier. In the scenario he hypothesized, his materialism and propensity to savage others for his own satisfaction were the vulnerabilities that would have led to his downfall.

"They could have used an undercover policewoman, a classy, good-looking one. Put her at Randy's with good clothes and a Rolex, but tell her not to cooperate," Escobedo said. "Or they could have watched me close enough to see where I shopped—I loved buying expensive clothes and ties. When they see me going to the mall, send her into the store. Then put her in a dating situation, but not willing to go to bed with me. I would have found her. I would have gotten her."

Throughout interviews, Escobedo sometimes balked at reciting facts even if they were matters of public record, and steered the conversation to topics he wanted to discuss, which, more often than not, involved some facet of religion. Later in the conversation, though, if the original question was rephrased, he frequently would answer it.

Discussing his feelings, however, was always difficult, plummeting him into pensive periods of silence and ultimately causing him to stumble in his thoughts or leave sentences unfinished. His answers, it appeared, lacked clarity less from evasiveness than from a void of understanding.

"The relationships I had, I just felt like they weren't enough," he said tentatively. "I hurt inside for some reason. Maybe . . . I don't know. I felt rejected. There was something I was looking for. I'd say it was love. I just wanted to be hugged and loved. I guess really what I wanted was to be *acceptable*. I don't know."

In some of the assaults, like the rape of Claire Miller, it was obvious Escobedo was seeking something beyond sex. Miller, according to the police report of her rape, "stated that suspect was very apologetic to her. Suspect and complainant talked casually for approximately 30 minutes after she was assaulted."

Several of his victims, Escobedo said, told him he didn't seem like a bad person. "Why didn't you just ask me out?" he quoted one as asking him.

It was clear that Escobedo never even entertained the possibility of asking the women out, opting instead to force them into sex against their will. As he pondered the question of dating versus rape, his feelings of inferiority and worthlessness surfaced.

"They wouldn't have gone, not these kind of women," Escobedo said. "And if they had, it wouldn't have worked out. They wouldn't have wanted to spend time with me."

But several of the women through the years, he maintained, didn't consider themselves victims at all, and didn't even call police.

"Some really got into it," Escobedo said. "I mean *really*. One in the Skillman area near LBJ said she liked having me inside her. She said, 'Do it one more time before you leave.'

"Another one, a very beautiful woman, she was incredibly lonely. She was so pretty that I thought there'd be guys all over her. She kept a diary and she wrote how lonely she was. I came one time, but her mother was visiting.

"I came back a week later. She told me how lonely she was. I thought, 'Well, I can't believe this.' I know she didn't believe she had been victimized."

Given the law of averages, it is not wholly inconceivable, over a five-year period with possibly as many as seventy-five to one hundred assaults, that a few of the women might have acceded to an intruder breaking into their houses and forcing them to have sex.

Sue James, executive director of the Dallas County Rape Crisis Center, recalls getting a bizarre referral for counseling from a convicted rapist.

"A woman came in and said the man who raped her had asked her to come in for counseling," James said. "She had gone to prison to see the man who raped her. And apparently she just kept going back and going back. She developed a very strong emotional bond with him. Finally, the rapist told her, 'You've fallen in love with me. You need help.'"

More likely among the women Escobedo mentioned, according to Marshall Touchton, is the fact that people under the threat of death will say and do just about anything to avoid being killed.

"A rapist might tell a woman to act like she enjoys it," the detective said, "and when she does it, under threat of death, the rapist actually believes it. In effect, he ends up believing his own lie.

"I interviewed a guy one time who told me that he didn't rape a woman because after they had sex, she had volunteered to fix him breakfast," the detective recalled. "He thought that made it consensual. The victim admitted she had offered to fix him breakfast, but it was only in the hope that she could get her hands on a knife and cut his damn throat."

Other than vague statements that he would like "to help the women I victimized" and to "apologize for what I've done," Escobedo never dwelled on the impact he had on the women he raped and deceived.

Of Lynn Stratford, the divorcée he met at Prestonwood Baptist Church and whom he had talked of marrying, Escobedo recalled her writing a check for $3,000 so that he could pay his delinquent business taxes.

"She told me that she didn't want me having to worry about that and be under any stress," Escobedo said, grinning at his good fortune. "She just sat down, wrote out a check for $3,000, and asked me if I was sure that would be enough. I took it right to the bank, and the teller said, 'Would hundreds be okay?' And she counted 'em out, bam, bam, bam.

"I told my dad about her and what she did, and he said, 'Boy, you better not let that one get away.' I really did think about marrying her."

Moments later, discussing Stratford's whereabouts, Escobedo said matter-of-factly: "She said that she couldn't go back to Prestonwood, that she was too embarrassed. Last I heard, she had moved to Florida."

There was no apology for disrupting Stratford's life or for the embarrassment he had caused her.

Nor was there any compassion when he discussed Claire Miller, the rape victim who later unwittingly became her rapist's lover and business partner.

"I caught her running around on me three times, having affairs, while we were seeing each other," Escobedo said. "Once was with one of our customers, a wealthy Hispanic guy who drove a Mercedes. She would lie to me, but I caught her red-handed. I couldn't trust her. She was bad news."

He related the anecdote self-righteously, an indignant edge to his voice as if he were the aggrieved party. That he had raped Miller appeared to elude him. Nor did he make mention of the fact that, during the period he and Miller had dated, he had raped at least five more women.

It was a curious revelation, one that implied a double standard by which Escobedo gauged the women in his life. More telling was that Escobedo apparently believed the rapes, notwithstanding their moral outrageousness and violation of criminal law, were not infidelities in his own personal relationships.

Never in his debriefing by police or during the interviews for the book did Escobedo ever inquire about the welfare of any of his victims. Though he claimed repeatedly that he never physically harmed any of the women—a not altogether accurate recollection—he seemed not to contemplate his capacity for causing the women severe emotional problems. It was clear that he believed any fear or trauma he instilled was limited to the hour and a half of the attack.

However he viewed the sexual attacks, Escobedo acknowledges that any satisfaction was short-lived.

"I felt satisfaction, I guess, but I also felt fear because I knew the authorities were after me," he said. "There's a self-satisfaction there, but it wasn't genuine. It was temporary satisfaction. The next day, it's all over.

"I don't know what I was really after. It was something, and I guess it had to be more than sex. I even called a couple of the women back just to hear their voice. I don't know what I expected them to say. I guess I was just possessed."

narcissism *(nar sis'iz em), n. 1 excessive love or admiration of oneself.* 2 **Psychoanalysis,** *gratification manifested in admiration and love of one-self, usually associated with infantile behavior and regarded as abnormally regressive in adults.*

—*The World Book Dictionary*

30

"People are born with a certain degree of narcissism, and depending on what happens to them, they take one particular path," says Dr. Jaye D. Crowder, a forensics psychiatrist. "If they have good structure and consistent parenting in childhood, they may become police officers or fighter pilots. This is aggression used in a positive way. If they had a more chaotic background like Escobedo did, then they're more likely to go toward the antisocial direction."

In Gilbert Escobedo's world, as interpreted by Dr. Crowder, Escobedo—vain, materialistic, selfish, and manipulative—stands alone and importantly as its axis, watching as people and events revolve around him. *He* is the center of the universe.

Dr. Crowder is a Renaissance man, of sorts, when it comes to ne-gotiating the murky passageways of the abstract world. He is a man of science, a forensics psychiatrist, and an assistant professor at the University of Texas Southwestern Medical School in Dallas. He's also a deeply spiritual man and an elder and lay minister in the Church of Christ. He walks the path between science and spirituality effortlessly as if the two frequently philosophically conflicting perspectives were, in fact, seamless.

By avocation, Dr. Crowder is a knowledgeable student of architecture and a serious collector of military memorabilia. By personality, the thirty-nine-year-old doctor is, not surprisingly, intelligent, straightforward, and quick to find humor.

The overwhelming majority of Dr. Crowder's time is spent trying to decipher, explain, predict, and treat the abnormal human behavior that makes people like Escobedo run afoul of the criminal justice system. A member of the American Academy of Psychiatry and Law, Dr. Crowder also is a consultant to the U.S. Secret Service Intelligence Division and Dallas County Jail's Inmate Treatment Department.

Modern American jurisprudence has it that, before justice can be dispensed, before right and wrong and guilt and innocence can be determined, the jury hears from experts. Dr. Crowder, as one of those experts, has testified countless times. In criminal cases, his testimony has been split about evenly, favoring the defendant about as often as the prosecution.

Because Escobedo chose to plead guilty to his crimes, thereby negating the need for a trial by judge or jury, the inevitable and exhaustive pretrial psychological and psychiatric evaluations of his personality became moot. As a result, there is nothing in the voluminous Escobedo public record that suggests *why* he did the things he did. Dr. Crowder was asked to provide the intangible, psychiatric motivations behind the documentably overt criminal acts that fill the record.

Dr. Crowder did not have access to Escobedo, not a totally unusual dilemma for a forensics psychiatrist. Escobedo equivocated in revealing himself to a writer, much less a scientist trained in unraveling deep secrets. Rather, Dr. Crowder based his opinions on police reports, my extensive notes and interviews with Escobedo, a videotape of police questioning Escobedo, rap sheets, chronologies, Escobedo's confessions, and letters Escobedo had written me.

The forensics psychiatrist spent weeks poring over the files of data, searching for the psychiatric explanation to Escobedo's lifetime of escalating crime.

The psychiatric profile that emerges is one of a highly self-centered personality with a strong bent toward antisocial behavior. Psychiatrists base their diagnoses on two fields, or categories: clinical syndromes and personality disorders. In the clinical syndromes, a person may have an organic or medically documentable impairment that causes, say, impulsiveness and lack of emotional control; if he has a personality disorder, he may generally feel all right with the things he does, but those things nonetheless bring him in conflict with the rest of society.

The clinical syndromes, dependent on testing and medical history, were difficult for Dr. Crowder to determine since he didn't have access to Escobedo. Signposts, however, include attention deficits, hyperactivity disorders, major depression, low-level depression that lasts over years and years, distractability, physical brain damage, and not being able to finish projects.

Interviews with Escobedo and others who know him well suggest that he frequently was hyperactive, a fact that became apparent to police almost immediately after they began surveillance on him. He worked ten- and twelve-hour days at the auto detail shop, then frequently came and went at all hours of the night. At times, Escobedo was mildly depressed and distracted, according to Angie Welburne and others who knew him intimately, and sometimes he put off plans about which he seemed genuinely excited, such as the expansion of his auto detailing business to a second location.

But whether the symptoms have an identifiable medical cause, in which the illness is termed an organic mood disorder, or whether the behavior exists without a definable medical cause, called a bipolar mood disorder, is a distinction that is somewhat academic anyway.

"All of them have chemical derangements, so it's kind of an artificial distinction," Dr. Crowder said.

"That general behavior goes with narcissism. These people can't defer gratification very well because they expect a great deal of praise and recognition for a small amount of effort on their part. They like it best when they can outsmart someone and do it quickly and easily. But they tend not to put the time in to be really as successful as their intelligence otherwise would have allowed them to be."

In personality traits, Escobedo meets the criteria for being both narcissistic and, based on his being sent to the Dallas County Boys Shelter at age thirteen, antisocial, according to Dr. Crowder:

"Antisocials are the ones who, before the age of fifteen, show a lot of antisocial behavior, like disregard for the truth, aggression toward other people, stealing with confrontation, forced sexual acts with other people, truancy, running away from home overnight, and stealing."

Beyond the psychiatric labels, the single dominant thread that runs throughout Dr. Crowder's portrait of Escobedo is the rapist's extreme self-centeredness and egotism.

There is, perhaps, no more telling factor in the rationale of Escobedo's progression of crimes than his recurring ambivalent feelings about his mother. Repeatedly, the conflicting feelings about his mother surfaced in prison interviews with Escobedo, and apparently in his personal relationships with women in his life, as witnessed by Angie Welburne and his wife, Shirley.

"His mother leaving the family and deserting the family while Escobedo was at any early age was a narcissistic injury to him," Dr. Crowder explained. "Here's a woman leaving him and, in a direct way, controlling his emotions.

"So he now has to control the emotions of other women, to be the aggressor rather than the victim. The passive victim role is injurious to self-esteem, and if he becomes the perpetrator, he then is active. The self-esteem associated with control is then restored."

In the fragile area of self-esteem, the psychiatric profile suggests that Escobedo was overwhelmingly dependent on what others thought of him for his own identity and peace of mind. It was why, according to Dr. Crowder, Escobedo vacuumed his apartment daily, drove a Porsche, dressed compulsively and expensively, wore gold jewelry and Rolexes, and why he chose only attractive women as targets for his rapes.

"These people are not chemically, neurologically the same as other people are," the psychiatrist said. "Another thing is that all this is an expression of his narcissisism. He wants everything around him to be the perfect prop for how perfect *he* is. He wants to see himself as perfect, and he wants everyone else around him to see him that way as well. They almost always want attractive women because anything less would not speak well of them."

That he chose only attractive women with striking body builds and upwardly mobile careers was an extension of his own need to be highly regarded.

"By recounting how wonderful the women were, by inference, he must be a very special man," Dr. Crowder said. "By asking them the positions they preferred, as he sometimes did, he wants to get inside their heads and know their feelings, almost like Hannibal Lecter [in the movie *Silence of the Lambs*] did when he wanted to get inside Jodie Foster's head. It's a measure of control over the person.

"Similarly, he doesn't want to compete with other men. That's an interesting element here. There's some inhibition about competing with other men and that's part of the reason he selected these people. His victims have jobs with responsibility; he wants somebody successful because that says something about how clever and wonderful *he* is."

Even when Escobedo was described by his victims as being curiously concerned about their welfare, telling them after the rape, for example, to lock their windows, he also was exhibiting signs of narcissism and control.

"He wants to keep them only as *his* victims and not have them victimized by someone else, because they're *his* territory now," Dr. Crowder said. "He also fantasizes that he is extremely powerful; he can give them pleasure and positive things as well as negative things.

"He wants to be the god of his victims. That's the way he sees himself and so he casts himself in the role as being omnipotent protector: 'But don't cross me, because you'll pay for that, too.'

"Plus, he probably wants to see if it has an effect. He probably gets off on it if it has any effect at all on the listener. After he's just done this horrible thing to her, he can see the surprise on her face when he becomes benevolent for a change. He probably enjoys that, too. It's just a form of emotional control over the victim."

Some of the same tendencies may have been at play when Escobedo stayed after the rapes, forcing his victims to hug him or talk with him.

"I think he wants to show that he can control them on both poles of the kindness-cruelty continuum. I think it also has to do with his desire to be reunited with his mother, in a sense, to get the affection he didn't have from her."

Escobedo's MO of covering not only his face, but also that of his victims, and never ejaculating inside them, may have transcended his concern for being identified and leaving evidence.

"It's almost as if he doesn't want to confront the woman in a direct sort of way," Dr. Crowder said. "He needs an indirect way to do it. In the dark, he ran. If a scream happened, he might have to deal with that person more directly. He covers his face, he covers her face.

"I'm just saying that Escobedo confronting women directly, because they were intimidating to him because of the situation with his mother, would have been difficult.

"It's hard to know if his not ejaculating inside women is his fear of leaving evidence or his reluctance in confronting women. It may be some of both. But I'm sure he had trouble with not being able to control them in other relationships, too. I doubt that he had meaningful and successful relationships with women. I suspect they were very superficial. . . .

"They do establish that he had availability of consensual sex, which is where the ideas about rape just being aggression come from. The idea that rape has to do with power and not sexuality is a reaction against an old and generally held idea that rape might result from a lack of sex or inability to obtain sex in a normal way.

"In that sense, rape is not that kind of phenomenon. It does have to do with power over women, but obviously it is still sexualized aggression. The view of perversion is that the aggression has become fused with the sexual drive."

The psychiatric evidence also provides a rationale not only for why Escobedo's crimes escalated from burglary to rape, but also helps explain even the time of morning they were committed and why the fear of apprehension wasn't enough to stop him.

"One issue may be that as time goes on, these highly narcissistic individuals seek stimulation because there's a vague depression in them, which may also go with the time he committed his offenses," Dr. Crowder explained. "People with depression tend to wake up several times through the night, and they tend to wake up about three or four in the morning. That's when the cortisol is highest."

Cortisol is a hormone produced by the adrenal glands, the same organs that produce adrenaline, which speeds up the heartbeat and, therefore, energy level.

"Depressed people have an exaggerated cortisol level at all times, and it causes them to wake up early and makes them unable to go back to sleep. . . . A fair number of these people don't have adequate supplies of neurotransmitters . . . and it makes them more irritable and aggressive.

"It also makes them seek stimulation, which will cause the neurons to secrete more of these neurotransmitters. Then they feel better."

The fact that Escobedo was aware police not only knew his name, but also were following him undoubtedly increased the stimulation.

"The underlying current is the narcissism. That's what makes things special. Sex without a narcissistic gratification isn't as much fun. This thread runs through everything, including the game he was playing with police.

"Whatever brain deficits they have tend to make them hyperactive. . . . It's kind of seeking stimulation to cover the neurotransmitter deficit."

That some of his victims were attacked while roommates or other people were asleep in their house at the same time actually may have been an added thrill rather than a logistical drawback or increased risk to Escobedo.

"It's kind of a turn-on to them when there's somebody close, and they can still do this without detection," Dr. Crowder said. "It lifts them to a higher plane of criminal genius."

Of Escobedo's indignation that a girlfriend like Claire Miller purportedly had affairs outside his relationship with her, notwithstanding that he was committing rapes at the same time, Dr. Crowder noted:

"These people view morals as merely an invention of someone to control other people. They view everyone as being on something of a con. Morals have no meaning to this kind of person. They're just a little set of rules that some people make you compete with. He preferred to be out of that whole system where he could directly control situations instead of having to operate on a level where success is not assured.

"Because success was assured with these women he raped, and it wasn't assured with these other women and, in a way, that's more intimidating to him. What he's afraid of is the narcissistic injury. It's not being caught. It's not being sent to prison. It's being defeated in some way."

That Escobedo would profess to have found God, to be cloaked in born-again Christianity, and to have been forgiven for his sins doesn't surprise Dr. Crowder.

"Who's to say he hasn't? That's the beauty of it, isn't it?" Dr. Crowder said. "Behaviors are so efficient and defense mechanisms are so efficient that one action accomplishes several goals."

Religion, according to the forensics psychiatrist, appeals to narcissistic people because they frequently operate on a sliding scale of depravity and salvation: "They'll go into fights with girlfriends, then rapprochement, then they'll go into more fights with the girlfriend. And then they'll go through these cycles of always moving closer and then farther away in their relationships, never just staying one distance.

"In the harshness of their superego, the conscience is such that the rather extreme morality and punitive nature of some religious systems appeal to them as well.

"Then it's an angle to control other people because they know people are sensitive to religion. As if, 'I've learned my lesson and you can let me out right now.' "

Do people with narcissistic tendencies respond to therapy?

Dr. Crowder paused momentarily.

"It depends on how bad it is. It depends on how much discomfort the person perceives. A person with this many deficits in his insights into himself usually is not uncomfortable enough to want to change anything. He just wants to go to another situation or find new people to relate to that will be easier.

"People will avoid changing in most cases. Some people are morally motivated, but they're not these kinds. They have to be specifically and immediately motivated with specific rewards in the near future. They don't anticipate negative consequences well at all. That's part of the problem. They physiologically do not respond with fear to things that normal people do. So you can't use negative things to get them.

"It seems like positive rewards and a lot of structure are the best ways to handle them. And that's why they become model prisoners, and why they tend to get out early by virtue of that."

And therein lies the vicious circle among sex offenders, one that accounts for perhaps the highest recidivism rate among all criminals: Behind bars, under scrutiny and locked away from women, they appear rehabilitated and excellent candidates for parole. Back on the streets, with unlimited access to women and little fear of consequence, they frequently pick up where they left off.

31

"I thought there would be more. It was so smooth, so easy."

Escobedo was talking about the first time he raped. There was no braggadocio and no arrogance this time, nor was there the usual spin that always had God forgiving him for the evil he had done. Escobedo's admission, delivered in the visitor's cell, was a defining moment of insight in two years of interviews.

He was leaning toward the wire mesh screen, his elbows locked on the desk, his palms supporting his cheeks. He was pensive, and his voice was barely above a whisper even though the visitors' area was virtually deserted in late afternoon. He realized where he was going, but he didn't embark on his usual detours. He had returned to the beginning of his madness.

The rape was before his incarnation as the Ski Mask Rapist, three years before he would lay siege and wreak terror in whole Dallas neighborhoods. He was married at the time, a grocery stock clerk, a dabbler in rebuilt classic cars, a weekend father to two daughters, and between burglary convictions at the Texas Department of Criminal Justice.

The rape was not a jolting aberration in a man's life with no context in which to measure it. Already he was out of control, having exposed himself in broad daylight from the seat of a new Corvette to people at a crowded shopping mall.

Escobedo had fixated on a lithesome college student who lived with her family in a simple frame house north of Love Field. A career burglar, Escobedo had found her window as he poked and prowled through other people's alleys and backyards in the course of his business. After happening on the young woman, he drove to her house for weeks, watching in the night through the window as she and her younger teenage sisters undressed and showered, and as their parents slept.

As circumstance would have it, the college student wasn't vulnerable enough to become Escobedo's first rape victim. By default, that dubious distinction fell to a woman who lived down the street from Escobedo's house on Larga Drive. She was a nurse, and the attack would be chalked with thousands of other crimes that year that went unsolved in the big city.

But Escobedo was nothing if not obsessive. He went back for the college student who had seized his fantasy, and he raped her in her house on Princess Street.

"I wasn't really afraid of getting caught," Escobedo said. "The main thing I felt was that I was surprised it was so easy. Getting in wasn't really any different than doing burglaries. No, I wasn't afraid. I knew then that it had to happen, you know, that they'd be others. I just knew."

Just as he predicted, his neurotic conviction reappeared some nine months later when he tried three times in one night, even as Dallas police cruised the Oak Lawn neighborhood looking for him, to break into two sisters' apartment. Only when he was arrested several days later in yet another frenzied attempt to get inside the sisters' house was he was returned to prison.

The criminal justice system obviously hadn't linked Escobedo to the rapes of the nurse and the college student, two attacks that were separated not only by geography, but also by MO from his monomaniacal assaults on the sisters. But to borrow from the legal system's own lexicon, prosecutors "knew or should have known" that Escobedo was out of control.

There was enough in his file to indicate he no longer was merely a cat burglar; the parolee had exposed himself at a shopping mall, been caught outside a woman's bedroom window, and, at his bizarre worst, had simply refused to be deterred from trying to rape the two sisters. Two of the three incidents had ended in Escobedo violently resisting arrest, and, in another, stabbing a woman.

Escobedo was the embodiment of the career criminal envisioned by Texas legislators when they created the Habitual Criminal Statute. But rather than prosecute him for a life sentence, prosecutors merely revoked his parole for attempted burglary and returned him to prison for less than three years. There, without any counseling for his sexual perversions, his chances of rehabilitation were virtually nil.

Escobedo was but another faceless recidivist in the clogged criminal justice pipeline, a man whose crimes hadn't killed anyone or created headlines that outraged. Dallas courts undoubtedly saw a hundred Escobedos a day.

But on the same day prosecutors severely underestimated Escobedo's propensity for violence and slapped his wrists, the system also doomed forty-eight—maybe as many as one hundred—women whose lives would be forever altered by the Ski Mask Rapist when Escobedo got out of prison.

Even if the criminal justice system was too disinterested or too negligent to understand that propensity, Escobedo did.

"One thing about sin," Escobedo said from the prison cell, "it always wants more. I knew there would be more."

Whatever the darkness in his psyche that led him to rape—narcissism, his relationship with his mother, his feelings of worthlessness—Gilbert Escobedo, purely and simply, was in love with the chase. He survived, even prospered as a rapist and burglar in the midst of a chaotic series of near-misses that would have scared normal people straight. In the end, those adrenaline-charged encounters only heightened his rush and propelled his fantasies.

Neither fear of arrest, his vivid recall of three prior incarcerations, nor even concern that he would be shot was sufficient to deter.

In each of his criminal enterprises, Escobedo relied on an abnormal collection of skills and instincts to preserve his freedom. He relied not on sheer intelligence—there is no indication that he was anything but average, if that—but on the street savvy he had gleaned in the process of compiling a five-page rap sheet of criminal offenses. He blended this dubious antisocial experience with an uncanny and instinctive ability to predict people's actions, and, always, with cunning to maintain his freedom.

"He was quiet, furtive, and sly," Touchton would say, not without begrudging respect, "and he had balls the size of television sets. He pulled it off for five years. We were damn lucky to get him."

Luck.

"It's not enough to be good," Escobedo conceded from inside his steel mesh cubicle. "I was good. Really. I developed a plan. You have to stay with the plan. You have to look things over, see how things work. You can find a way. You have to study it. I was good; I just ran out of luck."

Escobedo's personality and plan were chilling, even diabolical, in their manifestation. But it is in his recollection of close encounters that Escobedo unmasks the pride, guile, and arrogance that underscored his reign of terror as the Ski Mask Rapist.

Indeed, he acknowledged, it was a near-miss that led to perfection of his plan.

"I got shot at one night in an apartment," he said.

Fear, however, was neither as powerful nor as persistent as obsession: "I came back three nights later and got her."

The incident apparently was pivotal in reformulating his modus operandi. Compulsively, he took to entering targets' apartments while they were gone so that he could search for hidden weapons. The sound of gunfire was something he would never hear again. And while he maintained that his carrying a gun was solely to intimidate the victim, it was a practice he apparently began after the woman shot at him.

"I never intended to use it," Escobedo said of the pistol he carried in most of the assaults. "That's something I'd never do."

The daylight rape in November 1985 of Constance McIntyre not only was a daring departure from Escobedo's normal MO, it also triggered a series of panicked episodes that left the rapist momentarily harrowed and, perhaps, ultimately emboldened. The events of that day appeared to bear credence to the axiom that "anything that doesn't kill you makes you stronger."

After brazenly negotiating his way past a pool man in the backyard and a maid vacuuming in the next room, Escobedo raped and robbed McIntyre. But emerging from her house shortly before eleven in the morning, Escobedo couldn't find the Dallas Police Department ball cap he had hidden in the trash can in the alley.

"It gave me an eerie feeling like somebody might be watching me even while I was standing in the alley," Escobedo recounted.

Carefully, he walked the two blocks to his pickup truck, knowing that with every step police undoubtedly were getting closer to the neighborhood. The walk was a labored tribute to mind over matter: His heart told him to flee, but his mind forced him to walk casually, not wanting to be seen as acting suspiciously. The challenge in daylight, he knew, was slipping away without anyone seeing his face or license plate.

Once inside the pickup truck parked at the curb, Escobedo noticed a white business card beneath his windshield wiper, turned inward so that he could see the embossed police badge from his seat. Standing half in, half out of the cab, he retrieved the card, then slid back inside, started the pickup, and drove off, scanning the card as he moved farther and farther from his crime.

The business card belonged to a DPD investigator who had written a ballpoint note on the back: "Please call me." The rapist's mind raced and his legs felt like Jell-O. Periodically, his eyes scanned the rearview mirror.

Somewhere in the bowels of DPD was an investigator who could put Escobedo's pickup within two blocks of a rape scene. But, Escobedo reasoned, the rape wouldn't have been reported when the cop left the card, and, at any rate, he clearly wasn't a suspect or there would have been five cops camped out on his truck.

Still, the card unraveled him. He viewed it as the ominous precursor of apprehension. Fearing that police somehow had figured him for the series of previous rapes and worried that his home phone might be tapped, he pulled into a convenience store and dialed the number on the card from an outside pay phone.

The detective's tone was cordial and reassuring. The officer had been driving through the neighborhood and noticed the immaculately re-stored pickup truck.

"It's a beautiful truck," the detective said. "You interested in selling it?"

Relief swept Escobedo's body. Politely, he thanked the detective for his interest, but declined the offer. He vowed to keep his card in case he changed his mind, and hung up.

Escobedo only barely arrived at his condo on Woodbend Lane when the doorbell sounded. He opened his door to a uniformed female police officer. For the second time in half an hour, he fought to maintain his composure.

Had the detective had time to recall his truck near the rape scene and report him? Had someone else gotten his plate number? Wait, his mind told him: They wouldn't send a single female cop to arrest a bona fide rape suspect. *Would they?*

The officer was performing a public service. Motioning to the bag she carried in her left hand, she asked if Escobedo would like her to engrave his name and driver's license number on major possessions in the event they were ever stolen.

The rapist ushered the officer into his house. He kept her busy for as long as he could, dragging out TVs, VCRs, small appliances, and jewelry for her engraving tool. He chatted cordially and offered her something to drink. After the officer finished engraving his possessions, she inventoried them and gave him a copy.

Then he embarked on a ploy indicative of the cunning that typified his criminal career.

He asked her for a business card, explaining that he appreciated the service and would pass the card to friends, encouraging them to participate in such an important crime prevention technique.

"She gave me the receipt, but I wanted the card," Escobedo explained, an expansive grin covering his face, "for an alibi. She gave everyone a copy of the inventory. I don't think many people probably asked her for her card. She'd remember that. If they ever asked me about the rape, I was going to give them that card and say she had come an hour earlier than she did. She probably did fifty of those [engravings] a day. She wouldn't have remembered the exact time she came to my house. I would have a police officer for a witness."

The bizarre series of coincidences that day, Escobedo acknowledged, unnerved him. But only momentarily. Within a month, he was raping again. The next victim, Billie Jean Rider, he raped three times, unusual by Escobedo's pattern, which sometimes was marked by the fact he couldn't even get an erection. He appeared empowered.

At one point, Escobedo returned to a house where he previously had seen an attractive woman changing clothes. This time, though, he watched through the blinds as the woman's husband lay on the bed, counting a wad of what appeared to be $100 bills. The man stacked the bills neatly and stuck them in an envelope, which he placed in a jewelry box beside the bed. Impulsively, Escobedo's priorities changed.

The house was wired with a security system, the only obstacle that had prevented Escobedo from breaking in earlier. Now he had a new incentive. He waited until the couple was gone, and found a guest bathroom with a skylight in it. Peering around the skylight with a penlight, he couldn't find an electrical lead to suggest the window was wired to the security system. There was, however, another obstacle after he removed the skylight. The ceiling was vaulted; the bathtub was a good twenty-five feet below. He misjudged the drop, cracking his head on the side of the marble tub and temporarily knocking himself unconscious.

He was wobbly when he left and his head throbbed, but he carried with him $6,000 in cash and another $20,000 in gold jewelry. Just as easily, he knew, the couple could have found him unconscious in their bathroom.

The close encounters, as unnerving as they were at the time, and his ability to extricate himself from them only boosted his self-esteem and propelled his spree, leaving him with a feeling of invincibility.

Escobedo was half in a woman's apartment when she apparently heard the metal door slide across its railing. She let out a piercing scream, sending Escobedo outside. Leaning backward against the brick wall and contemplating escape, he knew she was dialing police. He waited. The scream apparently hadn't provoked any neighbors running toward her house. There was time to get away.

Instead, the thwarted rapist walked methodically across the street and into a large clump of shrubbery. Three feet into the huge flower bed, he lay on his stomach, positioning himself to watch the woman's front door. Within minutes, two police cruisers appeared simultaneously at the curb. Two officers emerged from one of the cars. One carried his pistol by his side, pointed at the ground; the other cradled a shotgun in the bend of his left arm. The other cruiser drove off, heading, Escobedo knew, to the alley behind the woman's house.

For more than an hour, the man who would have raped lay in watch as police attended his proposed victim. He was captivated by the activity. The scene, he surmised, was the same as he had triggered so many times in the past. He was enthralled with the police response and surprised, frankly, how quickly they had come. When finally police left, Escobedo emerged from the darkened bushes feeling important, no doubt, and, as Dr. Jaye Crowder would hypothesize, impressed at his own criminal genius.

Success, near-miss, a major score, then another close encounter, the manic cycle continued for five years.

"I got into the challenge," Escobedo would admit in prison. "There's something about doing something that nobody figures you can do, you know? It's like, don't tell me I can't do something. It makes me show you I can."

He once broke into a fashionable house and stole a Rolex he found on a bathroom lavatory. He also ripped out a blank deposit receipt from a checkbook he found in the woman's handbag. Dialing the phone number on the deposit slip a month later, Escobedo posed as a police detective and asked if she had had any more ideas on the disappearance of the Rolex.

The woman had been meaning to call, she said apologetically. She no longer believed the Rolex was stolen, but rather flushed down the toilet by her three-year-old. The insurance company had paid the claim, and her husband already had replaced his prized watch. She hoped she hadn't caused a problem, and thanked him for his interest.

Within days, Escobedo broke into the house a second time, taking the man's new Rolex and an expensive pair of matching Chinese vases he overlooked in the first burglary.

Escobedo controlled every variable he could. His precision not only ensured his success, but it separated him from the pack of sloppy, one-shot criminals who spent virtually all their lives behind bars. There was more than monitoring his victims' comings and goings and whether they kept weapons in their nightstands. Attention to detail, planning for any eventuality, staying within "the plan," that was the secret to Escobedo's longevity on the street.

"I preferred to do my burglaries and assaults on rainy nights," Escobedo explained. "I loved rainy nights. People don't walk their dogs in the rain. Joggers for the most part put off their runs until the rain stops. On rainy nights, I had the streets to myself."

Anything that gave him an edge, Escobedo embraced. Like his so-called "rape kit," the zippered, canvas athletic bag that he carried with him. Inside he stored a change of clothes, shoes, underwear, a towel, a flashlight, and a ski mask. In the dark, concealed in bushes outside his intended victim's house, Escobedo changed into the clothes he would wear during the attack.

After the rape, his habit was to strip to his underwear and immerse himself in a nearby swimming pool, seldom a problem at four A.M. in the luxury apartment complexes that lined North Dallas. Toweling off in the bushes, he changed clothes. If he were to be stopped, his clothing wouldn't come close to that described by a victim, even if she got a look, or any witness who saw him leaving. He would smell faintly of chlorine instead of sweat, and any trace evidence, like pubic hair or semen, would have been left in some North Dallas pool.

On one of his dark prowls, Escobedo almost literally bumped into a security guard apparently hired specifically to counteract the outbreak of attacks by the Ski Mask Rapist. Clad in black pants, a black sweater, black boots, a Dallas Police Department ball cap, and carrying a police scanner on his belt, his preferred outfit for window-peeking and scouting new targets, Escobedo was surprised by the security guard on the grounds of an apartment complex he had struck in the past.

"Can I help you, Officer?" the armed security guard asked.

He had come from nowhere.

"Uh, no, I'm fine, thank you," Escobedo replied in his most authoritative tone. "What I'm doing, I can do by myself."

"Doing some surveillance, huh?"

"Yeah," Escobedo said, turning up the squelch on his police radio. "Something like that."

"Well, if you need any backup or anything, just yell. I'll be here."

Occasionally, Escobedo misdiagnosed situations, a shortcoming probably attributable to his supreme self-confidence. Three or four times, he had watched an athletic young couple walk from their condo with a plastic bag of trash, deposit it in a Dumpster, and then continue on for a late-afternoon walk that consumed a good fifteen minutes. It was a quiet, closed-access neighborhood, and they never locked their door when they left on their jaunts. Equally important, Escobedo noticed during his window-peeking, the yuppie couple had an unusually large amount of jewelry.

Seeing the couple leave with the bag of trash, Escobedo darted from the edge of the house through the front door and into the master bedroom. He no sooner had opened the jewelry box, which played a little tune with chimes, then he heard the front door open. He shut the jewelry box quickly and fell to the floor even as he saw the man and woman headed for their bedroom.

Using his right elbow and foot, he pulled himself sideways toward the bed and tried to wedge his body underneath. With only half his body under the bed, his right shoulder and leg met with an obstruction. The couple had stored boxes beneath the bed from the other side. Escobedo lay there, the left half of his body exposed. Praying the couple wouldn't come to that side of the bed, he looked to his left. He could see himself in a wall mirror; more importantly, they would, too, if they glanced in the mirror.

Escobedo felt the weight of both man and woman collapsing onto the bed. He listened to their conversation. She had changed her mind about the walk. The man hoped she wasn't establishing precedent; walking was important, he said. They chatted aimlessly. Finally, she allowed she would take a shower. Halfheartedly, her husband mentioned a game on ESPN that he might catch.

Escobedo felt the weight lifting from the bed. He lay motionless. Eventually—an eternity, he thought—he heard the sound of a television, then a shower. Cautiously he edged from beneath the bed and peered over the mattress. He crept to a bedroom window, which he slowly raised, then to the dresser. Pulling as much air into his lungs as they would tolerate, he jerked open the jewelry box, dreading the obnoxious chimes. He emptied the jewelry into his pockets and lunged through the open window. Vaguely, he remembered a man screaming at him. He never looked back.

There also was another, less direct means by which Escobedo fed his fetishes. After watching a woman, he sometimes phoned her late at night, whispering vile things into the phone and taking pleasure in the revulsion and panic it created. Other times, he merely listened silently, taking in the woman's voice and committing it in his imagination with the naked body he had seen through the window.

The phone calls added sound to sight; the other senses—smell, taste, and touch—were dependent on physical proximity. He would add those pieces to the composite phantasm later.

But even after he extorted their intimacy and dominated them at gunpoint, his fantasy often demanded more. In some instances, he phoned victims after he raped them.

"It happens with these guys sometimes," Marshall Touchton said. "Several of his victims got calls from Gilbert before and after the rape. They're in search of the ultimate rape. But there is no ultimate rape. That's why there's always another one after that."

32

Early in the interviews, Escobedo mentioned writing letters to his victims in which he would apologize for what he had done to them. Over time, he discussed including the letter in this book. He liked the fact that he would be able to use his own words, say what was on his mind, and that, possibly, he would reach all those he had hurt. Later, he expanded the idea to add his "personal testimony," his story of how he had rediscovered God after confessing to the series of rapes.

But over much of the next two years, the "victim letter," as he came to call it, became typical of his indecisiveness. His inability to make decisions, frequently aggravated by pressure from his family, was only compounded by a new friendship Escobedo made in prison. The friend, a career criminal who also was a "writ writer," or jailhouse lawyer appealing his own conviction, suggested to Escobedo that police possibly had made errors in investigating his case. A letter, the writ writer noted, particularly one in which he made certain admissions, would not work in Escobedo's favor in the event of an appeal.

So, as deadline neared for the book, Escobedo wrote:

I decided not to write a victim letter to place in the book, nor a testimony. Reasons for being, I feel that the victim letter could

I prolonged looking at her graduation pictures and "flattered" with her accomplishment, and so proud of her!

The succeeding morning (Sunday, October 7, 1990) I was awakened by an officer and informed that the chaplain had called for me. I sensed that something was incorrect. The chaplain said, "Escobedo, I have some bad news for you. Your daughter Becky was killed this morning by drive by shooting. The victimizers were teenagers (15–16 years of age). As Becky stood with friends at a park one of the bullets from the drive by shooting pierced her back." I was totally crushed.

I cried, cried and cried and these tears were not of joy, for they were tears of sorrow and hurt and similar to what you victims experienced and still do. I was able to identify with the aftermath of sin, for it was "no fun." However, I forgave the victimizers for what they did to my daughter and continue to pray for them.

Continuing, God is my witness, I genuinely apologize to each of you victims for sexually assaulting you. I'm so sorry. Please find a place in your heart to accept my apology and to forgive me. Thank you.

I will continue to pray for each of you and your families and ask God to bring healing and comfort, for I know He will (in his timing) because He is a merciful God.

Thank you for reading my letter and allowing me to share my heart with you. May God bless you and your's.

In Christ,
Gilbert Escobedo

bounce back and be used against me, when and if legal action is tak
for the discovered errors the Dallas Police Department made in
case. I'm very cautious in all areas because I'm the one doing
time.

Secondly, I'm withholding in writing my testimony because I s
have sin in my life and my testimony wouldn't be pure and clean. I
only being honest and open with you and with God. . . . Anyw
thank you for giving me the opportunity. . . .

Additionally, I know that you will be using my mom in the bc
to bring out points of views when I was young, and I'm asking y
not to dishonor her in any way.

Months later, while the book was being edited, Escobedo unde
yet another change of heart. There would be no appeal of his case
it too late, he wanted to know, to still include his letter to the w
he raped?

In his letter, reprinted here as he sent it, Escobedo wrote:

Dear Victims,

Back in 1990 in the Dallas County Jail (single cell) I cried out
the Lord on my knees and repented for all my sins and rededica
my life to Jesus Christ.

Following, I prayed for each victim I had victimized and the ago
sting, ache, and woe I instilled within, along with the psychologi
disorder I caused. I asked God to please grant me a way to apolog
to you victims and I knew that He would (in His timing), but I did
know how.

However, God gave me this communication line (by writing
letter) to express my apology and I thanked Him for this opportuni

Before continuing, allow me to share this incident with you cc
cerning my daughter Rebecca (Becky). In October of 1990 on a S
urday night here at Ellis One Unit (Texas Department of Crimir
Justice) I inherited a letter from my daughter Becky with pictur
encompassed of her high school graduation ceremony. I was load
with "joy" and cried as I read Becky's letter.

I wrote Becky back that same night and managed to even mail

Epilogue

Late May 1994

Through a chaplain who had become a friend, Shirley Escobedo learned that her husband had been disciplined and removed from his job as a trusty for the prison major. Instead of working two hours a day running errands for the major and his administrative staff, Escobedo had been reassigned to the agricultural unit, the lowest, toughest rung in the prison pecking order.

Daily, he was hoeing weeds in searing temperatures under the watchful eyes of mounted guards who kept shotguns swung across their saddles. He also was moved from his trusty dormitory to a two-man cell in the maximum-security section of the prison, and he lost the benefit of earning so-called good time that only trusties can accrue.

It took two weeks for Shirley Escobedo to learn the reason for the abrupt disciplinary action against her husband. When she confronted him during a visit, he was meek and humble. Evasive at first, he finally related the events that led to his reassignment.

Sent on an errand for the major's staff, Escobedo happened upon a telephone; taped to the wall above the phone was a list of prison phone extensions. Through the barred window, Escobedo saw an attractive young blond guard standing on the platform of the tower in front.

"It was an impulsive act," Escobedo explained to his wife. "I didn't really think about it. I just picked up the phone and, uh, I, uh, well, did something I shouldn't have.

"I made an obscene phone call."

He already had prayed to God, he said, who had forgiven him for the lust in his heart.

January 1995

As he had twice before during incarcerations, Escobedo received a legal envelope sent from Dallas by certified mail. The top two pages inside, a petition for divorce sworn by Shirley Escobedo, contained standard legal boilerplate: "Irreconcilable differences," she alleged, had made their marriage "insupportable." A third page, submitted for Escobedo's signature, was a waiver acknowledging that he wouldn't contest the divorce.

Though Shirley had discussed the divorce with him on several occasions, a prison chaplain later told her that Escobedo had appeared "devastated" when he received the divorce petition.

In truth, the marriage had deteriorated in the six months since Escobedo admitted to making the obscene phone call to a female prison guard. Shirley, who had visited him at least twice a month, sometimes went six weeks between trips to the prison. Hard realities about her husband that she had worked to resolve—the crimes he had committed against other women, his being locked up until well into the next century, his domineering family that appeared to control his life even behind bars, his incessant jealousy—all became too much to bear.

Shirley was contrite in explaining the divorce. "It just wore me down," she told me. "I had to get out. I had to do it for me."

Escobedo signed the waiver, agreeing to the divorce. He enclosed it in a warm letter in which he hoped they could remain friends. Shirley sent her regards and wished him happiness.

It was the same thing Angie Welburne told him when she left.

Gilbert H. Escobedo appeared to have it all in 1987 as he prepared to embark on his third marriage. He owned a thriving downtown Dallas business, dressed in Italian suits, wore Rolexes, and drove Porsches. This photo was taken by his fiancée.

Ever the meticulous dresser, as shown in this photo by his former fiancée, Escobedo color-coordinated his wardrobe even down to the tinted sunglasses that matched his clothes. His obsessiveness carried over to other portions of his life.

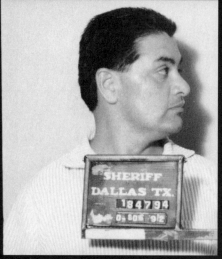

Even as he was caught outside a woman's apartment in April 1990, Escobedo professed to be the good citizen investigating a prowler. After being booked and threatened with consecutive life sentences, he changed his story.

Courtesy Dallas County Sheriff's Department

Incarcerated in Texas' maximum-security penitentiary, Escobedo claimed to have re-dedicated his life to God. Assigned as an orderly for a prison official, Escobedo lost his privileged status for disciplinary reasons and was reassigned to a field crew under armed guard.

Photo by David Woo, *The Dallas Morning News*